Syllables of Recorded Time

Other books by Lyn Harrington:

Manitoba Roundabout, Ryerson, 1951
Stormy Summer, Nelson, 1953
Ootook, Eskimo Girl, Nelson, 1956
Real Book about Canada, Doubleday, 1959
British Columbia in Pictures, Nelson, 1959
Encyclopedia of World Travel, Doubleday, 1961; Canada Section
Rangers' Handbook, 1962
Greece and the Greeks, Nelson, 1962
How People Live in Canada, Benefic, 1964
China and the Chinese, Nelson, 1966
Grand Canal of China, Rand McNally, 1967; B&S, 1974
Luck of the La Verendryes, Nelson, 1967
How People Live in China, Benefic, 1968
Australia and New Zealand, Nelson, 1969
Polar Regions, Nelson, 1973
The Covered Bridges of Central and Eastern Canada, McGraw-Hill, 1976
The Shaman's Evil Eye, Highway, 1979

Syllables of Recorded Time

by Lyn Harrington
Foreword by Harry J. Boyle

THE STORY OF THE CANADIAN
AUTHORS ASSOCIATION 1921-1981

Simon & Pierre

Published with the kind assistance of a Wintario grant and Alberta Culture.

We would like to express our gratitude to The Canada Council and the Ontario Arts Council for their support.

Marian M. Wilson, Publisher

From A LIFE IN FOLKLORE by Dr. Helen Creighton
Reprinted by permission of McGraw-Hill Ryerson Limited

MAPLE LEAF FOREVER
© 1964 by Gordon V. Thompson
Used by permission.

A SLICE OF CANADA by Watson Kirkconnell, © University of Toronto Press for Acadia University

Canadian Forum quotations © *Canadian Forum*

Excerpts throughout text:
Unless otherwise indicated, all quotations in smaller type are taken from *The Canadian Bookman* later *The Canadian Author & Bookman.* © Canadian Authors Association

ISBN 0-88924-112-0

1 2 3 4 5 • 5 4 3 2 1

Canadian Cataloguing in Publication Data

Harrington, Lyn, 1911-
  Syllables of recorded time

Bibliography:
Includes index.
ISBN 0-88924-112-0

1. Canadian Authors Association - History
I. Title

PS8005.C363H37   C810'.6071   C81-094657-2
PR9180.C363H37

Editor: Marian M. Wilson
Designer: Mario Carvajal
Assistant Editor: K.A. Chittick
Typesetting: Pickwick Type
Printer: Les Editions Marquis

Printed and Bound in Canada

Simon & Pierre Publishing Company Limited
Order Department
P.O. Box 280 Adelaide Street Postal Station
Toronto, Ontario
Canada M5C 2J4

To commemorate the Diamond Anniversary
of the
Canadian Authors Association
1921-1981

Acknowledgements

Material in this book has been drawn almost entirely from back issues of the *Canadian Author & Bookman*, published since 1919, and other Canadian Authors Association files.

In addition, the author used as a resource Susan Sills' M.A. thesis, *The Role of the Canadian Authors Association with Respect to the Licensing Clauses of Early Copyright Legislation and Canada's Adherence to the Berne Convention.*

Special thanks go to Dr. Helen Creighton, Bluebell Phillips, the late June Fritch, Cdr. C.H. Little, and Dr. Donald W. Thomson for their assistance and cooperation.

Foreword

To many Canadian writers and students whose development has taken place in the aftermath of the Massey report, it may come as a surprise to know that cultural self-consciousness did not spring up fully grown in the CanLit courses of the 1960s. Forty years earlier the Canadian Authors Association had 700 members and was a proportionately larger organization by comparison to national population, than the Authors League of America, which numbered 2,000 members. In a time of powerful lobbies and vested interest groups, the Canadian Authors Association remains a dignified and important agency of Canadian cultural life.

The Canadian Authors Association can take pride in what it has accomplished. Its restrained pleading may even have had a greater cumulative effect than some of the more militant intercessions. Its influence hasn't been confined to membership. It has helped all writers in Canada.

For sixty years it has persisted with the admirable notion that those who ardently desire to write are as important in their own way as those who write. This belief has extended to concern and help for many who over the years had contributed a great deal to the cultural life of Canada before there were formal grants and subsidies or even social security. Its inherent bellettrism has been rather out of fashion of late, but the unhappy effects of the succeeding trend to strict professionalism now seem likely to suggest the need for another tack again in our cultural life for the next sixty years.

There is an increased recognition of creative work in Canada. It should be much greater. It must be a contagious celebration by Canadians that we have powerful and sensitive voices that are now recognized internationally. How many countries can boast of having a Leacock, a McLuhan and a Frye in a scant span of sixty years? It's not only in the great universities that their literary and philosophical talents are recognized, for in those places where newspapers still regard culture as important these men are treated as natural celebrities, deserving serious coverage.

There's another reason for recognition. We need their insights at this time when an obsession for technology threatens us with facts, raw information and mindlessness. Only the examined life can survive the smothering deluge.

Communications technology broke the tyranny of space in Canada. Now it is rampant and it must be used in the cause of the human spirit and not allowed to impose its own imperatives. Our artists must remind us of thought, love, poetry, dreams, hopes, memory and the kindness that protects human dignity. This was recognized by the artists who set up the *Canadian Bookman* and the CAA. In 1919 they inveighed against:

> the merely sentimental, narcotic, idea-less books, miscalled books of the imagination, which have formed the literary food of too many of us who did not wish to be bothered with ideas.

They saw the need for a Canadian periodical which would discuss books

> not as masses of paper and binding, nor as so many square inches of type, nor as speculative adventures in search for "best-sellers", but as the vessels for the containing and the imparting of ideas — and of ideas suited to the uses of Canadian readers.

The key to these matters lies with artists. It is what they deal with all the time. They are the only true force that can restrain those who itch for the pushbutton of destruction in what they see myopically as self-defence. In a world where science has perfected the means of robbing individuals of their dignity and individual rights, we need the artists' concern for global fraternity.

"The poet" — as writer Norman Cousins speaks of all who have respect for and speak to the human spirit — "can help to keep man from making himself over in the image of his electronic marvels. For the danger is not so much that man may be controlled by the computer as that he may imitate it."

I do not suggest that Canadian writers alone will save our world. They are valuable however in reminding us of the power of better international understanding in the cause of fraternity rather than fratricide. One madman in this lifetime almost destroyed the world by suppressing individual thoughts and supplanting it with dogma; significantly today despots in many parts of the world are still attempting to do what he failed at. Where the rights of the state take priority, the first to be eliminated or silenced are the artists.

Can it happen here? It can, and it will be a supreme irony if the voices of the artists are rendered powerless by indifference rather than brutal suppression. The danger is that we can be lulled into such indifference by a deluge of soporific images and words in the mass of communications technology. What shall it avail us if we have an enormous gross national product and lose our sense of value as individual human beings with a responsibility to all mankind?

In future years the history of the CAA will undoubtedly be written in more detail, and the opening up of its archives to researchers will add to our knowledge of Canadian literary history. The valuable achievement of this account is that it is set down by someone who has participated in much of that history and that it can be published at a time when these events are still within the living memory of scholars and writers. Every decade brings its own analysis of literary history; in this sixtieth year of its existence, when comprehensive cultural review is an urgent part of Canadian life, the history of the CAA adds a significant perspective, that will help current writers to assess more fully our Canadian consciousness of a literary tradition.

Harry J. Boyle

Table of Contents

Preface

Catch: Preface

When an author starts out on a novel, he or she is rarely sure exactly how it will develop. The beginning and the theme are clear in mind, but the details, the development of plot and of characters are yet to be worked out.

So it was with the Canadian Authors Association. Founded in 1921 for a specific short-term purpose, it grew beyond the planners' most extravagant expectations, and the one meeting lasted sixty years.

Celebration of a Diamond Jubilee is a good time to look back over those six decades, to recall the beginning, and evaluate the progress. What has the CAA achieved for the countless hours of effort expended? Was it worthwhile? How did it benefit our fellow writers and our friends among the librarians, booksellers and publishers? What did individuals gain from association with other authors or would-be authors?

Scanning past records, it is obvious that the founders "builded better than they knew." None of them is alive today. They might be dismayed to learn that the meeting called in 1921 to correct unjust copyright legislation only partially succeeded, and the campaign is still being waged.

Yet they would be gratified to realize that their organization is winning other battles and still adheres to the founding principles of high endeavour and national unity.

Lacking the expertise and any funding, now available for the promotion of Canadian books and authors, the rank-and-file members of small branches across the country undertook to inform uninterested Canadians about the writing of their country. In doing so, through the boom-and-bust of the twenties and thirties, and through the long war years, they laid a solid base for the esteem in which Canadian literature is held today.

The charter members, and many more, were men and women of liberality of thought and generosity of action, who gave uncounted hours to the cause of Canadian cultural development. They did not attempt to form a professional writing group, for few could make a livelihood exclusively with their typewriters. But they strove to raise the standard of Canadian writing across the board. They offered encouragement and help to obscure struggling writers, and even to dabblers on the fringe.

"If humility, which is not mock modest is a sign of greatness, then greatness has more than once walked among us. We have done silly things in our day, and squandered hours on trivial things. But we have also had moments of achievements, and occasions of memorable brilliance," said Leslie Gordon Barnard.

If all this should sound like boasting, it is long overdue. Cecil Goldbeck, vice-president and editor-in-chief of Coward-McCann Inc. N.Y. on an author-hunt in Canada in 1943, could declare, "There is such a thing as being too modest. You Canadians have done a very small job of advertising yourselves across the border. It's time to forget that innate modesty and crash through! During my visit, I have made contact with more than a hundred Canadian authors, and I must say that never before either in Europe or in the United States, have I met such retiring and modest men." It was not meant as a compliment.

Many of the conditions which writers now take for granted had to be won by public-spirited authors who took time from their own work, and dipped deep into their own pockets to nurture Canadian writing and other copyrightable arts.

Thus the major goal was achieved in spite of amateur methods and the arrows of critics, despite the vicissitudes of enthusiasm and apathy, illnesses and the Grim Reaper. Some high objectives have not been attained as yet. Our Jubilee year provides an occasion to celebrate what has been accomplished, to take stock of the present, and to set up new targets for the future.

Lyn Harrington

Chapter 1
In the Beginning, the Word

It is generally assumed that the Canadian Authors Association fathered the *Canadian Bookman*. In fact, it was the other way 'round. The editorial committee of the magazine actually parented the CAA. The magazine was first published in January 1919, while the Association came into being two years later on March 12, 1921. But they had the same progenitors.

Canada had just come through a long and bloody conflict in Europe. Her raw resources, her factories, and her labour power had augmented the heroism of her men in the trenches. At the close of the Great War, the country was flexing its muscles with satisfaction and ebullience. Canada had earned the right to sign the Peace Treaty, and to sit in the League of Nations as an independent country, no longer a mere colony.

But in the process of growing, Canadians gave all honour to material progress, little to things of the mind and spirit. Culture had been neglected in the young country as not being practical. Everyone knew that artists starved in garrets, that poets died young of phthisis, and musicians led scandalous lives. What right-thinking Canadian would see his daughter married to such unreliable characters or becoming one?

Culture was necessarily secondary in a new land with a population of less than nine million, many of whom neither read nor spoke English or French. They were stretched thinly across a wide country where the only trans-continental communication was by rail and wire. Much of the land was still unsettled, with hamlets tucked beside the rails in bush country or naked to the sky on the prairies, or isolated by a ragged coastline.

First things first. Get a job, make a living. Then, maybe, education for sons. Few daughters got to university. Some won freedom by learning to type. Literary societies were all very well for city matrons with time on their hands, who might also patronize the rare stage drama or more frequent concert. But most entertainment was local, and not very worldly. Religion was strong, industry fledgling.

Still, since a few were interested in ideas, and books are the time-honoured vehicle through which ideas are expressed and preserved, probably there were many more just awaiting enlightenment. Why not start a magazine for them? A purely Canadian periodical which would impart ideas suited to the uses of Canadian readers, not ideas judged by the standards of any other nation. And so a small group of editors and "bookish" men in Montreal banded themselves together as the Association of Canadian Bookmen, largely at the instigation of B.K. Sandwell (later well-known as the editor of Toronto's *Saturday Night*).

Then aged thirty-two, English-born Bernard K. Sandwell had been head scholar at Upper Canada College and had graduated from the University of Toronto with first class honours in classics. After twelve years of newspaper journalism in London and Montreal, chiefly as dramatic and literary critic, he helped found the *Financial Times* in Montreal. By 1919, he was associate editor, a lecturer on commerce at McGill University, and a teacher of creative writing extension courses. He was also a practising freelance writer, selling his essays to magazines in England, the United States and Canada. In addition, he was an accomplished musician.

"B.K. was always a gentleman, in the finest sense of the word — notable for pouring out the oil of personal negotiation to solve crises which seemed about to wreck the machinery," old friend Kirkconnell remembered.

The ACB agreed with Sandwell that the time was ripe for a magazine devoted to the arts in Canada, and he was appointed as the first editor of *Canadian Bookman*, yet another sideline occupation for him. His first editorial discussed the place and concerns of the new magazine in contemporary Canadian culture:

> If this is to be an era of ideas, it follows that it is to be also an era of books, since books are the one great medium through which

ideas are communicated and perpetuated. Not the purely material books . . . nor the merely sentimental (miscalled books of imagination) . . . but real books, containing real ideas about the important things of life . . . ideas suited to the uses of Canadian readers. In this sense, the appearance of the *Canadian Bookman* at the very dawn of this new era is not a mere coincidence. The *Canadian Bookman* is itself one of the phenomena of the new era.

Evidences of the dawn of such an era are plentiful enough. . . . We can see them in the conversation of the social gatherings . . . in the growth and new vigour of cultural societies . . . as enough to prove that there is a widespread desire for the services we aim to tender.

The idealistic editor was backed by an editorial committee of equal conviction, among others: Capt. Frederick William Wallace, author of *Wooden Ships and Iron Men*, and editor of the *Canadian Fisherman*; John Murray Gibbon, publicity manager for the Canadian Pacific Railway and author of two novels; Dr. George H. Locke, Chief of Toronto Public Libraries; Dr. J.A. Dale, professor of education, McGill University; the Hon. W.S. Fielding, editor of the *Canadian Journal of Commerce*, formerly Dominion Minister of Finance. And others of similar ilk.

"With such cooperation," the publishers at Garden City Press, optimistically launched the *Canadian Bookman* on its long rollercoaster career, "In full confidence that it will serve a useful purpose, and will therefore achieve a deserved success."

At fifty cents a copy or $1.50 per annum, the slick bulky quarterly looked impressive, perhaps daunting to the average magazine reader. It had an ambitious editorial policy which was to include poetry, essays, reviews, biographical material (then in very short supply), photos and reproduction of paintings in monotone. Contributors were paid little if anything. The editorial board, nothing. It was a labour of love.

The first issue, January 1919, set the pattern. Its eighty-five large pages began with an editorial proclaiming its broad non-sectional attitude and a program that would examine the state of culture in one province after another.

The contents included: "A Need for more Bookishness in Canada" — a symposium of opinions from a dozen Canadian men outstanding in business, education and religion; "The Book Agent," an essay by Stephen Leacock; "Some Canadian Illustrators," by St.

George Burgoyne; "A Review of Historical Publications of the Year 1918," by W. Stewart Wallace, University of Toronto librarian; a bibliography of mining books; "Canada's First Publishing House" (the Methodist Book Room) by E.J. Moore, book steward of the Ryerson Press; "Twentieth Century Librarianship," by Mary J.L. Black (later outstanding librarian at Thunder Bay); as well as some verse and book reviews of topical interest. It carried many small advertisements for new books, mostly non-Canadian, since Canadian publishers were also agencies of foreign firms.

In a later issue, J.M. Gibbon's new novel *Drums Afar* was touted by his publisher S.B. Gundy of Toronto, as "the spiritual pilgrimage of a young Oxford student . . . who finally grasps the meaning of his life when his country calls to him at the outbreak of the Great War. Montreal provides a very vivid background for the most dramatic passages of the love story."

But the reviewer inside played no favourites, and condemned the novel as "dull and pedestrian." In compensation, the friendly editor tucked in the information that Gibbon was "the most important novelist domiciled in Canada," an overstatement indeed, although in education, John Murray Gibbon outranked many others.

The first president of the yet unborn Canadian Authors Association, Gibbon, son of Sir William, spent his earliest years in Ceylon, graduated from Oxford with a first class in *Literae Humaniores*, did post-graduate work at Göttingen, Sweden, in Sanskrit, and Greek archeology. His keen interest in folksong and Canada's ethnic origins produced several volumes more durable than his novels, particularly his *Canadian Mosaic*.

For all the tempting array, subscriptions for the magazine did not rush in on flood-tide. After publishing for two years, the editorial committee and the publishers admitted themselves baffled. They conceded:

> We have learned a lot. We imagined that there was an important place among the publications of Canada for a magazine devoted exclusively to Canadian arts and letters. We know now that there are not enough people genuinely interested in literature and the creative arts in Canada to support a magazine even so inexpensive as the *Canadian Bookman*. At any rate, we have put what money we had, and all th etime we could spare into this venture. But to survive, a magazine needs subscribers in larger numbers than we have been able to secure, more

advertisers than we have had, and rather more of a sporting leg up from the Governments of Canada. We hate to allow the *Bookman* to die . . . What we shall do next is not clear to us . . .

The demise of the *Canadian Bookman* was a major topic of conversation when Stephen Leacock (McGill Dept. of Economics) hosted a luncheon for Pelham Edgar, of the English Department, University of Toronto. Edgar had contributed to the magazine, and was well aware of its financial straits. B.K. Sandwell and Murray Gibbon were the other guests.

Contributors got some heated opinions off their chests, and words like "literary piracy" and "printshop iniquity" were some of the epithets cast at Canada's new Copyright Bill, which had had one reading in Parliament but had not yet become law.

Leacock, whose humourous essays had won a large international following, was particularly incensed, since the proposed clauses would give Canadian printers the right to reproduce any book by a Canadian, with or without the author's permission, and Leacock was an obvious victim.

"Those atrocious perversions of the right to copy were grafted in by a special interest lobby of greedy Toronto printers," he snorted.

"I'm confident that our Members of Parliament don't fully comprehend the purport of the clauses," Sandwell soothed.

"Then they shouldn't be making laws," snapped Gibbon, who rarely used three words if two would do.

"How many people understand perfectly the complexities of copyright? I'm sure most authors don't," said Edgar. "Including me."

"It really isn't all that complicated, and authors *should* know their rights." Leacock's humor went underground, and he was dead serious. "If we had a strong body of authors in Canada, we could make our position plain. But the Canadian authors are scattered all across the country, and scarce, besides."

"There are more than you might think," rejoined Sandwell. "We turned up quite a number when we were drumming up our subscription list. If we could assemble them for a meeting, we could explain copyright so they could understand it and what it means to each of them. Then we would have a forceful voice."

"Better plan for more than one meeting," Edgar commented with a smile. "It's likely to be a long fight."

"We'll have to act fast, or they'll slip the Bill through under our noses," urged Gibbon.

They decided to call an indignation meeting for Saturday, March 12, 1921.

"What about your March issue?" Edgar enquired.

"I really don't know how I can manage it," Sandwell replied. "It will probably be late, with all this other planning to do."

In fact, the March issue of the *Bookman* never did go to press. The editorial committee was too busy at the *accouchement* of the Canadian Authors Association, and by the June deadline, the masthead bore the words, "Official Organ of the Canadian Authors Association," a responsibility too heavy for such infant shoulders. Sandwell persuaded the publisher, J.J. Harpell, president of the Industrial & Education Press at Ste. Anne de Bellevue, to continue the quarterly as the official organ until the Association got on its feet. And for probably the first time in history, a Canadian Anglophone magazine carried part of its text in French. Thus the moribund *Canadian Bookman* became a pioneer in bilingualism.

Although the quarterly gained subscribers through the new Association, there were still too few to finance the *Bookman*. The magazine was sold in December to the Bookcraft Publishing Co. of Toronto, whose proprietor was Findlay I. Weaver.

Mr. Weaver felt the periodical should come out monthly to sustain interest. In January 1922, he sensibly cut the size to 7"x10", coated stock gave way to newsprint, and he reduced the price to twenty-five cents per copy. A coloured cover, graced by a Thoreau Macdonald woodcut, bore the words, "A monthly devoted to Literature, the Library and the Printed Book." It also carried pages for book collectors. For a year, it claimed to be "the Organ of the Canadian Authors Association," though the CAA only purchased three pages of space, at fifteen dollars a page, for news of its membership.

In short order, the Association began to produce its own *Authors' Bulletin*. The Association of Canadian Bookmen changed character to become a group of Toronto publishers. They advertised their wares in the *Bookman,* domestic (few) and imported (many) — and understandably didn't countenance unfavourable reviews, whether for Edgar Wallace's mysteries, or the popular homespun frontier fiction of Ralph Connor and H.A. Cody, both of whom were on hand for the birth of the Canadian Authors Association.

Chapter 2
The Canadian Authors Meet

"My private secretary is a rare one — she knows everybody and everything," Sandwell remarked one day soon after the luncheon. "She's already sent out a couple of hundred invitations."

"How many do you expect?" asked Gibbon.

"Oh, they won't all come, of course. She's including publishers, too. After all, it's in their interests as well."

"Where will you hold the meeting?" Gibbon was used to considering such details in connection with CPR hotels.

"Why, here at the Club, of course," Leacock offered.

Sandwell's indefatigable secretary dredged up some 800 names of Canadian authors living at home or abroad, writers of fiction and non-fiction, of poetry chapbooks or political treatises. Prime Minister William Lyon Mackenzie King was on the list. So were French-writing poets, historians and librarians. W.D. Lighthall, lawyer and littérateur, came up with a list of poets he kept in touch with for twenty years after his anthology *Songs of the Great Dominion* was published.

Frank L. Packard of Lachine and New York, author of the popular Jimmie Dale mysteries, was invited; Robert W. Service, who wrote *Songs of a Sourdough*, now living in France; Rev. Basil King, originally of Prince Edward Island, now pastor of a fashionable church in Cambridge, Mass.; Arthur Stringer, popular novelist and screenwriter, living in New York; Bliss Carman, outstanding poet, domiciled in Connecticut; Theodore Goodridge Roberts, war correspondent, living in London; and Dr. Charles G.D. Roberts, his more famous brother, roaming Europe where his animal books found ready sale in translation.

As acceptances and some 300 supportive regrets trickled back, the organizing committee was chagrined to learn that the majority attending were to be women. They could make the time for travel. This discovery was the more disconcerting when it was realized that the ladies' facilities of the University Club consisted of little more than a cubby-hole. And at least fifty women were coming!

"Perhaps we could obtain use of the Old Medical Building," Sandwell proposed. After all, he was teaching at McGill. So was Leacock. They advanced their best arguments to Sir Andrew Macphail, professor of the history of medicine at McGill, and he gave them leave. Not only that, but he attended the conference, being a writer himself.

Thus the first assemblage of the Canadian authors was held March 12, 1921 amid bunsen burners and blackboards. Authors present numbered from 96 to 150, depending on which report you believed. A close scan puts the figure at 110. Few outside Montreal had ever met before, and many durable friendships were quickly formed, and shop-talk buzzed.

The organizing committee held an all-male preliminary meeting on the Friday, the day before the conference. Dr. Pelham Edgar pointed out the need for committees, and the fact that if the organization proved permanent, it would need a draft constitution, subject to revision.

Half a dozen were appointed to this committee, including token females, and all looked at one another blankly.

"Who's had any experience with this sort of thing?" asked the chairman, John Murray Gibbon.

Dead silence.

"Well, I've got a copy of the Constitution of the Isaac Walton League of America at home," Gibbon said. "Perhaps we can adapt that."

Years later he recalled its beginnings for the CAA membership.

> When I got home I realized the difference between fishing and book-writing. All I could get out of that constitution was that it was broken into paragraphs and sections and sub-sections and by-laws. The result was that we had to work late, and I sat up all night to concoct something more to the point. The meeting was scheduled to start that morning at ten o'clock. At nine-thirty I received a telephone message to be sure to turn up, particularly

as the promoters had decided to put my name up as first President.

I still had to write that part of the constitution dealing with the French Section. Fortunately on arriving at the Old Medical Building, I saw a handsome French-Canadian, black-bearded, moustached, whose name I was told was Louvigny de Montigny, from the law department of the federal government. Instinct told me that he was an expert on constitutions, and so it proved, for he completed the document to the taste of his fellow linguists. In the afternoon session, he also proved to have the whole subject of copyright at his finger tips, and was a tower of strength to the Association in the ensuing battles on Parliament Hill.

My own selection as President, I soon learned, was due to the fact that I could travel on a CPR pass and organize the Canadian Authors at no cost to the Association. The real work was done by the secretary, B.K. Sandwell.

Despite the uncertainties, the provisional constitution was quite polished. It provided for a central office at each of four locations rotating on a two-year term, first in Montreal, then Ottawa, Toronto and Winnipeg; at least one branch in each province; a national president, a secretary and a treasurer; and twelve vice-presidents. These executive members, as well as a number of elected representatives, would comprise a Council whose number would not exceed forty. There was to be a self-governing French-Canadian Section, *La Section Française.*

The objectives of the Association were:

1. To act for the mutual benefit and protection of Canadian Authors and for the maintenance of high ideals and practice in the literary profession.

2. To procure adequate copyright legislation.

3. To assist in protecting the literary property of its members, and to disseminate information as to the business rights and interests of its members as authors.

4. To promote the general professional interests of all creators of copyrightable material.

5. To encourage the cordial relationships among the members and with authors of other nations.

Sir Arthur Currie, principal and vice-chancellor of McGill,

23

welcomed the authors to Montreal, "a fitting place in which to hold the first convention of Canadian authors, in that it is a city in which two people and two languages are blended."

The conference was chaired by Dr. George H. Locke, chief librarian, Toronto Public Libraries, and author of *When Canada was New France*.

The chairman first called upon the Resolutions Committee and B.K. Sandwell stood up, and introduced his resolution by saying,

> The size and personnel of the present assembly affords ample justification for any action it might take on behalf of Canadian writers as a class.

> Therefore be it resolved that in view of the great increase in books and other copyrightable material issued by Canadian authors, the interests of such authors would be furthered by the establishment of an association with branches in convenient centres, the object of such an association being mutual benefit.

This resolution was seconded by Basil King in an eloquent oration and heartily approved by the great majority of those present. Thus the Canadian Authors Association came into being with enthusiasm and optimism.

Dr. Locke left the chair to move that there be vigorous and increased effort to enlarge public reading by promotion and extension of libraries. Approved.

Moved by Dr. Pelham Edgar that the Canadian Authors Association extend a welcome to authors of other countries. Approved.

Moved by Col. Vernon Mackenzie of *Maclean's Magazine*, that an effort be made to have newspapers include more material concerning literature. Approved.

The Nominating Committee reported next, and the slate of executive officers was voted in by ballot. President: John Murray Gibbon; Secretary: B.K. Sandwell; Treasurer: W. Stewart Wallace. Vice-presidents elected were: Dr. Archibald MacMechan, Dalhousie University, Halifax; Canon H.A. Cody, Saint John, N.B., a prolific writer of backwoods historical adventures; Dr. Pelham Edgar; Prof. W.T. Allison, University of Manitoba, Winnipeg; Nellie McClung of Calgary, author of *Sowing Seeds in Danny* and many more; Isabel Ecclestone Mackay of Vancouver, noted for short stories, plays and poetry, as in the *The Shining Ship*; Basil King; Thomas Chapais of Quebec City.

A large Council of twenty-two included Hector Garneau,

Montreal Public Library; Louvigny de Montigny, Ottawa lawyer; Lloyd Roberts, Ottawa, son of Charles G.D. Roberts; Dr. W.D. Lighthall, Montreal lawyer and author; Sir Andrew Macphail, critic, essayist, of Montreal; novelists Frank L. Packard and Arthur Stringer of New York, and "Ralph Connor" of Winnipeg; poets Bliss Carman, Robert Service and Duncan Campbell Scott.

Here also was found room for women authors such as Jessie G. Sime (Montreal); Agnes Laut, New York historian; American-born Madge Macbeth (Ottawa); Judge Emily Murphy ("Janey Canuck") Edmonton; Lucy Doyle, journalist on the *Toronto Telegram*; poets Marjorie Pickthall (Victoria) and Florence Randal Livesay (Toronto).

Montreal newspapers covered the conference's shorter speeches, but ignored the serious ones on copyright and the resolutions. They gave special emphasis to the crowning social event, the dinner at Hotel Place Viger. Well-pleased with the day's accomplishments, the authors arrived in their finest attire, the men in dinner jackets and stiff wing collars, the women in long-waisted gowns of georgette spangled with beads. Some wore bandeaux across their foreheads. The chandeliers glittered on pince-nez, rimless glasses and the occasional monocle. It was a gala event, filled with a sense of virtue and nobility of purpose, borne out by the many short speeches of the evening.

Stephen Leacock, the real "begetter" of the enterprise, presided. He would, no doubt, have been the Association's first president, except that he planned to be in England for a year. He began with a toast, "To Canadian literature." Explaining that he had to leave early, he quipped,

> I had intended reviewing the whole history of literature in the Dominion, from the foundation to the top, . . . but a fortunate misadventure has intervened to deliver you from that infliction. I have to catch a train to Toronto.

On March 17, 1961, the Montreal branch held a fortieth anniversary dinner meeting, where Leslie Gordon Barnard recalled this inaugural dinner and even unearthed a menu of that historic occasion.

> It was a decidedly "posh" affair — preceded by lines of waiters bearing aloft trays of Malpeque oysters. These were followed by turtle soup, Paupiette of sole, Supreme of chicken, Filet of beef, and the whole works from then on. . . . I was a very immature

writer, just commencing my profession. I was soon to learn that this was not the style in which free-lance writers customarily lived!

No wonder Arthur Stringer's brief speech was a eulogy to the quality of refreshment in Montreal, and he expressed a hope to share there many anniversaries of the "birthday of Canadian letters."

Basil King maintained that the proper function of the Canadian writer was to act as a hyphen between the United States and Great Britain, so that American and Britisher might both learn to understand one another.

All the speakers expressed confidence in the new organization and its objectives. Louvigny de Montigny quoted Dr. Marius Barbeau (Ottawa) in commenting that three hundred years ago, the Indian tribes had a copyright law better than any at present existing in Canada. Every family had its family song, and no one dared quote from or sing the song of another family without acknowledging whose property it was. It was to be hoped that with the help of the newly-founded Authors Association, Canadian letters would soon attain that stage of advancement. Mlle. Margaret Gascoigne sang another of her French-Canadian folksongs, assuring the delighted diners that it was out of copyright.

The highlight of the evening came as a surprise to all. A tall lean figure in wide-brimmed black hat and long cape stood at the door of the diningroom. "Bliss Carman!" gasped those at nearby tables, and the entire assembly rose to its feet, clapping. He had been invited, but replied that he would be on a reading tour at the time. If he could arrange it, he would conclude in Montreal, perhaps in time to join the conference. And here he was, gaunt from a recent illness and travel-weary. But he took the podium with a flourish, told briefly of his tour through several Canadian cities, and of a gratifying response.

Bliss Carman read eloquently a short poem on Marshall Foch, "The Man of the Marne," and in response to enthusiastic applause, as an encore he read "Roadside Flowers."

But what did the writers learn about copyright, the very reason for coming together? Was there only de Montigny's glance at history? Far from it. Montreal coverage had not mentioned one word about copyright. Perhaps it was as baffling to them as to the politicians. The authors, however, came away with a thorough knowledge of the situation, after Louvigny de Montigny took them through the background of copyright in Canada up to the present time. It was a long afternoon session.

Chapter 3
Copy, Copy, Who's Got the Right to Copy?

It all began with piracy — legal literary piracy.

The invention of movable type made it easy to produce multiple copies of a piece of writing, with or without the writer's permission. Until it was clear who owned the right to copy literary output, there could be no security for the artist. Nor for his publisher. The battle between "What's good for the public" versus "What's good for the originator" began centuries ago, and keeps cropping up in various forms in various countries, and will continue in an increasingly technological world.

Oddly enough, the Canadian determination to enact their own copyright law was one of the first small rebellions against British Imperial rule, and the effort toward legislation was confused and uneven.

In 1921, the Hon. Hugh Guthrie, acting solicitor-general in the Meighen government, declared to the House of Commons, "I don't know any more complicated piece of legislation which comes before this house than this same copyright question. As far back as I have been member of this house, and long before I came into this house, it has proved a very very troublesome question."

As far back as 1832, legislators had yawned when the legislature of Lower Canada passed the basic rules of copyright protection. When Lower and Upper Canada became a single colony, the new Canada Act provided protection for authors living in the Province of Canada, with respect to books, maps, charts, musical compositions, prints and engravings. A few years later, the provisions

28

were extended to British authors — if their works were printed and published in the colony.

Originally each country or principality made its own laws to protect the interests of its citizens. All outsiders' writing was fair game to the literary pirates of another country.

Confederation became the occasion for a flexing of national literary muscle. Indeed, Confederation spawned "the headwaters of Canadian literature." Obviously, the powers of the new federal government needed to include copyright, patents at the very least. The first Canadian Act regarding copyright was passed in 1868. Books to be protected under the Act had to be published in the Dominion of Canada. This Act was disallowed by the Ontario Court of Appeal on the grounds that it conflicted with British Imperial legislation.

Colonial politicians were dismayed and frustrated, but they no longer bowed meekly to the Imperial voice. Wranglings and accusations hurtled back and forth by sailing packet and steamer, until 1875 when the Dominion Act was passed, and ratified that same year by Imperial statute. The squabble was by no means as dramatic as the burning of the Parliament Building in Montreal, but it served the same notice of independent action.

Nevertheless, an international spirit was rising. In 1886, a group of European countries showed a much broader vision by forming a copyright union and adopting a Convention in Berne, Switzerland, now revised every decade to keep pace with changing technology. Its purpose was to establish a uniform minimum grant of protection to the creators of copyrightable material — words, music, pictures, dance, sculpture — and ensure that the creators of work copyrighted in one country which subscribed to the Convention, should enjoy in all subscribing countries the same rights as granted to their nationals.

Great Britain joined on behalf of all her colonies and dominions.

The United States of America has never joined the Berne Convention, though it is a founding member of the Universal Copyright Convention, child of the United Nations. US printers' organizations insisted upon "the pernicious manufacturing clause" in its Copyright Act. This clause demanded that the owner of a book or periodical first published outside the US could receive protection for only five years. Yet if the owner imported into the US more than 1,500 copies — or failed to be printed in the US during that period — his US copyright protection ceased.

Canadian printers and authors railed against the iniquitous attitude of American printers, but could do little more until the Toronto Agreement of 1968 loosened the shackles somewhat for Canada.

Canada's struggle over copyright won for herself and for other far-flung colonies and dominions the right to enact legislation of their own. The other countries of the British Empire might simply adopt the Imperial Act. Not Canada. She wanted a new and independent Act.

One of the best-known examples of such insubordination was made clear in the judgment arising from *Smiles* v. *Belford, 1875.* Here the printing clause in Canadian legislation which required British works to be eligible for copyright only if printed in Canada, came into dispute.

Mr. Belford was an articulate fighter. In a scathing preface to a cheap edition of Mark Twain's *The Prince and the Pauper*, Toronto, Rose-Belford, 1882, he wrote caustically:

> The importers of this cheap edition of the *Prince and the Pauper* do not disguise their motives in placing it on the Canadian market. Their object is to show, by its importation into, and sale in Canada, *as a foreign reprint of a work which has secured British copyright,* how anomalous is the present law of Literature in the Colonies, and how injuriously and in an especial degree, this affects Canadian printing and publishing industries.
>
> It will be remembered that some weeks ago, Mr. Clemens (Mark Twain) issued by arrangement with a Montreal firm, a Canadian edition of the present work for which, on the plea of a temporary residence in the country, he sought copyright at Ottawa. This, for the reason that the author's brief sojourn in the Dominion while his book was passing through the press, did not legally constitute 'a domicile' was properly refused.

Twain easily got around that by publishing in England, which gave him access to the Canadian market, to the rage of Canadian printers, especially as his own government granted no reciprocal privileges. Mr. Belford practically frothed at the mouth:

> To extend an American author protection in Canada as the result of British copyright legislation, while the Dominion is the slaughter market for American piracies of English copyrights, seems the act of unwisdom. Yet as the English Act has jurisdic-

tion in Canada, Canadian publishers are restrained by fines and imprisonment from reprinting an American book which has happened to secure copyright in England. Fortunately by the provision of an Order in Council passed in 1842, foreign reprints of British copyright are free to come into the Colonies on payment of an author's royalty of 12½%, and the added fiscal duty imposed by the Colony.

What Canadian publishers are prevented from doing to supply their own market, an alien can do, and the native industries that might be aided have to give place to those of a foreign country in catering for whatever market exists in Canada.

Still, in the Revised Statutes of 1906, the Canadian government had gained little. It did not yet have exclusive jurisdiction over copyright, so that protection was still extended to all citizens of the British Empire and those "of any country which has an international copyright treaty with Britain," which included the United States of America. Such creators could thus obtain copyright in Canada, without conforming to the conditions of the 1875 Canada Act (disallowed) by which books and periodical material must be printed in Canada to obtain Canadian copyright.

Two years later, Twain was making sure that his latest book, *The Adventures of Huckleberry Finn* had full protection. It was published in England, and Twain spent an afternoon in Fort Erie, Ontario, while the book was being printed. Simultaneously, ten copies were produced in Boston to satisfy American copyright regulations.

The action we have taken (of importing a cheap edition) nullifies in great measure, the benefit which Imperial copyright affords the author in Canada; and this course we feel we are justified in adopting so long as United States government refuses to accord to British or Colonial authors reciprocal legislation, and while American publishers are free to flood Canadian markets with reprints of English books which native printers and publishers are restrained from themselves producing. In this course of action, the present importers feel that the Canadian public will, until these restrictions and anomalies are removed, heartily uphold them.

Mr. Belford's message reached many receptive ears, and it sounded only reasonable to Canadian printers and publishers, who were the chief victims of the US manufacturing clause. When talk

31

began about a revision of the Canadian Copyright Act, the printers were ready. Led by veteran printer Dan Rose, they lobbied for the inclusion of several retaliatory clauses, whereby they hoped to offset the loss of business to American printers and publishers. These three offending clauses in Bill 12 gave any Canadian applicant a license to print any book or magazine material, authored by a Canadian and first published outside Canada, with or without the author's consent:

> 13. (1) Any person may apply to the Minister for a license to print and publish in Canada any book wherein copyright subsists, if at any time after publication and within the duration of the copyright the owner of the copyright fails:
>
> (a) to print the said book or cause the same to be printed in Canada;
> (b) to supply by means of copies so printed the reasonable demands of the Canadian market for such a book.
>
> 14. (1) If the publication of a book is lawfully begun as a serial elsewhere than in His Majesty's Dominions . . . and the owner of the copyright has refused to grant a license to any person in Canada being publisher of a periodical, to publish such book in serial form, a license may in the discretion of the Minister be granted to any person in Canada . . . to publish such book once in serial form in the said periodical . . .
>
> 15. (1) Every license issued under sections . . . 13 or 14 shall be deemed to constitute a contract . . . between the owner of the copyright and the licensee shall be entitled to the like remedies as in the case of a contract.

Revision of the Copyright Act had begun years before but was interrupted by the Great War, and shelved until 1919. Hon. Herbert Mowat could declare to the House of Commons, "Canadian copyright legislation, which has been the despair of judges and lawyers for many years, will become more coherent only when all Imperial copyright jurisdiction is repealed."

That happened in Bill 12, which had its first reading in 1921. This Bill revoked all enactments relating to copyright passed by the British Parliament, and also wiped out the Canada Act of 1875.

Creators of copyrightable material were expected to be happy with the provisions of the new act, which was kinder to them than any previous copyright law. It extended the span of copyright from twenty-eight years to the life of the author plus fifty years after his death. No longer must an author publish in Canada for copyright protection. Even unpublished work was protected by statute. Intellectual property was recognized as part of personal property.

Further, the Bill gave more protection to playwrights, choreographers, to wordless drama (mime), and even to two new methods of communicating intellectual property — cinematography and radio broadcasting. Previously, a novel could be dramatized by anybody provided the result was sufficiently different from the original. Similarly with movie-making, or reproduction by mechanical means as on a phonograph record. Indeed, the new law expanded the old act to twenty comprehensive definitions.

One would have thought the authors would be content with an act much better than anything before, and considerably better than the US Copyright Act. And they would have been thankful except for those licensing clauses. These darkened relations between author and publisher (who often did his own printing in those days) since the authors (or composers or designers) felt that copyright should protect the creator, while the printer-publisher felt that copyright should meet public demand.

The Manufacturers' Association, the Trades and Labor Congress, and the phonograph recording companies supported the printers, and when the Canadian Authors Association popped up at the eleventh hour, it

> had to assault a Government protected within a well-walled, heavily fortified and plentifully munitioned city.

An editorial in the *Canadian Bookman* sneered at the argument that these clauses would eventually persuade the United States into a more generous printing policy with Canada.

> Canada has no power in this instance. These clauses are like a weapon too heavy for the bearer, and too short to inflict the slightest damage to the adversary.

The *Bookman* viewed with apprehension, the government offer to collect royalties for the author, wondering

> how much zeal and energy it would display, having no financial interest. Should the author be put to the trouble and expense of collecting merely to provide more work for Canadian printers? The whole proposal is nothing more than old-fashioned piracy; the licenses might not inaptly be described as letters of marque.

33

The Society of Authors in England considered the new act a legislative step backward, pernicious and unjust:

> The Canadian government is unwisely and short-sightedly subordinating the future of the author to the immediate interests of a small group of printers.

Le Droit d'Auteur, organ of the Berne Convention (as translated in the *Bookman*), regarded the compulsory licensing clauses as having evoked a dangerous situation. Such legislation would incline the USA to reach some kind of agreement with Canada, (thus delaying a longed-for universal copyright agreement), and perhaps to follow suit with its own appropriations of literary material:

> Piracy will be revived to the great prejudice of the authors of both countries, whose markets would undoubtedly be flooded with spurious editions.

In the House of Commons debate raged in unheard-of length and intensity. Discussions were heated and divided, particularly when the House met in committee on Bill 12, to amend the opposing claims of authors and printers. It was ironic that the new copyright act, which was meant to provide more protection to the author, should actually provide less. However, by attempting to protect the interests of the printers, the government had succeeded in alienating the authors at home, offending copyright institutions abroad, and created hostility between Canadian author and his printer-publisher.

The debate of May 25, 1921 was one of the most extensive ever recorded in *Hansard*, the official record of Parliamentary proceedings. It was a discussion that crossed party lines. Conservative Prime Minister Arthur Meighen and Liberal leader Mackenzie King were both on the side of the authors. King, in the Opposition, had earlier defended the rights of Canadian authors: "they have a hard enough struggle as it is to make anything out of their writings . . . and in an enactment of this kind, we should aim primarily at protecting them."

A Liberal from Nova Scotia took a forthright stand. "I want to enter my protest against Clauses 13, 14 and 15. I regard them as an unjustifiable interference with the rights of Canadian authors. They will certainly not receive as much for their work, as they would by being published outside Canada."

Several honourable members argued for retaining the compulsory licensing clauses, particularly 14, which allowed Canadian magazines eager to build circulation with popular writers, to lift articles or stories written by Canadians which appeared in US periodicals.

The Hon. C. Doherty, Minister of Justice, tried another tack. "Might we not appeal to the Canadian author . . . not to be absolutely selfish, but to have some thought for the Canadian printer or publisher who has contributed his part to the book? Such a financial sacrifice is surely not too much to ask from a writer who should, after all, be interested in the growth of his own country."

The Copyright Committee of the Canadian Authors Association went over the Act word by word, and reported the flaws they found.

> We quite realize that those who have had to draft this bill have been faced with the difficulty of securing adequate information, in the absence of any organization such as the Canadian Authors Association which would co-ordinate the experience of Canadian authors scattered throughout the Dominion and other countries as to conditions affecting their copyrights. We trust that now this information is available it will be accepted in the spirit in which it is offered, namely to promote the best interests of Canadian literature . . .
>
> This bill proposes to establish formalities in contravention of the spirit and letter of the revised Berne Convention; and would result in Canada being ranked as an outlaw nation in regard to international copyright. The licensing clauses deprive the author of his right to make his own terms with the licensee, hand over that right at an arbitrary figure under conditions which would permit the licensee to garble or abbreviate the work, to bring out a cheap edition without regard to appearance, and to prevent the importation of a correct or more presentable appearance for a period of fifty years.
>
> So far as serial rights are concerned, the clauses are drawn up in evident ignorance of the conditions governing serial publication today, would produce disastrous confusion and would inflict grave hardships on a very large number of Canadian authors without conferring any benefit on Canadian literature . . .

When the latter problems were fully explained, the clause regarding serial rights was withdrawn, especially as it would be unacceptable to the Berne Convention, which Canada was eager to join.

Louvigny de Montigny pointed out that:

Canada being a possession of the British Empire, the application must be presented by the British government, which would be obliged to support the request by a certificate that Canada has enacted legislation sufficient to qualify her for accession. Thus the question of conformity or otherwise of the licensing clauses to the Berne Convention will next come up to be passed on by the British government, which, if it sees fit, may refuse to grant any such certificate. It is obvious that this would create a very embarrassing situation between the Canadian and British governments.

Le Droit d'Auteur, expressed the opinion that

the licensing clauses could not apply to any books except those of Canadians themselves and of the citizens of non-union countries.

And the important non-union country was the United States, which had a private agreement with Great Britain!

De Montigny went on:

The authors of the clauses did not dare to press for the right of licensed piracy of *serial* publication, although they were ready and anxious to demand licensed piracy of *books* . . . simply due to the fact that they wanted to drive the largest possible coach-and-four through the spirit of the Berne Convention, and thought they had found a hole by which they could do so in the matter of books, while the same hole was carefully fenced up in regard to serial publication.

The Canadian government in 1922 passed an Amending Act — which repealed certain objectionable clauses as far as all other countries were concerned, but left them operative *against* Canadian writers. Lawrence J. Burpee reported wryly in the *Authors' Bulletin*, December 1928:

This satisfied the requirements of the Berne Convention because that treaty is designed to protect the interests of an author in countries other than his own. It was naturally assumed that no Parliament would inflict upon its own nationals burdens that it did not impose upon the citizens of other countries. Our Canadian Parliament demonstrated that that thing was possible.

Confusion still surrounded the copyright issue, as a humorous excerpt from *Hansard* on April 27, 1923 illustrates:

> Mr. Guthrie: ... I was satisfied when the Bill was brought before, and I am just as firmly satisfied now, that apart from the Minister himself (Robb) there is not a man in the Committee at this precise moment who understands this legislation.
>
> Mr. Robb: You might include me.

The battle seemed hopeless when Mr. Robb, Minister of Trade, determined to limit the debate. Ready or not, he set January 1, 1924, as the date for proclaiming Canada's new copyright law. The CAA Copyright Committee urged another six months delay, but to no avail.

The Act was passed. But there was still some hope of amendments to it. The Canadian Authors Association drummed up support in newspapers and from a few MPs, notably the Hon. Edgar Chevrier, until at length, Parliament set up a special committee to study the matter. Its report, an impressive and exhaustive 300-page document was presented to the House of Commons on May 29, 1925. The influence of the Association was evident throughout the findings, buttressed by telegrams from respected authors and speeches of leading members of the Association.

The first witness called was Dr. Lawrence J. Burpee, Canadian secretary of the International Joint Commission and a noted historian. As president of the CAA that year, he stressed the size and composition of the membership which included not only novelists, but historians and poets such as Bliss Carman; as well, it included some of the best-known artists, musicians and distinguished librarians. He submitted resolutions or letters from other notable and respected organizations and stated:

> The Copyright Act defines copyright as 'the sole right to produce or reproduce the work or any substantial part thereof in material form', yet it contains provisions that directly conflict with its definition ... Those compulsory licensing clauses are humiliating to the Canadian-born artist. After all, the poor devil of a Canadian writer is made the victim, while the mantle of justice is thrown over authors of France and England, Italy and Spain.

John Murray Gibbon, first National President of the Canadian Authors Association, fully supported Burpee's views, though personally he believed little use would be made of the licensing clauses, but they should be hedged with restrictions.

The third witness was Stephen Leacock, not droll but vitriolic:

> If you take away my copyright, you are stealing from me, and I will not listen to the idea that you are thereby helping to build up the printing trade; as if there was any comparison between the protection of literature and the purely mechanical material in the printing trade of a country. I am afraid that there are some people in this country who would measure out the greatness of Shakespeare according to the number of copies of his works, and the number of employees who would set the type.

Louvigny de Montigny brought the rhetoric down to a prosaic level from his own experience:

> Up to now, I have had only one book published, chiefly because the printing of that one book has already cost me $900. Had it been printed in Europe, it would have cost me merely one-quarter of the Canadian price. The book had to be sold for $1 a copy, to cover expenses, too high a price for a Canadian book of that kind.

The last CAA witness was Judge Edouard Fabre Surveyer (Montreal), second vice-president of the French Section, CAA who said firmly:

> The right of ownership is the most absolute, complete and purest right we have. These clauses not only will hurt literary production, but they have already done so. The sensitive author, thinking that his country no longer has any interest in protecting his works, will be offended and distressed and no longer interested in publishing in Canada. If the writer sees that he is disregarded even among legislators who are supposed to be well-informed of the needs of the country, he may well give up the profession.

The Senate displayed the same confusion, stubborness and boredom as the House of Commons. Several French-speaking senators, notably L.O. David, Dandurand and Belcourt were not intimidated by the nationalistic attitude of Sir James Lougheed who declared, "I am not in sympathy with the unrestricted protection which is sought by the authors. The public should have some rights . . ."

"But who are the public that these clauses endeavour to protect?" demanded Senator Belcourt. "They are the men who publish, the printers, the men who deal in phonographs . . . All this grand talk about the public is, in street language, just rot."

Canadian authors had one more string to their bow — the Rome Convention, which was being held in 1927 on its ten-year cycle of revising the Berne Convention. Canada had been eager for admittance into the union, even to the unheard-of-extent of penalizing its native-born authors. Canada, the last in the British Empire to accede to Berne, drew upon a little-known protocol (the only country to do so) and "slipped in by the back door."

"Canada should be directly and independently represented," read the CAA letter to Prime Minister W.L.M. King, "and not merely through the British delegation as in the past. Canada has copyright problems peculiar to itself."

The Canadian government sent two representatives to Rome. The Canadian Authors Association, funded only by its five dollar dues, sent Dr. Burpee, at a cost of $750.

When Bill 12 became the Canadian Copyright Act on January 1, 1924, Judge Fabre Surveyer's prediction came to pass. Some authors departed their native land in high dudgeon. One of these, Arthur Heming, popular author-illustrator of *The Drama of the Forests*, left for New England, complaining bitterly:

> This law is the last straw. The government wants me to starve to death so I can't write any more. I sell to twenty-six magazines; only four of them Canadian, and those four have paid me a total of $4,000 — spread over thirty-six years. US editors not only pay better but they are more businesslike. If I sell my work to American magazines, this law denies me the right to protect my work in Canada, although it grants the right for any German living in Germany to sell his work in the United States and pro-tect it in Canada; and it forces me to accept any ridiculous price that a Canadian publisher cares to set on my work. The only way a Canadian author can protect his work in Canada is to swear allegiance to a foreign country and then that privilege is at once granted to him.

Many more defections occurred less dramatically, as Cana-dians yielded to the twin lures of American publishing. Robert Watson, editor of the Hudson's Bay Company quarterly *Beaver* and prolific writer of northern adventures, abandoned Vancouver for Hollywood.

It was nothing new for authors to turn their backs on Canada for greener fields. After the Confederation euphoria subsided, Canadian nationalism had slumped, and with it the heady dream of a distinctively Canadian literature, despite a small upsurge in literary works in the 1890s.

Gilbert Parker left for England, bestsellerdom, a seat in Parliament, and a knighthood. Ernest Thompson Seton wandered from Toronto's Don Valley to the high mesas of New Mexico. Bliss Carman found Connecticut more cherishing of his genius, and Charles G.D. Roberts dryly summed it up in a rhyme in the *Bookman*, "The Poet is Bidden to Manhattan Island":

> "You've piped at home where none could pay,
>   Till now I trust your wits are riper.
> Make no delay but come this way
>   And pipe for them that pay the piper."

Roberts had found New York more receptive of his poems and short stories, and his animal tales proved very lucrative. Foreign translations encouraged his European wanderings. Frank L. Packard of Lachine accepted the invitation, and his hero Jimmie Dale romped through many popular mysteries in New York and California. Basil King, pseudonym of the Rev. C.W. King of Prince Edward Island, found enthusiasm for his novels, as well as his very popular *The Conquest of Fear*, in his fashionable congregation in Cambridge, Mass.

So the battle over copyright was lost after seven years, except for some small harassments. And what about those clauses which Stephen Leacock denigrated as "a dead letter which stinks in the nostrils of all right-thinking men?" They are still in the Canadian Copyright Act in 1981, but totally inert. The Ilsley Report on Copyright recommended their repeal in 1957. Nothing happened. Twenty years later, Keyes and Brunet in their *Copyright in Canada: Proposals for a Revision* urged their removal, pointing out that the clauses had never been called into use.

Murray Gibbon foresaw their worthlessness in a statement made to the Canadian Authors Association in 1925.

> The whole question is rather academic, because up to the present time, the only license that has been asked for or obtained is for a cookbook. That, I suppose, bears out the old rhyme:
>> "We can live without poets
>> Or painters or books,
>> But civilized man
>> Cannot live without cooks."

After seven years of altruistic struggle and expense, countless hours of unpaid effort, what had the authors achieved? They were organized into an articulate body, no longer too isolated and timid to speak up for themselves and their convictions.

Legislatively, they could claim some modest success. The clause regarding serials, which had been a great hardship to magazine writers, was withdrawn. The license term was cut from fifty years to five, and then only *at the discretion* (an important three words) of the Minister of Trade and Commerce; the author was assured of his royalties at a negotiated rate; he could buy as many copies of his own book as he desired; he could now demand the return of his manuscript and of the copyright which had originally been assigned to the publisher; he could register his work, but it was not compulsory as in the USA.

"Above all, the Canadian Authors Association had assisted in awakening many Canadians to the need for, and place of, a unique Canadian literature," wrote Susan Sills in her Master's thesis on the role of the CAA and early copyright legislation.

In 1931, it appeared that the Canadian Parliament had forgotten all it had learned about copyright, and its obligations under the Berne Convention. It passed a law, largely at the behest of the management of the Canadian National Exhibition, Toronto, exempting "agricultural fairs, schools, churches and charities not for private gain" from paying composers and song-writers for use of their intellectual property.

Since some members of the Canadian Authors Association were musicians, e.g. (Sir) Ernest Macmillan, and many more wrote lyrics that were set to music, e.g. "Duna" by Marjorie Pickthall, the Association went to bat again. These "confiscatory clauses" allowed the free use of a composer's art without even asking leave. The churches had never requested such privileges, and indeed the Archbishop of Quebec inveighed against them.

The CAA could not prevent the passage of the unfair legislation, but continued to make its presence felt. Composers and song-writers could not live on the royalties accruing from sale of their work, especially now that radio reception was almost universal, and consequently sales of sheet music and then of wax records had dropped dismally. Now the government was further discouraging the growth of Canadian music by an uninformed law.

We protest against the national dishonour of such legislation injurious to the musical composers of our own and of other countries whom our Government, by International Treaty, has pledged our country to protect.

Shortly after that, The Canadian Performing Right Society was established. Murray Gibbon pointed out:

> Not very Canadian . . . a collection agency that operates in Canada for British and American copyright owners, who have created a virtual monopoly. The Canadian composer would have to join one of these to gain protection in Canada.

In 1936, the "pirates" encroached still further by having industrial fairs exempted, and the phrase "without private profit" deleted, when the profit went into the pockets of the actual performers. Yet that same year, a concession was made — the composer and song-writer were awarded two cents (shared) on the public performance of any recording. Little enough in the days of 78 r.p.m. records, but paltry when the long-playing records came in. The law has not recognized them yet.

There was a tremendous amount of misinformation about the methods of the Performing Right Society. "Iniquitous" and "a racket" were among the less offensive phrases bandied about. Murray Gibbon soon admitted the value of a single collecting agency, provided that Canadian lyricists and composers received their fair share of compensation. He and National Secretary Howard Angus Kennedy had appeared before a Commission studying the PRS claims, and concluded that,

> if the Canadian Performing Right Society had a couple of Canadian directors to protect the interests of Canadian copyright holders, the CAA could find no objections to its methods.

The Board of Arbitration had no authority to modify the confiscatory clauses, but enough light had been shed to defeat a further invasion of rights. A Bill was introduced, and rejected by 91 to 58 votes, which would have made it impossible to collect through any society (and how much more impossible to collect without such a society!) any fees for the use of musical works through radio or gramophone "in any store, hotel, restaurant, skating-rink, lodge-hall, community hall, entertainment hall or other public place."

In 1938, Gordon V. Thompson (Toronto), music publisher and himself a song-writer, gave a splendid speech on the subject at the CAA convention in Vancouver. He pointed out that many CAA members were vitally interested in performing rights, which might indeed become the major source of their income, in view of the shrunken sales of sheet music and recordings.

> A country needs the writers of songs just as she needs mining engineers and manufacturers. Who would ever have heard of the Swanee River without Stephen Foster's lyrics?
>
> Only last week, I assigned the copyright of my song "Campfire Memories" to Irving Berlin, Inc. of New York. In view of the fact that I am a member of the Canadian Performing Right Society, I get immediate protection in the USA, England and forty-seven other countries where performing right societies are affiliated with our own Canadian Society. Once the public understands, criticism will give way to praise.

That, of course, was prophetic, because CAPAC, (the Composers, Authors and Publishers Association of Canada) and PRO (Performing Rights Organization of Canada, formerly BMI of the USA) now collect on behalf of musicians.

There may come a day when copyright will be settled once and for all, but not likely in view of changing technology. People quickly weary of the subject, because it grows more complex year by year, and is phrased in legal jargon.

The difficulty of assembling a committee to study copyright is illustrated in a small spate of correspondence in 1954. CAA President, Prof. Frank Stiling of the University of Western Ontario, was invited to submit a brief, detailing changes the Association would like to see made in the Copyright Act. Justice J.L. Ilsley had been appointed head of a Royal Commission to investigate copyright in Canada.

"If we miss this chance, it might be twenty years before there is another opportunity," Stiling wrote to Joe Holliday (Toronto), editor of the *Canadian Author & Bookman*. "This is the time we have to act. Where and when shall we meet? Unfortunately I am leaving for the west tomorrow for three weeks."

Joe Holliday was "up to his ears, getting out the final portion of an Xmas publication." He phoned Marjorie Wilkins Campbell (Toronto), always a good head, but she was going to be out of town all that week, could possibly spare a couple of hours on Saturday morning, but only if urgently needed. "Besides, I wouldn't know where to start such a discussion." Frances Shelley Wees (Toronto) had set aside ten days to give her attention to copyright and can-

43

celled appointments to be available, but when the date for discussion seemed to remain uncertain, she was 'browned off'. The rest of the CAA Copyright Committee lived out of town, and really met only at executive meetings. The Association asked and was granted a stay of deadline. The Brief was finally completed in plenty of time for the Ilsley Report of 1957.

Another small flurry arose in 1962, at a convention in Ottawa. An editor, R.B. Robertson of Clarke, Irwin, harangued the Association on the necessity of Canada's ratification of the Universal Copyright Convention, which the government had signed years before, but was now being pressured into ratifying. Since UCC signatories were not identical with those of the Berne Convention, Canadian authors would gain protection of their copyrights in additional countries. The Association was only too happy to pass a Resolution urging Canada to make it all legal and binding.

As a result of the renewed interest in copyright, and the fact that the Act would have to be overhauled sometime soon, the government created an Interdepartmental Copyright Committee and invited submissions. What did the Canadian Authors Association have to add to the Stiling Brief? What more could be said? Instead of repeating the challenges of the past, Carol Wilson and Lyn Harrington (Toronto) put together a "Brief on the Public Lending Right," the compensation to authors for the use of their books in public libraries. Four members of the CAA read the Brief (it was literally brief) aloud to the Committee, answered questions, and went home expecting to hear of results in the next session of Parliament. They had a lot to learn about the law's delays. This project was taken up by the Writers' Union of Canada, shortly after it formed in 1973, but even the higher profile of that organization has not yet effected legislation.

In 1965, the Canadian Copyright Institute was founded and eagerly joined by the Canadian Authors Association. Here the members could lay the burden down at the feet of men experienced in the field, men whose everyday business was copyright. The CCI interested itself in the Public Lending Right, though not strictly a matter of copyright, and in photocopying, a very tangled subject, which is far from unravelled yet.

Chapter 4
Branching Out

In June 1921, the *Canadian Bookman* announced the birth of the CAA:

> This must be regarded as a significant event in the history of Canada. It indicates that a new national consciousness is growing rapidly as one of the results of the Great War. Had there not been formed a League of Nations wherein Canada speaks and votes as an independent nation, it is not likely that we would have today this new League of Canadian Authors. . . . Before this War, Canadian writers were few in number, ill-paid, distrustful of their own powers, timorous to a degree. Recent events, however, have ushered in a new era of confidence and hope, the first fruits of which is the wonderfully well-attended convention of authors and their formal banding together in a national organization . . .

No sooner was the organizational conference of the Canadian Authors Association completed in March 1921, than its elected officials bestirred themselves to carry out the mandate of its constitution — to become Dominion-wide. Accordingly, they set up a series of meetings in major cities across Canada where it was hoped there would be enough interest and talent among local writers to establish a branch.

Montreal, naturally was first to hold an organizational meeting of local authors, and the French writers were particularly interested, but wary. The story of "Gathering in the Authors" formed a lengthy report in the September *Bookman*. It is reproduced here with spelling and hyperbole intact.

The wisdom of providing the Canadian Authors Association with a Constitution which would make the organisation Dominion-wide has been amply proved by the success which has attended the preliminary meetings of the various branches. The surprisingly large attendance at each of these meetings and the enthusiasm which developed as soon as it was realised that the branches were to be self-governing, leave no doubt as to the future of the new Association. It has come to stay and to create an interest in Canadian literature from Atlantic to Pacific on a scale which few would have ventured to predict so late as last February.

The life of the Canadian Authors Association depends not on the activity of the Central Office but on the vitality of its branches.

The first organisational meeting of the French-Canadian writers of Montreal to consider the advisability of forming a French Section in accordance with the Constitution was held at the Municipal Public Library of Montreal on April 17th through the courtesy of M. Hector Garneau (librarian). The chair was occupied by M. Victor Morin, and the objects of the Canadian Authors Association were explained by President J. M. Gibbon and Secretary B. K. Sandwell, both speaking in French. The Constitution was criticised at some length by M. Olivar Asselin, who favoured an entirely distinct French-Canadian Association. The meeting was adjourned until May 1st, when after further discussion, a vote was taken which gave a large majority in favour of joining the Association as a French Section, with M. Victor Morin as *président de Section*, assisted by a group of officers and a Committee highly representative of this most important branch of Canadian Literature.

The *French Section*, not a branch but a largely self-governing division of the main Association, elected the following officers: President, Victor Morin (who becomes ex-officio a member of the Executive of the Association); first Vice-President, Mme Huguenin; second ditto, Narcisse Arcand; Secretary, Gustave Comte; Treasurer, Edouard Montet.

The first organisation meeting of the English-speaking writers of Montreal was held on April 19 at the Royal Victoria College through the courtesy of Miss Hurlbutt. The ladies of the McGill Alumnae Association acted as hostesses to the seventy guests who attended. Mr. H.S. Ross, K.C. occupied the chair, and the objects and achievements of the Association were explained by the President and the Secretary. After a short discussion, those present unanimously resolved to support the Association by forming a Montreal branch, and Mr. W.D. Lighthall, K.C. was appointed local Chairman supported by officers and a Committee, as detailed at the end of this report.

Ottawa had its first organisation meeting the following evening, April 20, in the Chateau Laurier, at a meeting which showed an attendance of seventy. Mr. Robert Stead occupied the chair, and after the President and Secretary had explained the objects of the Association, Mr. Duncan Campbell Scott, Mrs. Madge Macbeth and others supported the proposal to form an Ottawa branch.

In the meantime, in Toronto Prof. Pelham Edgar held a preliminary discussion with a group of writers who had already joined the Canadian Society of Authors, formed a short time before. At this conference, which was entirely friendly, the more ambitious character of the Association was frankly recognised and the Canadian Society of Authors practically resolved itself into an Ontario organisation which would continue in order to maintain its charter, and in the hope that ways and means could be found of eventually merging with the Toronto branch of the Canadian Authors Association (and thus fulfill Edgar's ambition of becoming the largest branch.)

The organisation meeting was held in the Toronto Public Library, courtesy of Dr. George H. Locke, with Prof. Edgar in the chair. Again the President and Secretary explained the aims and objects of the Association, and the qualifications for membership. A number from the Canadian Society of Authors attended, and in spite of the high cost of living, joined both organisations, thus showing a public spirit which reflects great credit on Toronto.

The President, J.M. Gibbon was able to announce that the publishers had agreed to organize a Canadian Book Week for next November, and the practical character of the programme evidently appealed to those present. As a result the meeting proved highly successful, and arrangements were made for a later business meeting at which officers of the local branch should be elected.

Winnipeg was the next centre of attention. The Secretary was unable to travel West at this time, but Arthur Stringer and Captain J. Vernon McKenzie, editor of *Maclean's Magazine*, hurried up from Toronto, and joined the President on April 23, in facing the battery of press photographers and moving picture camera-men organised for this occasion by Prof. W.T. Allison and his enthusiastic fellow authors in Manitoba.

This was preliminary to a dinner at the Royal Alexandra, attended by one hundred and fifty-one Winnipeggers anxious to hear all about the Association. The local editors were there in force, headed by John W. Dafoe, who has since proved his prac-tical interest in Canadian literature by starting a monthly liter-ary Supplement to the *Manitoba Free Press*, the first of its kind in Canada, and so admirably done that it deserves the unstinted praise of every Canadian author. Mr. Dafoe made a telling speech at this dinner, and a characteristic touch was provided in the presence of two old-timer authors, Rev. George Bryce and Colonel George Ham, the latter of whom gave some fascinating anecdotes of the early authors of the West. The Winnipeg authors were keenly interested in the Copyright Bill, and Arthur Stringer had a busy time elucidating the hardships which that Bill proposed to inflict on the Canadian author. Not content with this one dinner, the Winnipeg Committee had also arranged with the Women's Canadian Club for a further meet-ing the following Monday. Arthur Stringer and Vernon McKenzie stayed over for this.

The President had to catch the train for Edmonton, as Nellie McClung and Judge Emily Murphy had arranged their organisation meeting for Tuesday, April 26. Their arrange-ments were truly admirable. Premier Stewart of Alberta, Pre-mier Oliver of British Columbia, the Lieut. Governor of Alberta; Dr. Tory, principal of the University of Alberta; the Hon. Frank Oliver, and Mayor Duggan of Edmonton were present at the inaugural dinner held in the Macdonald Hotel. There were seventy present at the meeting which followed, the President's address being followed by Nellie McClung, Judge Murphy, Prof. Broadus, Dr. Tory, and John D. Hunt.

Five delegates attended from Calgary and while they gave their whole-hearted support to the original plan of one general branch for Alberta centred at Edmonton, they urged the necessity of a local branch with local officers for Southern Alberta, centred at Calgary, in view of the distance between the two cities. This, of course was a matter for the Executive Com-mittee, but the President promised to address a meeting in Calgary on his return from Vancouver, which had fixed its opening date for Saturday, April 30th.

At Vancouver, Arthur Stringer was once more in evidence, having hurried on ahead of Vernon McKenzie so as to help in the good cause. Isabel Eccelstone Mackay had assembled a very representative gathering of writers for this inaugural meeting, with two delegates who had come over from Victoria. The local Editors and the University of British Columbia were fully represented, and after the visitors had spoken, very appreciative addresses were given in support of the Association by Mrs. Mackay, Judge Howay (author of a history of British Columbia), Bertrand Sinclair (author of *Big Timber* and many other highly successful novels), Robert Allison Hood, Professor Wood, Professor Eastman, Dr. Scott, the well-known literary critic; John Nelson, newspaper editor and proprietor; R.W. Douglas, librarian; Rev. R.G. MacBeth, a historian of the West; and Mrs. Julia Henshaw, a novelist and leading authority on the flora of the Canadian Rockies. The Committee selected covered not only Vancouver, but also the chief interior points.

The official representation from Victoria was left to a later meeting of the local writers on Vancouver Island. By arrangement with Isabel Ecclestone Mackay, CAA Vice-President who officiates for the whole of British Columbia, Vancouver Island eventually decided at a meeting on June 20th, to have its local branch with headquarters at Victoria, as that centre is more convenient for the authors of the Island than Vancouver on the mainland, the local branch to be part of the Provincial organisation, under the Vice-Presidency of Mrs. Mackay.

Calgary welcomed President J.M. Gibbon at an enthusiastic luncheon held in the Tapestry Room of the Hudson's Bay Company's store. Dr. G.W. Kerby, author of *The Broken Trail*, who presided, had written a poem for the occasion, and the spirit of the whole meeting was in keeping with its romantic setting. Sergeant Ralph S. Kendall, author of *Benton of the Royal Mounted* and Mrs. Frank Reeve (Onoto Watanna), author of *A Japanese Nightingale*, and nineteen other popular novels, were among the well-known novelists present, while one enthusiastic Calgarian claimed that that city had produced more famous writers of fiction within the last thirty years than any other city of its size in the British Empire; the list included Isabel Patterson, Robert Stead, Frank Houghton, Hulbert Footner and Willard Mack.

So splendid a response from the West must come as a revelation to our Canadian Authors in the East, and the activity of local branches such as Winnipeg in holding meetings is evidence that the enthusiasm is not ephemeral. Canadian literature is not merely a product of Eastern culture, but is just as vital and strong on the Pacific and in the Prairies as in the older Provinces near the Atlantic. Our Dominion-wide Constitution may have been ambitious but it was thoroughly justified.

OFFICERS OF BRANCH ORGANISATIONS

Montreal: Chairman, W.D. Lighthall; secretary, Mrs. E.J. Archibald; treasurer, Norman Rankin; executive committee: Miss J.G. Sime, Miss Lily E.F. Barry, Howard S. Ross, K.C., Mrs. Ramsden, C.W. Stokes, Mrs. Fenwick Williams, Miss A.D. Dickson, Miss Mary Brooks, Dr. Cyrus J. Macmillan, Hugh Cornerford, George Pearson, Leslie G. Barnard. The vice-president of the general Association for this district, Dr. Stephen Leacock, did not accept office in the branch for the present year owing to his expected absence in England.

Ottawa: Chairman, the district vice-president, R.J.C. Stead; vice-chairman, Duncan Campbell Scott; secretary, Mrs. Madge Macbeth; treasurer, Lawrence J. Burpee; executive committee: Lady Foster, C.M. Barbeau, R.E. Gosnell, Jules Tremblay, Dr. E. Sapir, Louvigny de Montigny.

Winnipeg: Chairman, the district vice-president, Prof. W.T. Allison; first vice-president, Canon Gill; second ditto, to be elected from Saskatchewan; secretary, Hopkins Moorehouse; assistant secretary, Will E. Ingersoll; treasurer, W.A. Deacon; archivist, Dr. John Maclean; executive committee: D.B. MacRae, T. Robertson, Norman Lambert, Miss Catherine Cornell, Miss Kennethe Haig, Mrs. Ruth Arakie Cohen, Mrs. H.R. Patriarche, J.D. Duthie, Prof. R.C. Lodge, Canon Bertal Heeney, Miss G. Irene Todd (Brandon).

Alberta (headquarters, Edmonton): Chairman, the district vice-president, Mrs. Nellie McClung; vice-chairman, John D. Hunt; second ditto, Major Kerby; treasurer Miss Edna Kells; secretary, Prof. Paul A. Wallace (University of Alberta); executive committee: Hon. Frank Oliver, Mrs. Joseph Price, Sergeant Kendall, Mrs. Frank Reeve, Rev. W. Everard Edmunds, Prof. Edmund Kemper Broadus, Dr. D.M. McGibbon, Charles Hayden, A.B. Watt, Prof. W.H. Alexander, Mrs. Justice Emily Murphy.

Calgary: Chairman, Dr. G.W. Kerby, Mount Royal College; vice-chairman, Mrs. Frank Reeve; Secretary, Frank Morton; treasurer, Miss Enid Griffis; executive committee: C.A. Havden, Mrs. J. Price, Mrs. Stavert, Consul C.S. Reat, Malcom Geddes,

W.M. Davidson, Sergeant Ralph Kendall, R.J. Deachman.

British Columbia (headquarters, Vancouver): Chairman, Mr. Justice Howay; vice-chairman, Mrs. Charles S. (Julia) Henshaw; second ditto, to be elected from Victoria; secretary, Bertrand Sinclair; treasurer, R.A. Hood; provincial committee: Charles Mair (Fort Steele), Frederick Niven (Nelson) Robert Watson (Vernon) Mrs. Evah McKowan (Cranbrook) Mrs. Shaw, Miss Marjorie L.C. Pickthall (Victoria) Major Langstaff (Victoria). Vancouver Committee: Dr. S.D. Scott, R.W. Douglas, John Nelson, Lionel Haweis, Prof. Larsen, Dr. Ashton, George Murray, Roy Brown, Mrs. Elizabeth Rebbick, Mrs. Lefevre, Rev. R.G. MacBeth, R.S. Somerville.

The enthusiasm of Dr. Archibald MacMechan of Dalhousie University made it unnecessary for President Murray Gibbon to make a formal organizing visit to Nova Scotia. "Archie" had returned to Halifax after the founding conference afire with zeal, and promptly set about planning a Maritimes branch, headquartered in Halifax. There was intermittent hope that a local branch might emerge on Prince Edward Island, but the province held only one known book writer at the time — not sufficient to form a branch, which required a base of five, later seven, professional writers. Prof. MacMechan sent out form letters to all the writers he heard of in Nova Scotia, inviting them to join the Association. It read, in part,

> The literature of Canada began in Nova Scotia. This ancient tradition must be upheld and our people must retain her literary primacy and should be stongly represented in this new organization.

Assembling and up-dating a roster in this restless society of ours is the bane of any organization. Prof. MacMechan was surprised and amused at one reply:

> I thank you very sincerely for having elected me as a member of the Nova Scotia Canadian Authors Association. Kindly find enclosed the sum of five dollars for the membership fee. I am very much honoured for having the title of Reverend conferred upon me in your letter of April 25th, but I must tell you that I have no right to it, being a simple layman. Yours truly, etc.

Prof. MacMechan invited the authors to meet in his own hospitable home, including authors who were already published, and those who were anxious and willing to write. Among the founding members were many who were distinguished in other fields of endeavour: Mr. Justice J.W. Longley, Prof. J.W. Falconer, Dr. H.L. Stewart, Mr. Justice Chisholm, Archdeacon Armitage, Miss Elizabeth Nutt. Meetings held in the MacMechan home were often devoted to poetry and book reviews, "all lightened by a flow of learning wit and wisdom," a veteran member recalls.

Though never one of the larger branches, Nova Scotia has out-shone all the others in service to the Canadian Authors Association, by contributing national presidents for twelve years of its existence. Six professional writers have taken time from their busy lives to take on the onerous task for periods of two years, and one, Dr. Watson Kirkconnell of Acadia University, did it twice. Dr. R.S. Longley, also of Acadia, served a single year. Dr. Helen Creighton, collector of folksong and folklore, and Donald Wetmore, playwright, happily survive the experience.

Like the Biblical parable of the sower, so were the missionary efforts of various presidents through the sixty years of the CAA's existence. In some places the seed sown sprang up quickly, but for lack of depth soon withered away. Some fell by the wayside on hard ground and produced no yield. Other seed fell on good ground and there took root and brought forth abundantly.

The Saint John branch has had a typical history of ups and downs. Rev. H.A. Cody brought home a glowing report of the founding of the Canadian Authors Association, where he was delighted to meet authors he knew only by name. He promptly formed a small branch and served as chairman. Probably because the province had few authors and they were dispersed in a province the size of Ireland, the branch did not flourish. However, it was re-formed in 1927, when National President Dr. Charles G.D. Roberts returned to the scenes of his youth. In celebration of Book Week, he and Dr. George Frederick Clarke of Woodstock, N.B., author of *Chris in Canada*, Ven. Archdeacon Cody and a few others held a public meeting in the Lord Beatty Hotel, which stirred up enough interest to re-establish the branch. A.W. Belding was elected chairman, Cody vice-chairman. The executive included Louis Arthur Cunningham, just beginning his very successful career in fiction, Major H.G. Christie ("Sirhindi") Rev. George Scott, and Margaret Lawrence, author of *The School of Femininity*, and a book reviewer.

The branch declined again during the Depression, reviving

briefly in 1939, only to relapse again until 1972, when it sprang up largely through the interest of Dan Ross and his wife Marilyn. The new branch held its organizational meeting at dinner in the Riverside Country Club, Rothesay, and National President, Commander C.H. Little spoke of the aims and progress of the Association to twenty writers.

In the election of officers, Dan Ross, in spite of the heavy demands on his time (a prodigious output of romantic and mystery novels unequalled in Canada) accepted the position of branch president. Jean Sweet, a life-member of CAA was named honorary president; vice-president, Dorothy Dearborn, novelist and journalist; secretary, Prof. Bruce Wright, Dept. of biology, UNB; treasurer, Will Connor, a Scot. Other founding members were: Dr. Stuart Trueman, Janet Macdonald, Eric Teed, and Dr. Fred Cogswell, poet and founder of the *Fiddlehead Press*, Fredericton. Almost at once, the New Brunswick branch launched a literary competition, acquired funding, and arranged with the *Atlantic Advocate* for publication of suitable winning entries.

Unfortunately, secretary Wright fell ill and passed away, a shattering loss to a small branch, not only for his sound commonsense, but for his outstanding nature writing. The scattered membership then decided to hold quarterly dinner-meetings in a variety of settings — Moncton, Oromocto, Fredericton — rather than attempt the more usual monthly meetings.

The Saskatchewan branch, headquartered in Regina, failed to take root in Saskatoon, but flourished for a few years in Moose Jaw while Joseph Schull was domiciled there. The Regina group held together for years under Mary Weekes and Adele McPherson, but was brought low by an over-zealous member who thought to publish poetry at the contributors' expense.

Brandon, Manitoba, had a branch very briefly as did Chatham, Ontario. Windsor was more durable, but when leading spirits grow old or tired or move away, they are not easily replaced. Yet branches can be revived, as happened in London, Ontario. It appears that the London branch was overloaded with university professors who talked over the heads of the members and had little concern for marketing — the chief interest of the aspiring freelancer. So the Western Ontario branch, headquartered in London, gradually melted away and the former members formed small independent groups to criticize one another's work, and exchange market information. The London branch was re-activated in 1971, thanks largely to the efforts of Eileen Edwards, and before long assembled a respectable coterie of producing writers. They found more stimulation and cohesion in the national Association.

An amusing anecdote arose in connection with the resurrection of the London branch. Ten years after its reformation, a relative of the treasurer who happened to work in a bank, queried a dormant account in the name of the long-gone treasurer. Lo, a nest-egg of $154.29 was added to the kitty. Later, upon the death of an energetic writer, the branch set up the Louise Plumb Award, annual prizes totalling $250 for the best articles submitted.

Sarnia had come briefly within the orbit of the London branch, but it was only in 1959 when the Creative Writers group decided to become part of a larger organization that a CAA branch was formed in Sarnia. It inaugurated one-day writing seminars at Lambeth College, and carried this on for several years, promoted literary contests, and produced a volume of poetry entitled *Polished Pebbles*.

Hamilton could boast some excellent members such as Jessie Beattie and Marjorie Freeman Campbell. Both worked assiduously and contributed to branch meetings when possible. However, Marjorie travelled a good deal as lecturer and in search of non-fiction material, whereas Jessie's health was never robust. Despite encroaching blindness, she worked on until into her eighties.

During the war, while Watson Kirkconnell was teaching at McMaster University in Hamilton, he was also National President and branch president. The national officers carried a heavy burden of deskwork, and Prof. Kirkconnell was a most diligent writer. He turned out volume after volume of translations from Icelandic and Ukrainian, an impressive list by any standards. He was too occupied to give the Hamilton branch much nurturing, and it slid inexorably down to the vanishing point. Vigorous writers such as Beattie and Campbell transferred their membership to the Toronto branch, forty miles to the east.

Still, the pitifully small leaderless Hamilton branch was not quite finished. Madeline Maeder, a public school teacher, got the notion that it could be resurrected, and with the encouragement of George Salverson, CAA office manager, started it up the hill again on shaky legs, struggling against the image projected during the slump, but winning through.

Membership in the Canadian Authors Association grew rapidly in the early years, but was even then far from embracing all potential members. "Regular" members were those who had published at least one book, half a dozen short stories or the equivalent in articles or poetry, or had had a play produced. "Associates" were aspiring writers, publishers or editors, or other creators of copyrightable material in other disciplines. Canadian painters and composers soon became valued members.

The executive decided to hold an annual meeting in Ottawa, April 28 and 29, 1922, with committee meetings before and after. Some mild debate arose over whether this was the first or the second CAA convention, since the first was a founding meeting, and the second meeting was the first "annual." It was a brief two-day affair, largely occupied with revision of the provisional constitution, and with copyright. The date indeed was chosen for when Parliament was in session. Delegates were keenly interested in the copyright situation. They didn't require kits and favours and excursions to attract them to the sessions in the Victoria Memorial Museum, nor to the closing banquet in the Chateau Laurier.

Certainly all members were urged to put in an appearance, if only to impress the government with a show of numbers, if not of strength. On the agenda was a meeting with Mr. Robb, Minister of Trade and Commerce.

For members from the extreme east and west who could not be present, votes could be mailed to National Secretary B.K. Sandwell with regard to the slate of officers, and revision of the constitution. It was not completely satisfactory, but in so wide a country, it was the best that could be done.

It may have been the following year that President Gibbon persuaded the CPR to grant press passes to delegates travelling to CAA annual meetings. This courtesy was matched in kind by Walter Thompson of the CNR. Press passes or reduced fares were never mentioned in CAA literature, but word got around, and critics suggested that such fares accounted for the size of the membership. Admittedly, they did help to dilute the high standards established. Thus for a decade, CAA members crossed the country happily, until the Depression forced the railways to curb their generosity in 1932.

Still, the railways received good publicity from the writers, who rhapsodized in print over areas of Canada they would never have seen otherwise. Since then members have reached into their own pockets to attend conventions in Halifax or Vancouver, though now most travel by air.

The 1922 Convention began with an address on copyright, by Louvigny de Montigny, who had found a new occasion for alarm. Under the previous Act, the term of copyright was for forty-two years. Many copyrights were due to expire soon, and once dead, they could not be resurrected. The term of copyright should be the life of the author, he declared, and fifty years thereafter for the benefit of his heirs, as the controversial new Bill agreed.

> Some rights are secured to the author by this new Bill, but many more are not, and cannot be until Canada joins the Berne Convention, which it cannot do with those licensing clauses in place. Until that time, those property rights remain in the public domain.

His audience was suitably awed, and when de Montigny mentioned moving pictures, there was a buzz of comment. Everyone knew that L.M. Montgomery had forced the company filming *Anne of Green Gables* for the second time to pay for the privilege. Musicians in the audience were shocked to learn that phonograph recording companies were using material without payment of any kind to the composer.

The Copyright Committee of the CAA had given a year's attention to Bill 12, and urged immediate adoption of its report. If endorsed by the membership, the report could be presented to Mr. Robb at noon. After limited discussion, the report was accepted unanimously, and the meeting adjourned, to proceed in a body to Mr. Robb's office. There they were joined by a number of senators and members of the House of Commons and other prominent Ottawa citizens sympathetic to the CAA stand.

President John Murray Gibbon briefly expressed the view of the Association. In reply, Mr. Robb declared, "It would be impossible for Parliament to deal with the matter at the session now in progress, but I can give positive assurance that the Act will be amended at the following session."

They believed him. What else could they do? The amendments occupied another year, and the Act was to come into force January 1, 1924.

Re-assembled in the Victoria Museum, members spent the afternoon in Association business, not least in reports from the branches — their progress, programs, plans, contests and Book Week activities, in which all were profoundly interested. A pall was cast over the proceedings by the announcement of the sudden unexpected death of Marjorie Pickthall (Victoria), just ten days ago. She had hosted the inaugural meeting of the Victoria branch, and was on the British Columbia committee. This gentle lyrical poet had already made her mark in publication, including a slim philosophical novel. She would undoubtedly have become a major figure in Canadian poetry. Interment was in the family plot in St. James Cemetery, Toronto, attended by many Toronto branch members.

Although Canadian fiction might not rate as first class in the eyes of the world and home-grown critics, Canadian poetry was respected. A large percentage of CAA members, at least dabbled in verse, and some wrote on a level with the best English and American poets of the day. Thus it was understandable that the premier Canadian verse — the unofficial (until 1980) national anthem, *O Canada* — came under fire. The English words with all their repetitions, were being sung in different versions across the country, none of them wholly satisfactory. What more patriotic gesture than to present one's country with a new version that would satisfy poets as well as patriots? A committee was formed to solicit new versions, and these poured in to the national secretary, Dr. E.A. Hardy (Toronto). Patriotic verse is difficult to write without falling into bathos or bluster, and the jaded committee members, Florence Randal Livesay and Prof. Pelham Edgar (both Toronto), asked for more time.

Joseph Dumais and Edouard Montet (Montreal) proposed an elaborate project: that of selecting the best English and French publications each year and arranging for translation and publication, and accompanied by a vigorous and wide-spread promotion campaign in this country and in the United States, at the expense of the Association.

All agreed that the idea was noble and greatly to be hoped for, but it could not be financed by the Association, which had no funds other than the five dollar membership fee. The proposal was withdrawn.

It was moved by J. Vernon McKenzie, associate editor of *Maclean's Magazine*, seconded by B.K. Sandwell (later, editor of *Saturday Night*) that:

> *Whereas* the Canadian market is now flooded with magazines, chiefly from the United States which do not inculcate Canadian sentiment and nationality; and *whereas* the large amount of

advertising in these magazines is detrimental to Canadian industry; and *whereas* this condition prevents the foundation of Canadian magazines and the growth of those that now exist, and thus restricts the market in Canada to the detriment of the interests of Canadian writers: BE IT RESOLVED that the Canadian Authors Association goes on record in favor of a duty to be levied on the advertising matter in magazines imported into Canada; and this meeting desires that copies of this resolution be sent to the Secretary of the Canadian National Periodicals and Newspaper Association, to the Minister of Trade and Commerce, and to the Minister of Finance. Carried Unanimously.

It was moved by Lloyd Roberts, seconded by Madge Macbeth that:

Whereas the purpose of this Association is to stimulate the production and improvement of Canadian literature; to encourage and support those struggling for literary recognition; to bring Canadian literature to the attention of other countries; and to awaken a more dynamic pride in the creation of a national literature among our own people; and *whereas* scholarships and prizes, notably those awarded by Nobel, the French and English governments and Academies, and the Province of Quebec, have proved of inestimable value in raising the standard in all the arts ... BE IT RESOLVED that this Association urge upon the Dominion government the establishment of a National Scholarship in Literature, to be awarded annually to a Canadian author domiciled in Canada, for the most significant work in either French or English, published or produced in any country during the preceding year; that this scholarship consists of a sum not less than Five Thousand Dollars per annum; and that it be awarded on the recommendation of a board of three members approved by this Association. Carried with one dissenting vote.

An idea which proved to be ahead of its time was moved by the Rev. Dr. Abbott-Smith (Montreal): that the time was ripe for the preparation and publication of a Canadian dictionary of national biography, covering the whole period from the time of the early explorers to the present day, and that such a work might well be produced by the Candian Authors Association. This proposal was regretfully turned down by the Resolutions Committee as being too great an undertaking for the Association in its present stage.

The idea was excellent, but the time was not to come for

another forty years, when the University of Toronto undertook the task. Funding was provided by an imaginative and public-spirited bequest of the late James Nicholson, a Toronto business man who left the bulk of his considerable estate for this very purpose. Volume One appeared in 1967, covering the period 1000 A.D. to 1700. With all the goodwill in the world, it could never have been accomplished by a volunteer organization, as the foresighted clergyman proposed.

It was moved by J. Castell Hopkins, seconded by Prof. Pelham Edgar and carried unanimously that $200 be set aside for publication in French of part of the Association's news pages in the *Canadian Bookman*.

It was moved by Robert J.C. Stead on behalf of the Calgary branch, that editors of magazines be petitioned to pay for contributions on acceptance rather than on publication. (That battle is almost but not quite won, even now.) Carried enthusiastically.

It was moved by Mr. Justice Howay (Vancouver), seconded by W. Stewart Wallace of Toronto University Library, and carried unanimously that:

> The CAA prepare and publish a periodical bibliography Bulletin, giving the titles of all new books or reprints of Canadian character, with the name of the author, price and publisher, and where possible a brief synopsis of its contents, both in French and English, and that the authors be invited to send two copies of each to the Secretary of the French or English sections.

This resolution was carried out for several years informally, until the Toronto Public Libraries did it more professionally. Later, the project was taken over by the National Library in Ottawa, in the form of a monthly list entitled *Canadiana*.

The 1922 Annual Meeting then moved on to amendments to the constitution. These proved to be minor refinements, for the provisional constitution proved reasonably workable, despite the haste and inexperience of the committee. The major change was simply an affirmation and definition of a clause. The original premise had been that the Association should include creators of copyrightable material in any discipline, either as Regular or Associate members. The first Annual Meeting specified that composers of musical works and designers of illustrations (not necessarily fine art) be included. And that affiliated guilds of musicians and artists might be admitted.

Broadening the membership of the CAA did not sit well with some members, in particular author/artist Arthur Heming. Miffed, he founded the Writers' Club of Toronto in 1923, "for the benefit of the few writers to whom writing is a vocation, not an avocation." But when the Copyright Act was proclaimed, Heming crossed the border in disgust, "driven out of his homeland."

The Association's decision to report news of the French Section was implemented directly, in forthcoming monthly issues of *Canadian Bookman*, the official organ of the Canadian Authors Association until December 1922. Thereafter the CAA bought space in the magazine for CAA information, supplemented by an annual *Authors' Bulletin*.

Welcome but startling news came up, in that the provincial government of Quebec was about to make an annual literary grant of $5,000 mostly for works in French, but also in proportion to English writers of the province. How much inspiration was provided by *La Section Française* is not recorded, but its membership was distinguished and persuasive. Athanase David was Provincial Secretary, and the Prix David is still honoured in Quebec in tribute to Sen. L.O. David.

It gave the English-speaking members pause to think with provocation: if Quebec could do this, why not richer Ontario? However, the *Bookman* wryly noted,

> The request got short shrift from Premier Ferguson on the plea of economy. The authors are trying to harmonize this with the substantial increase in the salaries of the ministers, and in the sessional allowances of the members.

Donald G. French (Toronto), chief editor at Macmillan, conducted a Writers' Corner in the *Bookman* and also gave writing courses to students. He established the Canadian Literature Club of Toronto, hoping it would spread. It didn't, but it brought an awareness of Canadian literature to the Toronto public, and until the 1960s, encouraged established authors through its programs, and collaborated with the CAA in celebrating Book Week.

The burning question in 1922 was whether to repeat Canadian Authors Week in the coming November. Booksellers admitted that it had boosted their sales and not only of Canadian books. They offered more cooperation a second go-round. "Their cooperation is not to be despised," Gibbon reminded the delegates, and the motion was passed, almost unanimously.

The final bit of business was the election of officers, and the Nominations Committee presented a slate which was approved:

> Hon. President, Her Excellency Baroness Byng of Vimy, wife of the Governor General; President John Murray Gibbon, setting a pattern by serving a biennium; Secretary B.K. Sandwell (until he moved to Kingston); Treasurer Dr. G.R. Lomer, McGill University librarian; Vice-presidents: Archibald MacMechan (Halifax); Jessie G. Sime (Montreal); Victor Morin (Montreal French Section); R.J.C. Stead (Ottawa); Sir John Willison (Toronto); Dr. W.T. Allison (Winnipeg); Austin Bothwell (Regina); Dr. G.W. Kerby (Calgary); Nellie McClung (Edmonton); Isabel Ecclestone Mackay (Vancouver); R. Sheldon-Williams (Victoria).

Business being completed, the delegates repaired to the Chateau Laurier where most were lodged at four dollars per day (with bath), to prepare for the Annual Banquet.

Asked for a backward look twenty years later, a delegate from Vancouver, Robert Allison Hood, author of *By Shore and Trail in Stanley Park*, recalled:

> In considering the benefits from membership in the CAA I should like to testify to the pleasure I have received from the Conventions, in the friendships I have made and the treasured memories that remain.

> I was down at the very first Convention in Ottawa, a lively and successful event indeed, largely due to the personality and efforts of Madge Macbeth who was the life of it. She composed a playlet which was presented at one of the luncheons. The banquet was a brilliant affair. George Ham (Winnipeg) the darling of the Canadian Women's Press Club, certainly had a way with the ladies. Onoto Watanna (Calgary) a novelist with a colourful personality spoke. Among other speakers were Mrs. George Black, M.P. from Whitehorse, and our own Judge Howay (Vancouver).

> One of the highlights for me came the next day, when I spent Sunday afternoon and evening at Lloyd Roberts' home on the Ottawa River. Elizabeth Bailey Price (Calgary), Vernon McKenzie (Toronto), Hopkins Moorehouse (Winnipeg) were of the company. Martha Black recounted stories of her early hardships in the Yukon in '98 and afterwards. Lloyd read one of his poems, but said he would never fill his father's boots. He was a charming host.

Two books came out of that social evening. Elizabeth Bailey Price interviewed Martha Black at length, and ghostwrote *My Seventy Years*. Two decades later, Whitehorse journalist Florence Whyard completed *My Ninety Years*, by Martha Black, a tribute to a lively and lovely woman.

Conventions are always times for creating and renewing friendships, in addition to absorbing information and inspiration. Madge Macbeth (Ottawa) and Canadian historian Agnes. C. Laut of New York, arranged to spend most of the summer at Jasper National Park, "where two typewriters will do their utmost to disturb the majestic silence of the Rockies."

The Rockies also featured in a plan devised by John Murray Gibbon, Public Relations director for the CPR. A memorial to explorer-fur trader David Thompson was to be officially unveiled at Lake Windermere, B.C. on August 30. How splendid if western members of the CAA should meet and hold a Campfire as part of the celebrations! Any who felt so inclined could join a packtrain through the Rockies over the new road to Radium Hot Springs, and meet the B.C. authors at Lake Windermere for the Indian pageant. (Perhaps this was the forerunner of the famous Trailriders of the Canadian Rockies which Gibbon founded.)

The Campfire was a tremendous success with not only Western members but a distinguished handful from the East, including Bliss Carman in cowboy hat, W. Stewart Wallace, Dr. Lawrence Burpee, J.B. Tyrrell, Col. J.S. Dennis, and of course Murray Gibbon, more rumpled than ever, and certain of good publicity. It was a joyous occasion under sunny skies. And amid the fun and laughter, what were they thinking of? Why, the second Canadian Authors Week, naturally.

Chapter 5
The Annual Book Week Skirmish

The idea for Canadian Book Week probably evolved from the American Library Association's Children's Book Week which was celebrated the second week each November, nicely in advance of Christmas gift-buying. The propaganda in the library journals and in the *Publishers' Weekly*, unquestionably had some effect in Canadian libraries.

Perhaps Dr. Locke, head of Toronto Public Libraries, looking for new ideas with the rest of the executive of the newly-formed Canadian Authors Association, remarked how very few Canadian books were published for children. President J. Murray Gibbon, always alert to promotional opportunities and full of optimism over the new coast-to-coast literary links, considered, "Why not a Canadian Authors Week?"

"How could we bring that to the attention of a wide public?" queried Sandwell, National Secretary. "The next *Bookman* won't be out until December, too late for most Christmas shoppers."

"Make it a project for the branches. Get them involved. Suggest they could make up posters for libraries and bookstores, and slogans, say 'Read a Canadian Book' or some such thing. Have displays of books by Canadian authors. People will be startled. Most of them couldn't name a Canadian author to save their lives. Likely the book publishers will cooperate. I'll try them out."

"We could suggest members contact local service clubs, offer to provide speakers for that week."

"They could send speakers into schools if the local school board agreed. The bigger branches could put on an Author Night, open to the public. Maybe with a display of Canadian books."

"If they do anything dramatic or unusual, they needn't worry about getting attention from the press." Gibbon was accustomed to placing news and press releases on behalf of the CPR.

One after another made suggestions. But publicity outlets in 1921 were limited to newspapers and a few periodicals, and public relations was a new idea to unfunded organizations. There was talk of booklists and bibliographies, scarcely feasible before Gestetner and Xerox.

"The fact that we'll be promoting Canadian-authored books won't mean we want people to buy or read *only* Canadian books. Let's make that clear. But no one will boost Canadian books if Canadians don't. The motion pictures and stage plays spend a lot of money advertising their wares. They compete with reading. Well, we haven't got resources like that, but we should encourage people to read, and show that Canadians write on all kinds of subjects."

The executive decided to set Canadian Authors Week in November 1921, immediately following Children's Book Week.

"Our critics will say that we are forcing Canadian literature down their throats," murmured one. "We've got to make it plain we're not tooting our own horn — just reminding the public that there is such a thing as Canadian literature."

"Shouldn't we make a selection of the best books?" queried another. "We don't want to recommend Canadian books indiscriminately."

"The Association is not a private literary club, nor an Academy to weigh the virtues and demerits of a country's literature," replied Gibbon. "A frontier story of action and adventure may be just as valuable in winning readers as a treatise on Milton or Flaubert to a college professor."

Late that summer of 1921, Gibbon was invited to address the publishers' section of the Toronto Board of Trade, along with Frederic Melcher of the *Publishers' Weekly*, who spoke first. He dwelt on the success of various Book Weeks held in the States,

> notably Children's Book Week which has become an annual affair and is rapidly developing the reading of more and better books by the children, who are the booksellers' customers of tomorrow.

Gibbon was then called to outline his plans for a more intensive cultivation of Canadian reading by celebrating Canadian Authors Week, and promised the cooperation of branches and members-at-large across the country.

F.F. Appleton, secretary of the publishers' section could report:

As a result of the meeting a new kind of cooperation between author, publisher and bookseller is promised, and with the cooperation of these three groups, the Canadian Book Week (the name preferred by the book publishers) should be a tremendous success this fall. The proposed campaign will get more newspaper and magazine publicity than anything in the history of Canadian bookselling, and needs the cooperation of everyone concerned to realize the full benefit. Cooperation is the least expensive and most important item of the whole campaign. After all, look at how cooperation benefitted the paint companies when they adopted their cooperative advertising scheme, and everybody used the slogan 'Save the Surface and you save All.'

Appleton then suggested a general meeting in Toronto for all the booksellers and clerks in the city, as well as the publishers or their representatives. Possibly a dinner could be held, followed by a business meeting with the same two inspiring messengers. A window display competition might be held. John McClelland, Sr. proposed a Book Fair to be held in Massey Hall during Canadian Book Week, as a means of stimulating interest in Canadian writings, a pattern that could be tailored to suit smaller communities. This idea came to fruition only seven years later, when Canadian Book Week had become an established event, and booksellers and publishers had overcome their skepticism.

Later, in discussion with Mr. Melcher, Gibbon commented wistfully,

Canadian authors have an attitude of timid respect for foreign authors, regarding with bated breath the author from London or New York. If they did acquire the energy to move out of the bush, it was to go to the States or London, and become known as American or British authors.

Returned Melcher,

Yes, our American authors were like that, too. Before our Civil War, the selling value of an American book depended on the stamp of English approval. Why, Fenimore Cooper actually pretended to be an English author in order to find a publisher for his first novel!

Now to my mind, the national consciousness of Canada has received since 1914 as great an impetus as the United States received in the Civil War and the Spanish-American War combined. Canada stands now very much where the United States stood in 1900. Since then a distinctively national school of American fiction has grown up, distinctive in language and method, from Edith Wharton and Willa Cather to Kathleen Norris and Zane Grey. They found a public among their own people. ·Book readers in the United States were glad to read about themselves and their life, to find characters in fiction who talked like them. These authors are appreciated by their own people because they expressed, perhaps unconsciously, the national spirit of their day, and no longer an imported spirit.

Gibbon said:

I believe the same kind of spirit is arising in Canada, and Canadian publishers and booksellers are wise to recognize it, and encourage Canadian authors to consider the Canadian market. Quite a few of our authors have achieved a good reputation in other countries, partly through lack of market at home. In a recent volume on Contemporary American Literature, out of the 240 names selected as worthwhile American writers, five were born in Canada.

Still, only a few publishers got behind Canadian Authors Week. It was new and untried, and publishers and booksellers were at least as cautious as the next Canadian. Besides, they had more imported books than Canadian to unload on the market. Most publishing houses were branch plants of established US or British or French firms, or held agencies linked to foreign publishing firms. Relatively few had taken out "corporate Canadian citizenship" to the point of publishing and promoting books by Canadian authors. Large print runs made the imports so much cheaper, and thus easier to sell. There was also the considerable advantage of the promotion and salesmanship stemming from the parent plant.

The Association of Canadian Book Publishers did, however print and distribute to bookstores and libraries, with the willing cooperation of the Canadian Authors Association, a poster that read:

> **700**
> **Canadian Authors**
> **in our**
> **Wonderful Canada**
> **Have you read their Books?**

Cloke's Book Store in Hamilton won the cash prize of $75 awarded by the ACBP for the best window display.

Later, National Secretary Howard Angus Kennedy, came up with practical directives for celebrating the occasion and enlightening the populace:

> It may be possible for a small Branch to hold a public gathering, as larger Branches do ... some kind that will even catch the casual newspaper reader's attention. Amateur dramatic talent might be enlisted; even reading in parts by their own members might be enough to convince the incredulous that good Canadian plays exist. Selections of good Canadian music naturally commend themselves for performance.
>
> Originality might be employed in arranging shows in store windows — not only in book stores — and not of books alone. Relics, or other objects, pictures, costumes, models, maps, etc. illustrating the adventures of famous characters in our annuals, along with relevant books. A large proportion of our distinctively Canadian books, including fiction, naturally springs from the thrilling history of our explorers, traders, missionaries and pioneer settlers.
>
> Our Nova Scotia Branch last year by decorating Halifax with original posters produced for the occasion by a College of Art set an example which other Branches might follow.
>
> It is through our schools that we can do our most fruitful work. Some of our Branches have acted on this knowledge with great energy and wisdom, and all have the power to do so, either —
>
> by pressing for the active cooperation of provincial and municipal authorities — they are generally more than willing.
>
> by reaching the individual teachers through their conventions and periodicals.
>
> by interesting addresses in schools, when we have the members available for this agreeable duty.

by offering prizes for essay or story competitions; or by such other methods as the ingenuity of the Branch can devise.

To promote the general adoption of this young people's scheme by our Branches, the National Executive will add a special prize of $20.00 for the best of the first-prize-winning essays or stories in all the Branch competitions, and $10.00 worth of books for the best of the second-prize-winners. It is suggested that competitors be asked to write on a phase, event or character in Canadian history.

One example of enthusiastic "boosterism" came in its first autumn, when John Murray Gibbon received a panic note from Margaret McWilliams, wife of Manitoba's Lieutenant Governor, and president of the Winnipeg Women's Canadian Club. She had arranged a poetry reading tour for Bliss Carman through the West, before she discovered that few Western Canadians had ever heard of him. He was a member of the Canadian Authors Association, wasn't he? And so, could the Association help with publicity?

The CAA President did what he could; (though sixty years later it looks deplorably coy). Gibbon recalled:

I therefore called a meeting of the Montreal Branch, at which we decided to give him a send-off by crowning him with maple leaves as Poet Laureate of Canada. We had no authority but our own, but we did the coronation in style. I wrote a song for dancing which Harold Eustace Keys set to music, and we engaged the ballroom of the Ritz-Carlton Hotel for the ceremony. We needed children for the dance and these, after a refusal from a select English school, we obtained from the young Hebrew New Canadians. They were dressed in costumes of crepe paper decorated with maple leaves (cost $1.00) and they danced beautifully. The crown was presented to Bliss (height 6 ft 2) by a little tot half that height, and he accepted his new dignity with great good humour. That launched his tour with favourable publicity, and the lecture tour was a great success in Western Canada. The wheat growers had never seen a Poet Laureate in Canada. before.

A Calgary paper carried the story, where it was read by a young admirer of Bliss Carman. The editor of the Normal School paper, Wilfrid Eggleston, lined up fellow students to sell tickets to the poetry reading. Some of them knew so little of the distinguished poet, they called him "Carman Bliss." Still, they sold a hundred tickets, and young Wilf got to meet the poet. He also ran a

Book Week editorial urging readers to extend their familiarity with Canadian literature. A later encounter with Bliss Carman at Queen's University changed the course of the young man's life, when he was advised to "take the path of journalism rather than of teaching, which did not blend well with writing." The result — a lifetime of reporting and a dozen books.

B.K. Sandwell could rhapsodize after the Big Week:

> Never in his history has the Canadian author had so much attention from his fellow-citizens as during the week Nov. 19-26, 1921. This is the outstanding achievement of Canadian Authors Week, the first great undertaking of the Canadian Authors Association. Attention is the first thing the author needs ... The Canadian author has done enough good work to justify all the attention, enough to ensure that attention will speedily be translated into appreciation and active support of the best in Canadian literary products.

> In some quarters, the campaign has been viewed, wrongly, as a sordid commercial undertaking carried out in cooperation with sales agents, and having nothing higher than sales of a larger number of Canadian books. We have the highest regard for the *Canadian Forum*, which is the accredited intellectualist organ of this country, but we feel it has failed to perceive that a sale of a book may become more than an enjoyable transaction, may in fact be followed by spiritual consequences ...

> It is surely something to have diverted an appreciable fraction of the purchasing power and also the attention of Canadians for a brief time from phonographs and movie shows, and have them directed towards the very creditable, if not always genius-marked products of the Canadian writer.

J.M. Gibbon, addressing the Booksellers of Canada in Montreal a year later could report,

> The demand for information about Canadian authors and Canadian literature was astonishing. Over 300 influential clubs and institutions in Canada asked for speakers on the subject during that week. The Canadian Clubs surely represent the best element in Canada. Practically every Canadian Club arranged for a speaker on Canadian literature in 1921, and is doing the same for 1922.

(The Canadian Clubs for many years carried on a program of sending literary figures, Canadian, British and American across the country on speaking/reading tours, lectures patronized by the Canadian Women's Press Club, the Dickens Fellowship and other culture-hungry organizations.)

Gibbon went on,

> Speakers are all very well, but you may ask if Canadians are buying more books? Publishers assure me they are. For instance, although Bliss Carman has been writing good poetry for over thirty years, no Canadian publisher had the courage until last year to bring out a Canadian edition. The edition was comparatively large, but sold out within two months.

> The last thing we want is to overload the bookseller — or unload third-rate books upon the Canadian public just because these books are labelled Canadian. Unless books offered you by Canadian authors are worthwhile, for heaven's sake don't waste your time or energy upon them. This morning I received from George Locke of the Toronto Public Libraries, the advance proof of a catalogue of current Canadian books popular in the circulating division. These total 169 books and cover every phase of literary activity.

That catalogue in itself was an achievement, spurred by the enthusiasm generated by the founding of the CAA and by the impetus created by Book Week.

Such commercialism was a stench in the nostrils of the *Canadian Forum*, founded in 1920, which never desisted during its first decade from misreading the *Canadian Bookman* and misjudging the Canadian Authors Association, accusing both of uncritical acclaim of everything Canadian-authored. Admittedly, *Bookman's* reviewers did lay themselves open to derision at times, yet throughout the few years of the *Bookman's* links with the CAA, it ran constant reminders that "patriotism is not enough."

The *Forum's* attitude wounded deeply, and the scar tissue still throbs. For the contempt poured out upon the ingenuous Association spread to others, who discovered that criticism is a comfortable form of one-upmanship. In time, the Association began to believe itself unworthy, apologetic for its existence.

The unkindest cut came from the Montreal poet Frank R. Scott in his satiric poem "The Canadian Authors Meet." Alone of his verse, it has been anthologized often, too often to need repetition here. He portrayed the CAA as an effete and posturing nationalistic group of authors who spent a good deal of time at tea parties admiring one another, and dithering over how to promote Canadian writers. Obviously they should have been sipping absinthe in a Paris bistro, imitating Ezra Pound's cantos, or in a Montreal tavern quoting T.S. Eliot, rather than perpetrating their own amiable mediocrity. He conjures up a picture of a covey of matrons in pouter-pigeon corsets and ornate hats swapping compliments with elderly poets, all "springing to paint the native maple."

Scott and others of the Montreal Group were bright, impatient, idealistic, scornful young men, sniggering at their seniors' earnest endeavours. Their satire was cruel and biting and so funny to their undergraduate peers. But then, nurturing is rarely a virtue of youth, and nationalism is a ready target. They were after international standards and contemporary styles. Canadian readers were not ready to make the transition, as the young men found when two of their literary magazines folded after brief outings. But they did force a new approach to writing that has had a strong influence.

The *Canadian Forum* ran an article in their December 1926 issue, by Douglas Bush, entitled "Making Literature Hum": "It would seem incredible that intelligent people who were abreast of the contemporary movement could hold the opinions which most of our literati exuberantly express about their own work and their friends. Every year one hopes to hear the last of our windy tributes to our Shakespeares and Miltons, and every year the Hallelujah Chorus seems to grow in volume and confidence . . ."

Cast down but not destroyed by disparaging comment, the CAA continued to dream up new ways of bringing Canadian literature to the masses. They were almost virgin territory, in view of the scant publishing record of the past. In 1917, Canada had published twenty-six books; in 1918, forty-three; in 1920, seventy. Other Canadian titles were published abroad and imported.

The *Canadian Forum* was not alone in its ivory tower. Thomas B. Roberton (Winnipeg) writing in the *Literary Digest International Book Review* in February 1926 denounced Canadian literature as "uninspired, pedestrian, imitative, complacent, elementary and conventional." To which, Ella Julia Reynolds (Hamilton) made meek reply:

> Is his charge not painfully true? His array of adjectives stings . . . yet there is hope. Everyone who contributes sincerely to the world of Canadian letters is a stone of foundtion, upon which those greater ones who will follow us shall build.

Frederick Philip Grove could pronounce categorically, "Culturally, the people on this continent are only on the threshold of life." Was he condemning utterly, or did he hint at some faith?

T.D. Rimmer, a frequent reviewer in the *Bookman* added his two-cents worth and flouting the editorial policy.

> In the field of fiction, we have a few distinguished names, but the rest is mediocrity. We have other novelists, of course, distinguished merely by the circulation of their books. The general standard of Canadian fiction is not literary.

(This is undiscriminating self-glorification? He no doubt referred to Canada's all-time best-seller, Ralph Connor (Winnipeg) whose books by 1926 had sold over six million copies.)

Dr. Lorne Pierce (Toronto), editor of the Ryerson Press, agreed sadly.

> Even many best-sellers lack ballast, and are headed for oblivion. A new race of novelists and of two-fisted critics is needed to bring out the best in our literature.

Nor was the general public entirely happy with Book Week admonishments, as a letter to the *Vancouver Province* by H. Cheriton-Hilgate attests. He wrote, in part:

> The great danger attending the steps of a young nation is that of confusing patriotism with a petty parochialism. It frequently happens, particularly in young and crude countries where tradition enforces little or nothing in the way of safeguards or standards, that a movement in itself so desirable, is sometimes liable to be diverted from its legitimate path into the wandering by-ways of self-interest and vanity which, wherever they may ultimately end, lead never to the high goal pointed out in the use of a national title.

> We are directed to consider the finest literary work of Canadians as our models. We are urged to write in Canada, of Canada, for Canada. We are implored to talk about our Canadian writers, to buy their productions and send them to the Old Country, in other words to "boost" the works of Canadians.

> What would have been the measure of Shakespeare's production if he had refused to write except of his own immediate surroundings? How feeble, how self-conscious, how petty . . . if he had written with one eye on the gallery and the other on the bank?

To this purblind exile, novelist Robert Allison Hood (Vancouver) made tart rebuttal:

> Shakespeare, from what we know of his life had a keen eye on both gallery and bank. Great literature is inspired by the spirit of its age, is starved or nourished according to the quality of its reception.

> In an age where every trade and profession finds it necessary to organize for protection and mutual betterment, are the writer folk to be branded as mercenary if they organize too? The Canadian Authors Association does not urge its members to write solely of Canada, but it encourages them to think that there is good, and for them perhaps the best literary material because it is closest to their experience. Is not this a desirable thing? It is just what Walter Scott, Thomas Hardy and R.D. Blackmore did for their own regions of Great Britain.

> In Canada our literature is in its beginnings. But it will never be great if Canadians themselves refuse to take an interest in it. The CAA is a trade guild, formed primarily for the benefit of the craft, and only indirectly for that of Canadian literature. What helps the one, however, must necessarily build up the other. In this, our Association is similar to the British Authors Society, which devotes practically all its energies to the help and protection of its members in a financial way. Fortunately for them, it is not necessary for the Society to urge upon the British public the desirability of taking greater interest in the work of its native writers; otherwise I daresay its leaders would not consider it improper to do so.

Having chortled over the success of the Canadian Authors Week, National Secretary B.K. Sandwell was even more jubilant over the 1922 Canadian Book Week, and paid tribute where it was due — to the branches.

> It is in work of this kind that the unique constitution of the Association, with its central authority for dealing with national questions, and its constant emphasis on local autonomy in all other matters, is seen at its best.

> In organizing Book Week, the head office could do little except determine the date, enter into understandings with one or two national bodies (booksellers, publishers and library groups), offer a few suggestions as to methods, and give the word "GO."

> The real work was done by the locals. Probably from four to five hundred persons participated actively in the campaign of

oratory, library exhibits, bookstore displays, and other devices by which the Week was carried on. The newspapers were literally loaded for three weeks or more with articles on Canadian books and Canadian authors, and with reports of speeches on similar subjects.

The Week was launched in the highest circles of the land — Rideau Hall itself. The wife of the Governor General, Baroness Byng of Vimy had graciously consented to become the first Honorary President of the Canadian Authors Association. Her Ladyship laid on a reception at Government House and invited Robert J.C. Stead, president of the Ottawa branch, to give a short talk on the Week and its objectives.

Stead, as second National President, the following year pioneered in the new medium, local radio, and the third National President, Dr. Lawrence J. Burpee, reached a much larger audience over a radio network.

The retail book trade, under the leadership of bookseller A.T. Chapman (Montreal) cooperated judiciously, with some misgivings over two Book Weeks in less than a month. As years went by, Children's Book Week was displaced by Canadian Book Week, though it revived as Young Canada Book Week much later.

The chief share of head office participation consisted of booking tours for speakers, notably those of Basil King in the Maritime Provinces, and of Dr. Archibald MacMechan in Ontario. (Could it be that they paid their own way? There is no record of travel expense drawn on the CAA's slender means.)

> The Rev. Mr. King was given an extraordinary welcome on his return from Boston to the land of his boyhood and youth, and left a deep conviction that literature was something going on in the hearts and minds of the people, and not of authors alone.
>
> Dr. MacMechan brought to Ontario the story of the early and intensely native development of a literature in his adopted Province of Nova Scotia. Ontario also had the advantage of addresses by H. Gerald Wade (Winnipeg) and of Judge Emily Murphy, whose presence in the East was not strictly due to Book Week.
>
> We cannot refrain from mentioning three branch officers who achieved surprising results. Any association which can enlist the services of such executives as Madge Macbeth (Ottawa) Jessie G. Sime (Montreal) and Hugh Eayrs (Toronto) can count

on getting things done. The latter, once a writer and now a publisher, has shown exceptional enterprise in bringing out the works of new Canadian writers.

Heartened with this cooperation from the authors and other well-wishers, the Canadian publishers took up courage in the exuberant 1920s to produce half a dozen histories of Canadian literature. All were pondered by librarians to their amazement, and proved immensely useful to teenagers tracking down material for "oral compositions."

Not so the hefty volumes of the *Makers of Canadian Literature* and the *Master Works of Canadian Authors*. They told you more than you wanted to know. But new editions of Canadian classics made it possible to follow up on interest-provoking leads in the histories.

Another unanticipated result of this burgeoning interest in Canadian books came in 1924-25, with the British Empire Exhibition at Wembley, England. CAA members among the publishers, and two notable librarian members had a great deal to do with the Exhibition. Dr. George Locke (Toronto) and Dr. Victor Morin (Montreal French Section) prepared annotated booklists in two languages to accompany the display of Canadian books. But it was largely due to one man, novelist Robert J.C. Stead, that any of the arts had been allowed space amid Canada's customary spread of mines, forests and farms products. The Canadians also exhibited a certain delicacy — or stupidity — revealed when the Australians set up their display. Not only did they tout their fewer titles more vigorously, but they had the foresight to take along stacks of copies which sold well. "Next time . . ." vowed the Canadians.

Canadian Book Week having been officially designated as "the first clear week in November," the various branches of the Canadian Authors Association annually put their shoulders to the wheel. 1927 showed the typical response across the country, with two exceptions — Edmonton flagged, while Saskatchewan rose to new heights with Regina leadership.

The Saskatchewan government prepared some eighty coloured slides of twenty eminent Canadian writers, their homes and the setting of their plots. The Department of Education furnished lecture material, including extracts from an author's writings, and made them available to any responsible committee in the province, to make programs more interesting. By cooperation of the press, librarians, teachers, and many organizations including the Women's Christian Temperance Union and the Rebekahs, more than a hundred Book Week programs were offered, while school societies, literary clubs and bookstores had a share in the success.

Winnipeg branch reported

> Some very fine editorials in our dailies as well as articles in the Manitoba weekly papers. At a number of teachers' conventions, reference was made to Canadian literature, and at two, several papers were given on the subject. Several radio addresses were given by Professors Kirkconnell and Allison, by Crawford Maclean and E.K. Marshall. The clergymen of the city and the larger towns were all asked to make special reference to Book Week. Quite a number complied. The larger stores of Winnipeg had special displays during the week.

Toronto branch was able to arrange for addresses in practically all the collegiates and high schools, and in several private schools and colleges. Several lectures were given to private groups, such as the Junior Council of Jewish Women. Speakers of the week included John Garvin, J.W.L. Forster, C.W. Jeffreys, A.E. Smythe, Fred Jacob, Wilson MacDonald, Florence Randal Livesay, Louise Rorke and John Elson.

Ottawa branch declared:

> Book Week is an established institution in the education of young French-Canadians here. Prizes are offered every year in the essay competition dealing with some aspect of Canadian literature, French or English. (The English schools had refused to bother.) Separate schools, convent schools and students of Ottawa University took part in the competition this year. Book prizes were offered, and the competition was keen. Several bookstores made displays of Canadian books, and stressed them in their advertising.

In Montreal:

> The outstanding feature of Book Week in Montreal this year was the *Gazette*'s traditional special edition, with four pages given over to carefully prepared articles on Canadian literature.

The newly revived New Brunswick branch made a beginning at celebrating Canadian Book Week with window displays of Canadian books, and a public meeting in the Admiral Beatty Hotel. Speakers included Dr. Charles G.D. Roberts, Dr. George Frederick Clarke of Woodstock, Rev. Canon Cody and others.

The Nova Scotia branch reported:

> We had a number of attractive posters printed and mailed to all booksellers and colleges in the province. The *Halifax Chronicle* published a Canadian Book Week page, to which Dr. Archibald MacMechan, president of our branch, contributed a three-column article, including short reviews of Canadian books. He also gave a radio talk. Two leading bookstores carried advertisements on this page and had special window displays.

In addition, National Secretary Dr. E.A. Hardy (Toronto) wrote to the heads of the English departments of the universities of Canada, asking them to devote at least one lecture to the subject of Canadian literature.

He got some very dusty answers. Who was the Canadian Authors Association to tell the learned professors what to teach? It appeared that this upstart organization was hobnobbing with publishers and booksellers in a crassly commercial way, and the universities were above all that. Besides, they didn't admire this grassroots "boosterism" of an almost non-existent subject.

It would seem that they didn't care to display their ignorance. A *Bookman* survey of 1924 showed as poor a record of acceptance of Canadian literature as a legitimate subject, as had Canadian history a generation ago.

In fact, Findlay Weaver, editor of the *Canadian Bookman* had made a survey of the universities four years before, inquiring about their courses in Canadian literature. It wasn't encouraging. UBC reported no study of the subject at all; Manitoba one hour a week in the fourth year; UNB had had a course but none now; U of Toronto included a few Canadian poems in a textbook; UWO studied a little Canadian poetry in the fourth year; Dalhousie reported a course on "Literary Movements in Canada"; only Acadia had a full-term course, and had for the past twenty years given courses in Canadian literature and was developing the department. Small wonder the universities were not about to take on the occasional lecture.

The Canadian Chatauqua Institution blithely hopped into the breach in 1926, advertising "The first Summer School of Canadian Literature," a week-long holiday combined with culture. It was held outdoors in June in Muskoka, with classes morning and afternoon, conducted by Dr. Charles G.D. Roberts on "The Method and Technique of Prose and Poetry"; Wilson MacDonald on "Canadian Poetry, early and recent"; and John Garvin on "Explorers' diaries and early fiction." Few took advantage of the learning experience offered, and Chatauqua did not repeat the experiment.

Book Week reached a pinnacle in 1928 in Toronto, when an immense gathering filled and overflowed Convocation Hall, University of Toronto. At least a thousand enjoyed the free program presented by the Toronto branch in cooperation with the Literature Club, of which John Garvin was president.

Dr. Charles G.D. Roberts, fifth National President of the Canadian Authors Association read his poem of the Diamond Jubilee of Confederation just past, plus an encore. L.M. Montgomery, author of *Anne of Green Gables* Canada's all-time favourite juvenile, was greeted with an ovation.

> Laughter followed her humorous sallies. In conclusion she tried
> to recite a poem in answer to about five minutes of applause,
> but forgot it before she even started. She good-naturedly con-
> jured up another.

Tall handsome Arthur Stringer, poet, novelist and screenwriter came up from New York for the occasion, and entertained the audience with reminiscences of his first rhymes. The very first was scrawled on the bathroom wallpaper, to his mother's annoyance. More permanent, but even less popular was his second, finger-printed in wet concrete on the wall of a Chatham pickle-factory. "I Love Bee and Bee Loves Me" — the amused passersby promptly learned that couplet. Stringer finished by reading recent poems, to a clamour of applause. B.K. Sandwell, up from Queen's University, fulfilled advance billing in an urbane address to the enthusiastic crowd, who had scarcely suspected authors of being alive, much less lively.

Stringer, Roberts and a young poet, Nathaniel Benson bore the news of Book Week to Western Ontario. In the course of his address to the London branch, Stringer proposed erection of a memorial to Archibald Lampman, "Canada's greatest poet," and that it be set up at nearby Morpeth, the poet's birthplace. He would contribute the first fifty dollars to the fund. Roberts supported the motion, though he demurred over the characterization. Personally, he believed Bliss Carman outshone Lampman. With boyish charm, Nat Benson said he enjoyed the little debate, but his own nomination as the major Canadian poet was right here, Dr. Charles G.D. Roberts.

The meeting closed with moving pictures taken at the CAA

convention in Banff in midsummer. The next day Stringer went home to Chatham, and Benson was Book Week ambassador to the Rotary Club in Welland. The Rotarians voted his speech a great success.

Book Week continued to grow in the consciousness of Canadians, even in spite of the Depression. After all, it cost almost nothing. Speakers were never paid, while schools and clubs enjoyed the occasional outside fare, especially on patriotic subjects. Newspapers were happy to report something more cheerful than breadlines. Authors, publishers and booksellers loved the priceless publicity.

The Canadian Authors Association became somewhat locked-in to Canadian Book Week through another literary incumbent of Rideau Hall. John Buchan, Lord Tweedsmuir, became Honorary President of the Association even before reaching Canada late in 1935. The new Governor General cabled a lengthy message to ninth National President Dr. Pelham Edgar (Toronto):

> I am delighted to hear that Canada is having a Book Week. It is a plan which we have tried in England with real success. As a writer I have naturally a special interest in the promotion of the habit of book buying. But my welcome to your venture is based on something much stronger than any professional partiality. An extension of the reading habit is vital to the future of a nation, for how else can you have a diffusion of thought and knowledge in the widest commonality? I especially hope that the Book Week will stimulate interest in Canada's own literature, for which, in my belief there is a great future. Demand creates supply; an intelligent and interested public is the best hope for the production of good books.

However, from 1945 on, when the *Canadian Author & Bookman* took to the newsstands, Association affairs were no longer reported in much detail. The end came in 1957. Enthusiasm of CAA members was waning, and besides, was there need for Book Week any longer? Authors were making promotional tours across the country, their works were being read over the radio, and now that Canada had television, viewers could see and hear them without stirring a foot to a bookstore or library. Surely it was time to call it quits.

As far back as 1925, Prof. Watson Kirkconnell, then National Secretary in Winnipeg had warned that

> a diet of copyright porridge and Book Week applesauce, good as
> they both are, do not form an adequate diet for this Association.

Now in his presidential address of his final year of a second term as
CAA National President, Dr. Kirkconnell announced the termina-
tion of the Association's participation in Book Week, and asked the
Publishers' branch of the Board of Trade, Toronto to assume full
responsibility for the annual event.

> It has been essentially a publishers' project, with the Authors
> Association fronting, gratis, for the publishers. But at a time
> when scarcely any of them even so much as advertise in the *Ca-
> nadian Author & Bookman*, the arrangement is almost completely
> one-sided. The best we can do is to assure the publishers that
> local branches will co-operate in any Book Week program, if
> called upon.

The establishment of Canadian Book Week was therefore daring, even foolhardy, yet it lasted as an annual event for 36 years,
and withered when the CAA in 1957 declined to be patsies for the
publishers any longer. It was resurrected in the late seventies as
two events, the Children's and the National Book Festivals, both
handsomely funded by the federal government.

Chapter 6
Who's Writing What?

Montreal branch celebrated its fortieth birthday at a dinner-meeting in the Ritz Carlton Hotel in March 1961. Dr. Leslie Gordon Barnard, tenth Past President and still a prolific short story writer shared reminiscences of his own forty years with the Canadian Authors Association. The dapper writer was always popular as a speaker, whether in serious dissertation on fiction techniques or on more general topics. He glanced around the dining hall, and began,

> Through the years, we have taken — and survived — much criticism. We have been the butt of many jokes, some good, some unpleasant. We have been accused of many things, for instance of being *merely* a social group, which is a complete falsity. What is more nearly the truth is that we are reasonably social and gregarious — but no more so than those who gathered at the Mermaid Inn, or in Bloomsbury, or indeed in our Press and Faculty Clubs.

> Certainly our convention frolics won more press coverage than our Resolutions or our services to authors. That's understandable. Nor could the media report the intangible benefits, that to my mind have mattered most:

> —the encouragement of an older writer to a younger
> —the shared excitement of a creative idea
> —the market tip that pays off
> —the word of timely advice
> —not least the linking of mind with mind, of province with province, so that the Canadian scene is dotted with friendships.

81

The Annual Meeting, or convention (until the term came to suggest whoopee, when it became 'conference') was held at various venues across the country, at the invitation of different branches who would then take on local responsibilities. An effort was made to alternate between East, West and Central, to make it possible for members to get to at least some of the gatherings, and also in a determined effort to acquaint members with their country and fellow Canadians. At first, the conventions were held centrally — Montreal, Ottawa, Toronto — as being most accessible to the majority. But thanks to a decade of railway passes, the more distant branches were able to play host.

The National Treasurer forwarded a cheque for one hundred dollars repayable if the convention showed a profit. If it showed a deficit, the Association made up the loss. Any profit went to support headquarters, until 1962, when Edmonton arbitrarily retained twenty-five percent, a practice now routine. The programs were the responsibility of the executive, chiefly the National Secretary, who thus carried a tremendous load.

Conventions opened with the appointment of committee chairmen — Resolutions, Nominations, Credentials. Despite the quips that absolutely anyone could get into the Canadian Authors Association, acceptance was stricter than outsiders guessed, or than it is today.

Then followed the President's address, a roundup of what had transpired since the previous meeting. Reports of the National Treasurer and National Secretary ensued, according to *Robert's Rules of Order*; reports of committee chairmen, and branch reports. The latter were heard with keen interest in the early days, for the stimulation of ideas and news of colleagues. Some reports became tedious, listing every speaker, every winner in every competition. If there were internal tiffs, the branch secretary obviously edited them out to present a picture of serenity. In later years, the reading was dropped, and written reports were filed at headquarters. But how could Halifax learn the variety of programs presented in Victoria, then five days distant by the fastest train? Or discover new methods of celebrating Book Week, say?

Selected items were picked up by the *Bulletin* and later, the *Canadian Author*, but these naturally diminished when the *Canadian Author & Bookman* went public in 1946 and lost its house-organ character.

A smattering of items from branch reports of the mid-twenties indicates what branch secretaries considered important, and conveys the Association's interest in other copyrightable arts, especially music, which was included in some form at all meetings.

The Toronto branch hosted the 1923 convention in the Arts & Letters Club, where the banquet also took place, "a comedown from the palatial Chateau Laurier of last year," sniffed William Arthur Deacon, recently arrived from Winnipeg to be literary editor of *Saturday Night*. (M.O. Hammond was then literary editor of the *Mail & Empire*, where Deacon succeeded him.) Robert J.C. Stead (Ottawa), second National President was in the chair.

Edmonton listed its first meeting as being addressed by Judge Emily Murphy ("Janey Canuck") on "Some Canadian Writers." At another meeting, Howard Angus Kennedy, a local homesteader, formerly a journalist in London, England, read his short story "Cinderella Takes up her Pen." Prof. E.A. Corbett spoke on Joseph Howe. December featured "Picture and Story in Music," by Vernon Barfoot. The January meeting was cancelled because of a blizzard and low temperature. February's subject was "Alberta's First Citizen Army in the Rebellion of 1885." In March came the first appearance of Prof. W. George Hardy, of the Department of Classics, U of Alberta, where he was notorious for liking to shock his students. He spoke on "Oedipus Rex and Conditions Governing Greek Drama," illustrating his remarks with lantern slides. It was a small beginning to more than half a century of service to the Canadian Authors Association. Another Corbett, P.E., visiting from Oxford University, closed the season with an address on "Canada's Place in the League of Nations."

The Edmonton branch had sponsored a series of fortnightly lectures during the autumn months. It had joined with the Canadian Women's Press Club in honouring Katherine Hale (Toronto), Laura Goodman Salverson (Calgary) and helped to entertain travelling Bliss Carman. (Such hospitality toward touring literati was very prevalent during the twenties, especially in the western provinces. Even though, as Isabel Ecclestone Mackay (Vancouver) commented ruefully, "Literary lions and liabilities have more in common than mere alliteration.")

The Saskatchewan branch was centred on Regina, with an offshoot in Moose Jaw, some forty miles east. The latter's most distinguished novelist was Ethel Kirk Grayson, but in later times young Joseph Schull quite surpassed her. In Regina, Mary Weekes was active in writing historical books, and guiding the branch. "A population of only 35,000 restricts our membership," she apologized.

The February 1927 meeting of the Maritimes Branch, held in Halifax, combined the reading of members' poems and prose selections. Dr. Archibald MacMechan read a series of poems about Nova Scotia, and a short story, to an enthusiastic audience.

Montreal's February 1927 meeting held at the Ritz Carlton was attended by both the French and the English Sections. B.K. Sandwell in introducing the program said that the Montreal Branch lived in a profound realization of the importance of the French language, and then introduced Dr. Frank Oliver Call of Bishop's College, Lennoxville, who spoke on his recently published book, *The Spell of French Canada*. Mr. Murray Gibbon spoke of his volume of *French Canadian Folksongs*, English words composed by Mr. Murray to the music of old French *chansons*. He used gramophone recordings to illustrate his talk. As often at CAA meetings, there was a vocalist, to indicate the nature of the Association's interest in all copyrightable material.

The Calgary branch devoted its February meeting to the one-act play, beginning with an instructive yet humorous treatise on the subject. Louis Parker's *Minuet* was then read, followed by Frank Skelhorne who read one of his own one-acters. Nellie McClung gave a summary of *The Changeling* by Isabel Ecclestone Mackay (Vancouver).

The Calgary branch welcomed the visit and address of Dr. Lorne Pierce at another meeting, and of Dr. Charles G.D. Roberts in March, which was celebrated with a dinner and dance.

On the west coast, the Victoria and the Islands branch crowded its February meeting with goodies, beginning with an amusing presentation by H.O. Litchfield of some impressions of short-story writing, and gave some older plots modernized. Alfred Carmichael gave a brief resume of his experience in collecting *Indian Legends of Vancouver Island*. He read the Nitnat story of the Flood as given to him, partly in Chinook jargon by an Indian at Clo-ose. H.S. Henderson read a delightful paper on the romance of the Northwest Passage. His present work is chiefly historical, dealing with the North Pacific coast. Major Langstaff showed a fine collection of lantern slides of various types of historical ships. C.C. Pemberton reviewed two government publications, one being *Songs of the Copper Eskimos*. Mrs. J.L.O. Cameron, president of the Ladies Musical

Club then read a most interesting paper on Eskimo music, "It is significant that even in a desolate land lacking warmth and vegetation there should be music which seems to require only harmonization to bring out its latent beauty."

"Four years ago, Regina librarian J.R.C. Honeyman originated "Literary Nights at the Library," free weekly meetings, and our branch gave receptions for travelling authors, Katherine Hale, Wilson MacDonald, Laura Salverson and Bliss Carman. The secretary, George Palmer, gave two talks on dramatic arts, which developed into the Regina Community Players. There were five public meetings, three of readings and three dramatic productions with scenery and costumes."

During the twenties, the Victoria & the Islands branch brought out a limited edition (three typed copies) of a miscellany of western verse, short stories, Indian legends, a couple of articles and photos.

Sales by CAA members included: "in the *Canadian Magazine*, Katherine Hale, James L. Hughes, Adrian Macdonald, L.M. Montgomery, Elizabeth Roberts Macdonald, Baldwyn Acland, Beatrice Redpath, W. Everard Edmunds; *Queen's Quarterly* published Watson Kirkconnell, Vincent Massey, Carleton Stanley, Prof. J.A. Roy, Duncan Campbell Scott, (who also made the *Dalhousie Review*)."

And there was other publishing news: "Basil King of Cambridge, Mass. is starting a new serial in *Harper's Magazine* which printed several of his preceding books. W.D. Lighthall's *Old Measures: Collected Verse* is published by Chapman of Montreal. W.A. Fraser's (Vancouver) *Caste* is published by Hodder & Stoughton. George Ham's *The Miracle Man of Montreal* — was published by Musson. McClelland brought out *The Return of Blue Pete*, by Luke Allen (Lacey Amy). Cape published Phil Moore's *With Rod and Gun in Canada*. Thos. Allen published A.L. Fraser's *God's Wealth and other Poems*, while J.W. Dafoe's *Laurier* was brought out by the University of Toronto Press."

"*Maclean's Magazine* continues to use a large quantity of fiction, including stories by Beatrice Redpath (Montreal), N. de Bertrand Lugrin (Edmonton), Alan Sullivan (Montreal), Archie McKishnie (Vancouver) and articles by members J.K. Munro, Guy Morton, J.L. Rutledge, H. Glynn-Ward, Dorothy Barlow. J.E. Middleton has again a regular column now in *Maclean's* entitled 'Between Friends'."

The Quebec City branch of *La Section Française* invited the CAA to hold its fourth convention (third annual meeting) in the historic city in 1924, where delegates were welcomed graciously, and the annual meeting began with prayers in both languages. The City Hall was the setting for the two-day business meetings, and delegates even from the extreme West added a few French phrases to their vocabulary.

It was decided that the executive should publish a quarterly *Authors' Bulletin* to replace the CAA section of the *Canadian Bookman*, (cost not to exceed $500 per annum including mailing) and the first issue should carry a full report of the Quebec convention.

The Secretary reported, inadequately (no names, no titles) on correspondence with the Authors League of America about a case of plagiarism. A resolution from a Montreal member proposed that when seeking names for new stations or railway cars, the CPR and CNR might well honour the most eminent deceased figures of Canadian literature of the past, such as Thomas Chandler Haliburton, author of *Sam Slick*.

Among the few speeches recorded — apart from lengthy discussion of the Copyright Act which had become law on January 1, 1924 — Madge Macbeth, a vigorous American woman, married to an Ottawan, gave her testimony in her usual warm-hearted forthright way:

"For the first few years of my writing, I did not know a single fellow craftsman. When at a luncheon of the Authors League of America I first met half a dozen struggling writers, I learned more in an hour than I had during all the years I had been writing. Authors must have a common meeting ground. The author who does not need the stimulation and the practical assistance of his fellows is very fortunate — or the reverse. Any member of the Association who is not receiving both pleasure and profit from association with fellow workers is not putting enough good fellowship into it."

(In his autobiography *One Damn Thing after Another*, the late Hugh Garner, determinedly a loner, took a battering-ram to authors' societies. He told of attending one meeting of the Toronto branch CAA, after which he went away disgruntled, and never joined any group, but felt free to castigate them all on the strength of one disappointing visit. Yet obviously his early struggles could have been eased greatly by even a few sentences from experienced writers.)

At this time news of members ran:

Basil King has just completed a novel which under the title *Caught* is to run in *Good Housekeeping* during eight months of next year, and is now at work (despite crippling arthritis) on a sequel to *The Conquest of Fear* to be published next year by Doubleday & Page.

Frances Fenwick Williams' (Montreal) novel *Viking's Rest* (Century) is getting good reviews and good sales.

Thomas Robertson's *Fighting Bishop* (John Strachan) has recently appeared as a series of articles in the *Manitoba Free Press*.

George Bugnet's (Edmonton) book of poetry *Lys de Sang* has been selling well in Montreal and Paris. He has completed a second volume.

Marius Barbeau (Ottawa) is at work on a companion volume to his *Indian Days in the Canadian Rockies*, this one on the Skeena River area.

John Garvin (Toronto), president of the Radisson Society, plans to bring out an ambitious series of Canadian reprints, to include Paul Kane's *Wanderings of an Artist*, and Dr. Grant's *Ocean to Ocean*.

In 1924 we read:

Dr. Archibald MacMechan has produced *Old Province Tales*, and *Headwaters of Canadian Literature* and Prof. John D. Logan, (both of Halifax) *Highways of Canadian Literature*, with D.G. French (Toronto).

Robert Stead's *Smoking Flax*, which has already appeared in England and USA is being published in Canada by McClelland & Goodchild. Mr. Stead has also completed a biographical and critical study of Ralph Connor for the *Makers of Canadian Literature* (Ryerson) and is now engaged upon a new novel of the Canadian West for publication next year.

Perhaps the busiest member of the Canadian Authors Association was president-elect Lawrence J. Burpee (Ottawa). He edited for John Garvin Paul Kane's *Wanderings of an Artist*, and Charles Heavysege's poetical works; prepared a biographical and critical sketch of James de Mille for the *Makers of Canadian Literature* series; the introduction, translation and notes of La Vérendrye's *Journals* for the Champlain Society; prepared a paper on the International Joint Commission for the World's Power Conference in London; a paper on Pioneer Transportation for the British Association Handbook; a paper on the Beaver Club for the Canadian Historical Association; and one on Quebec Books for the Royal Society of Canada. He is now working on a book, *On The Old Athabaska Trail* and preparing a short sketch of the Northwest Company for the series *Outline Lectures in Canadian History*, which the Historical Association is to issue in collaboration with the Public Archives of Canada.

(At the same time, Mr. Burpee was a civil servant, Canadian Secretary to the International Joint Commission and chairman of the CAA's Copyright Committee. What a work addict!)

> Among the new books by Toronto members are Marshall Saunders' *Jimmy Goldcoast*, a story of a Monkey. *Eager Footsteps*, a book of verse by Anne Elizabeth Wilson, and *A Gentleman Adventurer* by Marian Keith.

> A short talk was given by W.T. Allison (Winnipeg) on "Our Literary History," in which he pointed out that both Artemus Ward and Mark Twain acknowledged inspiration from *Sam Slick*, which was very popular in the US and also in Britain. The resemblance of the relationship between the Judge and Sam Slick and that of Pickwick and Sam Weller is so marked, that unquestionably Charles Dickens too, was influenced by Thomas Chandler Haliburton.

In his presidential address, Robert J.C. Stead nimbly skipped over the CAA's achievements of three years, and quoted a Toronto critic who declared that "Canadian literature must not be satisfied to be only as good as the literature of other lands. It must be better before Canadians will accept it in competition with the foreign-made article." To which Stead replied,

> Why? Does this criterion apply to other Canadian products? We must walk before we run. How shall we learn to run if our critics do not allow us to walk first?

(This rational query drew testy response from the literary editor of the *Manitoba Free Press*. "Writers are born with the gift to write. Keats wrote verses at nineteen and twenty that had nothing to do with literary perseverance and industry — they sang themselves out of him. Mr. Stead reduces literature to the level of a trade in which marketable articles are produced ... Learning to walk may produce books, but not literature.")

President Stead touched on the Wembley Exhibition presently in London, and the French Exhibition Train (with no further explanation of the latter). He went on to speak of the work of the Adjustment (Grievance) Committee. Most of the complaints against editorial delinquency came from outside the Association, but they were dealt with, as far as possible.

> It is only by associating with one's fellows in the craft that one learns to avoid pitfalls. Most disputes rise out of unfair or ambiguous contracts. I am convinced that the Association might render a great service by framing, in cooperation with the Canadian publishers, a standard contract in which the interests of the author as well as of the publisher would be explicitly protected.

President Stead then turned to finances.

> Our membership fee of five dollars is a very small charge — of which one dollar per capita is returned to the branch, but even so, our activities could be extended if only the fees were paid promptly.

He was not poor-mouthing the national executive, when he observed that,

> Owing to our financial limitations, members of the executive who live outside the headquarters city (in this period, Ottawa) not only give their time in attending executive meetings, but actually defray their travelling expenses out of their own pockets. You can appreciate the sincerity of their interest in the welfare of the Association.

(This situation still holds true of the CAA. Travel costs are awarded only to the President, and a small stipend to vice-presidents, for parochial visits. Capitations have increased.)

> Your executive is constantly aware that the service they are rendering to the membership and the cause at large is circumscribed by our financial exigencies. Yet our fee is low compared with the twenty-five dollars a year of the Authors League, which does not remit capitations, since it has no branches.

The National Secretary, Jules Tremblay (Ottawa), of the high forehead and waxed mustache, reported on the volume of correspondence handled: 2388 items received, 2457 mailed, 7 executive meetings attended, 79 new members, total membership 865. With all this, he didn't get enough mail! Branch secretaries failed to inform him when members died, moved or resigned. He concluded his report by requesting part-time hired help for secretary and treasurer, both offices having become almost full-time tasks. It came later.

The big address of this convention was again on copyright, a burning issue even though the Act had come into effect on New Year's Day, still including the "poisonously dishonest" clauses which protected printers more than authors.

When the Nominations Committee asked Stead if he would carry on for a second term as National President, he demurred. It might not be prudent for a civil servant to hold this position in view of such denunciation of the Canadian government. Dr. Lawrence J. Burpee, a civil servant of higher profile, had fewer qualms, and accepted the nomination. It must have stunned the members like the abdication of royalty. In his valedictory, Stead told them:

> The rewards are not in money but instead in fellowship with other writers. In my opinion the greatest service this Association is rendering its members is the acquaintanceships established among them. A bond is woven which knits together the literary interests of Canada, and inspires every individual member to efforts which will bring credit upon himself and his fellow craftsmen. Speaking for myself, the treasures of friendship which have been unlocked to me through my connection with the Association more than repay any small effort I have expended on its behalf.

It was a graceful speech from a normally silent Scot. He rather marred the effect by quitting his post, though not his membership in the CAA.

The third national president, Lawrence Burpee, presided over the first convention west of the Great Lakes, held in Winnipeg in June 1925. A female news reporter, Kennethe Haig, from the *Winnipeg Evening Tribune* covered events — and personalities:

> We spent time looking up Burpee, Lawrence J. in *Who's Who*. He writes essays and poems and articles and novels, and is president of this and that, and Fellow of other sorts of things, has achieved eight letters after his name, and contributes to the *Encyclopedia Britannica*. That's the sort of person Lawrence J. is. . . . We can't think why he didn't allow his photograph in the record. It would have raised the average.

Starting his address, President Burpee declared he would keep his remarks to a minimum. He didn't. He touched on a barrage of snide comment that accused the CAA of

> "whooper-upism" for the works of its own members, and sundry unworthy aims. Such exaggerated and ill-natured statements have their uses if they prod us into a jealous scrutiny of our actions and of our viewpoint as a national Association. If it is still our purpose 'to act for the mutual benefit and protection of Canadian authors, and for the maintenance of high ideals' — as it must be — we can afford to treat with good natured amusement the mis-directed shafts of the phrase-makers.

At the conclusion of the address, Murray Gibbon (Montreal) was disposed to discount such darts:

> For an Association to last four years and then show a cash surplus of fourteen hundred dollars is surely a record. The future of the CAA will depend on a worthwhile literature; it must have something to function for. If nothing important is written, it will die. The upbuilding of a Canadian literature must be a long slow performance.

More dangerous to the Association than detractors were unreasonable expectations, President Burpee believed. Some members felt they were not getting adequate return for their fees, low though they were; he pointed out the difficulties of a small under-financed association as compared with large memberships in Britain and the United States.

> The work of our Association has to be carried on by three National officers, all of them very busy men who have to steal away from their other occupations the time they devote to your interests. They have not accomplished all that you or they would wish, but they have achieved some things of value.

He instanced the copyright battle waged this past year, when E.E. Chevrier, M.P. introduced a Bill in Parliament, and it got as far as committee.

> Day after day, Mr. Chevrier, Dr. de Montigny and one or two others (including himself) sat in the committee rooms and listened to the clever arguments and appeals to prejudice of these influential people. Yet we won — the Committee passed the Bill. The first round was ours, but we lost the bout. One senator commented cynically, "Well, there are more printers than authors."

91

An important small matter would come before the membership. It was vital to maintain communication across the country. Could this be done best by publishing the *Authors' Bulletin* from time to time, or by staying with the *Canadian Bookman*? In either course the members should elect an editor to relieve the load on the National Secretary.

President Burpee applauded the broad-minded example of Quebec in awarding the David prizes, and felt it was time that the Canadian government should be no less generous in encouraging the Arts and Literature. During his visit to Canada last year, Captain John Buchan had discussed the matter with the Governor General (Lord Byng) and Prime Minister Mackenzie King, and the suggestion received a good deal of interest. But that was as far as it went at the time. Nonetheless, advances would be made again shortly.

Peppery redhead Robert Watson (Winnipeg) dredged up a curious situation. Canadian writers paid income tax to foreign countries on their copyright royalties — 22½ percent in Britain, only eight percent in the USA. Did foreign writers pay similar income tax to Canada? If not, it was peculiarly short-sighted on the part of National Revenue, since the sums involved would be far greater than Canadian writers coughed up. In addition, when the reduced cheque arrived in Canada, Dominion tax took another bite of four percent, and provincial tax a further two percent.

A committee was earmarked to investigate, and report at the next convention in Vancouver. It was there announced that through our friendly links with the Society of Authors in Britain, a Canadian author published in Britain was no longer required to pay income tax there, on the grounds that his British agent paid a percentage of his/her profits into the coffers of the British government. The threat of retaliation in Canada stirred the British authors and government into unusually prompt action. It took a quarter-century to reach a treaty with the USA, which was ratified only in 1966. The author would pay income tax in only one country, and the choice was his.

The Treasurer's report in 1925 showed a total budget of $3,772 entirely from fees collected. The fee which had been three dollars for an Associate member proved self-defeating, since it did not encourage a member to meet the output required to become a Regular member. All fees became a straight five dollars and remained so for decades.

It makes an interesting comment on costs, to look at the expenses of Canadian Authors Association, and note the severe economy practiced. Only the hired stenographer drew a salary.

Here then are the disbursements in 1924-25:

Capitation to the branches	$ 639.50
Salary of assistant	625.00
Publishing Bulletins	344.00
Secretary's expenses	166.26
President's travelling expenses	125.00
Stationery and stamps	169.92
Printing and engraving	79.32
John Buchan dinner	16.27
Regina branch booklets	3.96
Winnipeg Convention grant	100.00
Post Office box	6.00
Bank charges	20.16
Sundries	55.48
Balance, cash on hand	1,421.69
	$ 3,772.56

The Winnipeg reporter gave thumbnail sketches of various other participants on the program.

> There was Charles G.D. Roberts with the shutters of his face all down, but his eye-glass ribbon guard. There was Frederick Philip Grove, with thought in the process of evolution and no hurry about it. Murray Gibbon maintaining his expression of complete disillusionment, and Prof. Allison with the smile that refused to be effaced.

The reporter found something to please when Nellie McClung (Edmonton) took the platform.

> Nellie McClung comes home! She says so and the audience believes her. Same beautiful voice, same flavour of dramatic instinct, same rollicking wit, "wild men of the West and wise men of the East." She told of a dear old soul in Ontario who had three children living and two out West. Mrs. McClung's audience grins with her, chuckles, agrees with her that authors who can contribute to "Canadians all" have the gift of life for Canada. Nellie McClung — born with the gift of laughter and the sense that the world is a little mad, a little kind, a little cruel, — made up of human beings.

> Dr. George Locke, *the* Dr. Locke of Toronto Public Libraries, is

not so much a speaker as a monologuer, a large person, a large voice. He has the courage of his association of ideas. On the talk ripples, slipping from crest to crest easily, effortlessly, glimmering with gentle wit. Biff! he touches on libraries, and instantly becomes mantled with his profession. That is why Toronto and Canada owe so much to his fine work in showing what a library may mean to a community.

A French-Canadian who looks like an English squire, such is Judge Surveyer. He comes right out and announces he has a Message. Alarm in the ranks. Slight scurryings to and fro, this way to the exit! But there is no need. The judge is not being instructive nor unduly uplifting, just charmingly carrying Quebec's best *devoirs.*

Officers elected at this fourth Annual Meeting were: President, the hospitable Prof. Wm. Talbot Allison of the University of Manitoba; Treasurer, Robert Watson, tiny dynamic editor of the Hudson's Bay quarterly *Beaver,* and prolific fictioneer ("My books are nothing wonderful but they are clean out-of-doors virile stuff, and they seem to be liked by Canadians, Americans and British alike."); National Secretary, Prof. Watson Kirkconnell of Wesleyan College, a prodigious worker, both in literature and in the service of the Association.

With the three officials conveniently in the same city, the files were shipped west from Ottawa, the bank account transferred, and the three settled into harness. Even with half a stenographer (paid) each, the work piled up for the treasurer, and especially for the National Secretary.

Chapter 7
Getting Down to Business

Vancouver & Mainlands Branch hosted the 1926 convention in early August. Most of the delegates stayed in the Hotel Vancouver, next door to the Vancouver Court House where the plenary sessions were called, President W.T. Allison (Winnipeg) in the chair.

Beaming, he announced that the bank balance stood at $1,600, "for the very good reason that our Treasurer Robert Watson was born in Scotland."

Referring to Book Week, Dr. Allison declared,

> I am persuaded that this educational feature of our work as an Association has amply justified our existence.... As we look back on five years of corporate existence, we can see that owing to our efforts, there has been a distinct improvement in the attitude of the Canadian reading public towards Canadian letters. While it must be admitted that we have to face much indifference to native books and expressed hostility in certain quarters where nothing is judged worthwhile unless it is English or American, there has been a decided change for the better.

> I can best illustrate this change for the better in the literary life of this country by sketching the career of one of our own CAA members, the Rev. Charles W. Gordon (Winnipeg).

> It was in 1897, a generation ago that the man known the world over as "Ralph Connor" wrote his first story, *Black Rock*. At that time, he still vividly recalled his own experiences as a young missionary preacher in the Canadian Rockies, and took to fiction to stir up interest among church people in the East. He ped-

dled his manuscript round to the two or three publishers in Toronto and to many in New York, but each and all failed to see any popular appeal in a story about a sky-pilot in a Rocky Mountain mining camp.

Ultimately *Black Rock* was published by a little Toronto group of Dr. Gordon's personal friends who were no doubt as surprised as he was when it became an immediate success. In fact so large a sale was achieved in Canada and so favourable were the reviews far and wide that the New York publishers realized that they had made a decided mistake in judgment. Within a year, fifteen pirated editions of the story were published in the United States, and Ralph Connor had become famous. Since then he has produced a story every other year, and as everyone knows, his books have sold by the million. No writer on this continent has had such a large or steady sale for his books. In England, Australia, South Africa and India, his stories are to be found on every bookstall and many of his books have been translated into foreign languages, including Russian and Icelandic.

Now the significance of Ralph Connor as far as Canadian literature was concerned is two-fold: first, he opened up a new field in world fiction, our Canadian West, the broad land of prairie and mountain, where a young and vigorous people is building an inland empire. In the second place he opened a new era of Canadian authorship.

Until the publication of *Black Rock* in 1897 no work of fiction by any Canadian writer attained a circulation of three thousand copies. And even after Ralph Connor had started his meteoric career, there was little activity in the publishing business in Canada. The Canadian people were skeptical as to the quality of homemade fiction and there were comparatively few who were prepared to spend their money for poetry or history or any kind of book of the heavier sort if it came from the pen of a native-born.

From the year 1885, when Charles G.D. Roberts published his first volume of verse, *Orion, and Other Poems*, Canada has never been without poets who have sung melodiously of her romantic past and of her glories of lake and forest and stream. Some of those poets, for example Bliss Carman, William Wilfred Campbell, Duncan Campbell Scott and Archibald Lampman have won international fame, but it is doubtful whether any of them ever sold more than one thousand copies of any volume of his verse in his own country. Until within recent years, a Canadian publisher would not dream of issuing a book of verse unless the cost was advanced by the poet.

Few members had known these facts, and they were enthralled by the address. National Secretary Prof. Watson Kirkconnell brought them back to business with his lengthy hard-hitting report. The annual *Bulletin* had been published in December, and the Commissioner of Taxation had promised consideration. An exhaustive investigation into musical copyright had been made by Dr. E.A. Hardy and John Elson (both Toronto), with no final results. The motion of Leslie Gordon Barnard (Montreal) asking federal subventions for literature had been acted upon:

> In view of the imminence of a celebration of Canada's Diamond Jubilee of Confederation, your Executive recommended strongly to Prime Minister King and to the committee in charge of the solemnities that in the name of Confederation they endow in perpetuity an annual prize of perhaps one thousand dollars to be awarded for the most notable work published each year by a resident Canadian. It seemed that such a permanent memorial would have a more abiding value to Canadian nationhood than a present orgy of demonstration. The Confederation Prize for Literature was warmly supported by enlightened editors from Nova Scotia to the Pacific. Its concern with the intellectual welfare of Canada instead of with mere mob combustion commended it to many thoughtful citizens in all provinces.
>
> The Diamond Jubilee Committee has given our proposal a courteous hearing and has reserved it for further consideration. Should the present venture be void, it is to be hoped that continued importunities from succeeding CAA executives will press the claims of Canadian literature upon a government which abandons authorship to the Department of Trade and Commerce.
>
> It is perhaps significant that an otherwise admirable book published by the Jubilee Committee on Canada's national achievements has not a word to say about Canadian painting, sculpture, music or literature. It is to be hoped that the birthday of the Dominion may yet be associated with a memorial which stands for the cultural rather than the material side of civilization.
>
> The question of a larger capitation may be answered by a simple reference to arithmetic. In 1925-26 our surplus of income over

97

expenditure was only $213.72. The present year reports a small deficit. To hand over an extra dollar per member to the branch would mean a deficit of about $500.00 per annum. Even fifty cents would put us on the road to bankruptcy.

At the same time expenses have been whittled down to a minimum. The national officers give their services free, although I myself have handled 10,000 items of mail in the past two years and my predecessor, Mr. Tremblay, reported 12,000 for his biennial term. I have been providing an office rent free. Virtually our only expenses have been fifty dollars a month for a stenographer for the treasurer and myself and several hundred dollars for postage, printing and convention expenses. The surprising thing is that we have been able to run a nation-wide organization on so little.

The frequent suggestion that the membership fee ($5) is too high is thus answered at the same time. Our dues are really ridiculously low, probably lower than those of any similar society in the world. American authors pay $25.00 a year to the head office of the Authors League of America, while the British Society charges thirty shillings (about $5) a year with a membership of many thousands.

Finally, there is the question of branch autonomy in admitting members to the Association and determining their status. This is of course, directly opposed to the Constitution which, in Articles 3 and 4 assigns such powers exclusively to the national body. An informal practice of having branches endorse local applications in order that they might be recommended from local knowledge and guaranteed as *persona grata* has created a vague impression that this implies branch authority to make and unmake members. The dangers in such an arrangement are exceedingly grave. Membership in the Association is obviously a national affair. To delegate the power of admission to thirteen local bodies, many of them small and haphazard, would be most impolitic. Consider, for instance, the heart-burnings and bitterness over the determination of status or even possible rejection by local citizens instead of by an impersonal national executive.

But beyond all this, the suggestion indicates a disquieting tendency towards sectionalism and disintegration into a mere group of literary societies scattered across Canada. For effective survival, the Association needs to move in the opposite direction and make itself more definitely felt as a national organization. In this it needs to devise new national functions and extend its field of national usefulness. One such function, would call for the creation of a national committee or bureau which would be available as a consultative mediator between the Canadian author and the cinema producer.

The same or a similar committee might be available for editors desiring information as to sources for special articles on Canadian subjects. (A "brain bank," as it were.)

Other new activities might look towards the artists and composers of Canada, who are eligible for membership but are not likely to come in of their own accord. We might even think seriously of raising our fees to $25 and hiring some skilled lawyer as a permanent full-time secretary located in the Dominion capital. But whatever steps are taken to build for the future, it is to be hoped that the welfare and existence of the national organization as a whole will be carefully guarded.

I have said farewell at some length, and with some candour, for during my two years of hard and often thankless ("No, no") work I have gained a somewhat intimate knowledge of our present general problems, and I feel that that knowledge should be placed at your disposal. Moreover, there is a sense of freedom that comes with release from duty, and at the end of a hard day, I hope you will forgive a tired horse for shaking himself as the harness is being taken off.

(But, in fact, Prof. Kirkconnell was not out of the shafts yet. He ended his service as national secretary at the 1927 convention in Ottawa, and felt sure he had done his stint. Far from it. He had two bouts as national president ahead of him, to say nothing of filling-in during the absences of Ralph Connor. He fully earned a "reputation for patience, integrity, hard work and administrative competence, in other words, for being a nice tame dray horse who would not run away with the milk-wagon" as he described himself later.)

After a morning of business, the male members were guests of the Men's Canadian Club, with Dr. George Locke as speaker. He reversed the customary opinion in speaking on, "The Influence of Canadian Literature on that of the United States." Dr. Locke cited Haliburton as the precursor of Mark Twain; Roberts' animal romances as inspiring Ernest Thompson Seton (who was also a Canadian); and thirdly, stories of the great West inaugurated by Ralph Connor had given a distinct direction to literature on this continent.

The female contingent missed this dissertation, being entertained to lunch by the Women's Canadian Club. On reassembling in the Court House, members heard Arthur Heming open a general discussion on the question, "Can Canada support the Canadian Writer?"

"In a word, no. Or rather it wouldn't. He described his early income from freelance writing and illustrating, then how vastly it had improved after he had departed to live in New Jersey.

My experience has been that authors and artists, if they really tried, could be better business men than the business men themselves. I myself have never employed an agent, yet I have been able to negotiate free camping outfits, free rifles and painkiller (smirk) and huge advance cheques for work as yet unwritten. In connection with one of my books, working independently, I succeeded in selling eighteen different rights. (And this before radio and television!) My general view is that a Canadian author would starve if he sold only to the Canadian markets but that he can, even though remaining in Canada, make a living selling his work abroad."

Robert Watson heartily agreed. He valued his editorship of *Beaver* not only for his living but as a source of endless stories of Hudson's Bay Company trading areas.

> I must have other employment to assure a living. A writer has to gain the goodwill of newspapers that run fiction. I sent out synopses of four of my most successful novels to *thirty-three* different Canadian newspapers, suggesting the same price as they were paying for similar American material. Few of the newspapers bothered to reply, and none accepted. I believe we need a syndicate to handle articles and fiction in such volume as to assure the newspaper world of a steady flow of contributions.

(Watson took off for Hollywood shortly thereafter, only to learn the faraway fields were not so green as they looked from Winnipeg. He found himself not so much a scriptwriter as part of a committee, where 'compromise' was the key word. Then one foggy evening, he was fatally injured by an automobile.)

A little diversion was laid on for the evening, by way of a steamboat excursion up the North Arm to Wigwam Inn.

> This charming rendezvous at the head of the mountain-girt fiord was reached after a sail of two hours. Here a regal banquet was followed by a delightful program of song, address and recitation, including clever verse by P.C. Luce (who often contributed to *Saturday Night*), and a witty song in French by Judge

100

Surveyer. A moonlight sail back to Vancouver completed the spell of the outing.

The Saturday afternoon was scheduled for literary dissertations, but was pre-empted by a late invitation. Would the authors care to ride up to the new Grouse Mountain Chalet, and take high tea at a very scenic viewpoint? The Grouse Mountain and Scenic Resort Company of Vancouver would happily play host. Who could resist?

The revised program did not please all the delegates. How could the CAA request the austere Frederick Philip Grove to prepare a speech for his fellow-members, and then they flitted off on a frivolous excursion! Kirkconnell, who was largely responsible for the convention program was chagrined. Grove was outraged. Here he had been at pains to write out an intellectual lecture for an audience who snatched the first opportunity to duck out. Grove would not again travel two thousand miles in his rickety old car, to find his words ignored in this cavalier fashion!

On returning home, Grove wrote out his indignation in an essay entitled "A Neglected Function of a Certain Literary Association." That function he held, "was to present the young author with fundamental standards of art and thought, based on the great classics of European literature and not on the popularly successful work of E. Phillips Oppenheim, Zane Grey and Arthur Stringer." Kirkconnell later wrote, "At the time of the 1926 convention Grove was known only as the author of two gifted volumes of prairie essays, although Arthur Phelps and I on a weekend visit to his home in Rapid City, Manitoba, had seen the manuscripts of a dozen full-length novels awaiting publication."

(Perhaps it was as well the delegates were up on Grouse Mountain on a beautiful August day, rather than sitting in the Court House being nagged or bemused by standards beyond their grasp.) Arthur Stringer took fifteen years before presenting the case as a dialogue between a veteran author (himself) and a youthful idealist.

The cameraderie of the Vancouver convention spurred Calgary branch to renew its invitation to the Association to hold a convention in the Foothills City. Its executive admitted themselves nervous about getting together a program that would impress Easterners. The invitation was accepted for 1928, on the sensible grounds that 1926 having been held so far west, the next convention should be central, in Ottawa. In the meantime, the national executive would muster a program, enlisting cooperation of various branches. At least ten contributed a speaker or some feature. The result was an exceptionally rich fare, to the point that some members felt a touch of indigestion.

In his opening address, National President, Dr. Charles G.D. Roberts (Toronto) expressed pleasure in the growth of every branch, and the revival of the Saint John branch, thanks largely to a turnout of some 600 listeners to a poetry reading by Bliss Carman and Roberts himself. In his year of office, the sixty-seven-year-old president had visited all the branches from Ontario to Victoria, some of them en route to the University of British Columbia where he was a special lecturer for the winter term. He hoped to visit the others within the next few months.

> For the branches *are* the Association and it is upon their healthy activity individually that the usefulness of the Association mainly depends. We are in effect a Guild of Workers. We include not only those who have arrived, but those who are arriving, and those who are striving earnestly to arrive. It is our business to be broadly and liberally inclusive.

The President spoke feelingly of the loss of several members by death during the past year: Sir John Willison (Toronto), Dr. Jules Tremblay (Ottawa), Austin Bothwell (Regina), and only a few days ago, Basil King. He paid tribute to Charles Mair, "the father of Canadian literature," dead in Vancouver, aged eighty-nine. He touched on the Book Fair in Dayton, Ohio, where as representative of the CAA he had been invited to speak several times to audiences of authors and publishers. Their interest was gratifying. He referred to awards and prizes, particularly the Royal Society's Lorne Pierce Gold Medal for Literature conferred upon Bliss Carman.

National Secretary Dr. E.A. Hardy (Toronto) gave his report in detail and seriatim:

1. The *Bulletin* was late in being mailed because vital data had not been received sooner.

2. The biographical/bibliographical questionnaire had been mailed to all members. Some 200 had already replied, and their value is established. The secretary is often asked for information about authors, and with a membership of over 700, it is impossible for one person to keep all the informa-

tion in his memory.

3. Book Week. See branch reports. Your executive hopes to secure much wider cooperation through other organizations interested in this work.

4. The *Canadian Bookman*: Continuing the arrangement of last year of three pages at $15 a page each month. The secretary has supplied material covering the activities of the national executive and of the branches.

5. Committee meetings: 7, including one on copyright.

6. Branches: 13, including two in the French Section.

7. Copyright: see Mr. Burpee's comprehensive memorandum.

8. The Calgary Convention: Every branch was asked to make some contribution to the program in the form of a paper or an address, or readings. A tribute should be paid to Elizabeth Bailey Price and her committee, for the completeness of their arrangements, and also to our two great railways for their assistance in transportation and hotel arrangements.

9. Membership: we had 706, lost 6, gained 95. Total 795.

10. Office detail: My correspondence has been heavy and continuous. At least 1,000 letters have reached me, and at least 2,000 pieces of printed matter have been mailed. The national treasurer and I share clerical help @ $50 a month, which is fairly satisfactory, but not really sufficient.

11. Expenditure: Naturally these have been heavier, because of the larger services we undertook; for example, the larger *Bulletin*, the copyright matter (sending Dr. Burpee to the Rome convention).

12. The Future: For the coming year there are matters left over from 1927-28, which we were not able to complete: a) a larger membership of artists; b) establishment of strong working committees of artists; c) establishment of a committee on scenario rights; d) establishment of new branches; e) formation of a card index of membership; f) a monthly list of Canadian contributors to Canadian periodicals; g) compilation of members' biographical data; h) lists of competitions in Canada and elsewhere; i) appointment of an Honorary Solicitor; j) study the question of incorporation and a national headquarters.

13. Your Executive believes that the National Body should render a more intensive and extensive service to individual members, and to the branches. The branches might be of more service to one another through exchange of papers and addresses.

But it became evident that the Association had already bitten off more than it could chew, when the report of the Resolutions Committee recommended that:

1. The invitation to hold the 1929 convention in Halifax be accepted. Carried

2. The correspondence with motion picture studios be left to the national secretary to advise scenario writers.

3. Any action on the proposal of the Performing Right Society be deferred until Mr. Burpee's return from the Rome Conference on copyright.

4. Correspondence with the Australian Literature Society be referred to the national secretary.

5. Correspondence with the League of Western Writers had resulted in the official visit of the president at their meeting in Portland, Oregon.

6. Action on the invitation of the International Confederation of Authors and Copyright Societies, to attend its annual convention in Berlin await Mr. Burpee's report.

7. Arthur Stringer, who is president of the Metropolitan District of New York offer his services as a liaison between the CAA and the Authors League of America.

8. In view of the interchange between the CAA and the Society of Authors (Great Britain) active cooperation and exchange membership privileges be implemented.

9. The incoming Council revise the constitution so that the offices of secretary and treasurer, either separately or together be made permanent, instead of bi-annual as at present. (Impracticable. Deferred to 1929.)

10. The CAA strongly recommends the appointment of a qualified representative of the prairie provinces on the Dominion Historical Sites board, in view of inaccuracy in certain tablets.

In the interests of the historical records, and as a contribution to the work of historical writers ... that surveyors working in areas of historical interest shall endeavour to locate lost historical sites, and that aerial photographs of such areas be made available to historical writers.

Finally came the treasurer's report, with John M. Elson (Toronto) beaming as he informed members that the budget for the year came to a whacking $4,037, and there was a balance of $1,171 on deposit. The only unusual expense was $750 (less a refund of $100) for Mr. Burpee's brief visit to Rome for the revision of the Berne Convention on Copyright.

Years later, a National President scanning a proposed convention program that glittered with hoop-la, had to demand, "But where's the meat of the program?" Not so at Calgary in '28. One speaker after another sparkled with humour and inspiration. Their words still read well after fifty years.

Margaret I. Lawrence, author of *The School of Femininity* (about women writers) had interviewed Major Christie ("Sirhindi") (both Saint John) on his opinion of critics. The crusty ex-army major began by quoting Coleridge's sour comment:

Reviewers are usually people who would have been poets, historians, biographers, etc. if they could: they have tried their talents and failed. Therefore they turn critics.

Coleridge indulges in generalizations ... and implies that a critic and reviewer are the same thing. Critics there have been since the first artist scratched on an auroch bone and his friends sneered.

But the reviewer is a modernity. The critic is like an autocratic dashing and debonair surgeon in a military hospital ... probes without restraint, slashes away the unhealthy tissues, to heal if he may by dressings that oft-times smart horribly. The reviewer is like a mild consulting physician who accidentally has strayed into a surgical ward filled with patients whose rich relatives refuse to countenance an operation ... He is deserving of much sympathy. He must daily wade through oceans of bilge. His metier is to interest a public noted for its lack of taste and aversion to thought, and to inform it as to what new publications it may read with pleasure and profit. He is not required to criticize. He is constantly tempted to degenerate into a mere ad writer. (That comparatively few succumb to this temptation may account for the low estimate placed by authors on the mentality of reviewers.) While literary critics are becoming rare, recruits aplenty fill the reviewers' ranks.

The reviewer is the guide, philosopher, and friend of the book reader. He is the servant of the periodical in which his material appears, and most valued assistant to the publisher.

Margaret I. Lawrence herself took up the role of the book reviewer, as she was for the *Saint John Evening Telegraph*, and began by quoting the young Goethe: "Kill the dog — he's a reviewer," and went on to say,

> Many new writers are so intolerant of the critic as to merit the phrase: "they desire not criticism but uncritical praise ..."

> There has always been the question of finance. No one considered the book reviewer worthy of a salary. Yet the reviewer is a hopeless optimist and accepts the conditions for sheer love of his work, even knowing that most newspaper editors regard book reviewing as "a frill," and that column is the first to be squeezed out. What is needed is guidance in the technique of the review. Very little has been written to supply this need. Recently Mr. William Arthur Deacon has moved to the *Saturday Night*, and opened its pages to the reviewer who can qualify according to his "Theory of Reviewing." Mr. Deacon sets forth the ideal book review as: "The truthful record of the impression made by a certain book upon a well-read man who has been stirred by it. It should reflect the personalities of both author and reviewer and hold the attention of its readers. It is then at once a narrative, an exposition and a judgment, and is in itself, literature."

> Authors as a rule are rather a helpless lot when away from their desks, and refreshingly grateful to those who really like and appreciate their work. One stands abashed before the courteous little note that follows a review whose only merit lies in its sincere desire to see the thing from the author's point of view. Nor can I agree with Sirhindi's assertion that publishers appreciate nobody except insofar as they bring him profit. Business is business of course, and it would be folly to neglect the big and little steps that make for success in the publishing of books.

> And yet I have found the publishers to be the most approachable and agreeable of mankind. My years are filled with the most redolent memories of publishers ... Again and again there is a line from some publishers — a few words that make of us, reviewer and journal, author and publisher a united firm engaged in an effort to promote greater knowledge, a greater

love of and for letters.

The terrific volume of books, largely fiction, that is at present pouring over the public leaves a member of the older generation a bit breathless, yet how exciting and worthwhile it is; that while there are more books to read and criticize, there is a corresponding increase in those you want to keep.

Carroll Aikins (Vancouver) of Penticton, B.C. drew on his wide experience in amateur dramatics to instruct, inform and inspire would-be playwrights. Montreal Branch had launched a playwriting competition, with meagre prizes and abundant response. It was the era of little theatres and one-act plays, and Mr. Aikins' advice was timely as well as sound. His talk was charmingly illustrated with parables, as he pointed out flaws in material that had been thrust upon him at times.

Few plays written by occasional authors can be accepted for production. First, because their subject is *undramatic*, does not lend itself to the sharp, resolute and pungent treatment the stage demands. Second are dramas with religious or racial enmities or sexual perversions, or any theme or treatment tending to arouse ignoble or malicious feelings.

Third, some subjects are too obvious, such as the prairie wife or the Mounted Police. Theses about world peace or prison reform or vegetarianism are quite alien to the ends of art. And there is the would-be mystical drama, and of course many others that are unsatisfactory.

Turning to defects in treatment — the commonest is an extravagant use of materials — too much talk, too many scenes, too many people. I had this year the script of a very distinguished publisher, a thoroughly lively and engaging drama, good fun and good sense, but not good practical theatre-stuff. For instance, the first scene called for forty actors dressed as sparrows to be discovered twittering and preening on a gigantic dung-hill. Intriguing.

Another but less common mistake is to be led into bathos. As an awful example, I recall a manuscript in which an abnormally virtuous young hero, was done in by his enemies at the end of Act Two, and loudly and explicitly forgiving them from the vantage point of a heavenly mansion. The setting required for this act was a billowy cloud with a hole to talk through, and certain conveniences for a chorus of female angels. Altogether it was a perfect sample of what not to ask of the actors, the director and the stage carpenter.

Another type of failure, the most common, are plays written to a formula — plays of algebraic certitude, of calculated advance and retreat. Of such plays there is not much to say except the rather equivocal comment that the authors must have enjoyed writing them. In direct contrast to these mannerly efforts are many (a great many) which while lacking every amenity of form, and thus impossible to produce, have nevertheless quite a vigorous life of their own. Of these one can only regret that the authors failed to submit themselves to the rigorous discipline which play-writing demands. And it does demand, I assure you, great efforts of patience, suppleness and humility. I should like to mention Merrill Denison of Toronto who writes of the Ontario backwoods with great good sense, humour and authority. He is I think, the only Canadian dramatist whose work crosses frontiers and deserves to do so.

Miss Donalda Dickie, of the Provincial Normal School, member of the Calgary branch, and author of several books of Canadian history for children, spoke of the importance of reading early and quickly. She pointed out that great authors such as Barrie and Kipling did not disdain to write for young readers.

Almost all the supplementary reading we have for children ... has been written by English or American authors for English or American children. Canadians have as yet written scarcely anything for children. Yet few countries provide richer sources — romantic, historic, geographic, industrial. Moreover, writing for children pays — The need is great. The field is wide and almost virgin. It waits for you who will enter in and possess it.

Miss Georgina H. Thomson of Calgary Public Library was detailed by Librarian Calhoun to prepare a talk on Canadian books for Adolescent Girls. She had protested, "I don't know anything about it." "Yes, but think how much you will know when you get through."

Her list, she admitted, was not exhaustive, but the search was exhausting.

Probably the logical place to start is with *Anne of Green Gables*. My sister and I spent our childhood on a prairie farm, far from circulating libraries and bookshops. The modest stock of books we brought from the East, mostly classics, were read and re-read, and passed around the neighbourhood until they were worn out. It was a genuine thrill to get hold of a book about a real girl like ourselves, so that Anne had a royal reception from us. I have also included Nellie McClung's trilogy *Sowing Seeds In Danny* and Marian Keith's small town Ontario stories. Ethel Hume Bennett wrote *Judy of York Hill* (a girls' boarding school in Toronto) and her summer camp books. May Embree wrote *The Girls of Miss Cleveland's*, the first Canadian schoolgirl story.

Another librarian, Evalyn Srigley (Edmonton) declared,

In fact there was little Canadian fiction for the adolescent girl — and even less for her brother, once you got past the animal stories of Ernest Thompson Seton and Charles G.D. Roberts (originally meant for adults).

Gentlemen the Authors, the boys are not reading the books — that's your fault. You haven't written them. When a young Englishman asked me for titles of books he might send home to teenage nephews that would introduce them to a real Canadian boy, there was only one book of the kind he wanted, E.W. Thomson's *The Young Boss*. Here's hoping he finds what he wants . . . I've been trying to find such books for fifteen years. You see, he didn't want hyphenated types — Scot, Irish or French — excellent though they are, but tales of lads as essentially Canadian as is *Anne of Green Gables* . . .

We have some thoroughly good historical fiction — written for adults. I am not pretending that the Boy will be particularly easy to write for. He doesn't like "fine writing," but he does appreciate a meaty idea. He won't accept fakes and scorns inaccuracy. Tell him the stories of the Pioneers, and their pride and endurance and hardships. And the boys of 1812, when males of sixteen to sixty were called to defend their country. Tell today's youth of them, alluringly.

Who can do it?

Men who are just out of boyhood themselves, and those who are old enough to take joy in remembering how they used to feel. Middle-aged minds will muddle the work; women cannot do it at all.

Here's one tip. People, even boys, used to have a constant consciousness of God.

It was not an academic but the secretary of the London & Western Ontario branch, Ruth Higgins, who gave the most impassioned address at the Calgary convention, on Canadian history and biography. An American, she met her Canadian husband at McGill University, and adopted his country enthusiastically. As an outsider, she could see the gaps and the flaws. She spoke forcefully.

> Our (Canadian history) textbooks are DRY AS DUST! . . . Yet Canada is full of Drama, Romance, and Human Interest, as Dr. Frank Underhill states in a recent issue of the *Canadian Forum*.

Mrs. Higgins quoted Underhill at some length, a severe arraignment of Canadians' written history, as compared with the liveliness of American textbooks. She felt that biography offered most, but it was in the old laudatory mode, nothing like the human interest of Lytton Strachey's new biographies.

> What an ideal subject for some Canadian Strachey would be Sir John A. Macdonald! Sir Wilfrid Laurier has been well done in Sir John Willison's great work, but we still lack the biography that will vividly create for us the picturesque figure of "The White Plume" with all his little tricks of manner, his characteristic figures of speech, his knowledge of men and their weakness. Let's have a Strachey for Laurier too.

> Biographies of the railroad magnates, Strathcona and Van Horne or Mackenzie and Mann could scarcely be dull. There are rumors that some of our political leaders have in mind to contribute an account of their times. All will be welcome when they appear. One biography most needed is that of Edward Blake, an enigma. Why did he fail to marry, then marry in haste? Blake was leader of the Liberal party 1880-87, and his word gave Canada young Laurier, when the party was deliberating between short-tempered Richard Cartwright and the philosophic David Mills.

> There is Antoine Aimé Dorion "one of the noblest figures in our political annals" and there is Israel Tarte, who organized Quebec to victory in 1896, but is remembered chiefly as an inveterate intriguer. Another who should attract western writers is the weird figure of Louis Riel. He will never be forgotten, but what is the truth about him?

> History is the record of *all* the people — men and women. The lives of our leaders *belong* to us, part of our national wealth. This then, is the point — a plea for the books that will give us intimate and more sympathetic contact with the past through interesting and humanizing records of the lives of men and women who make our history.

(It is gratifying to note that many of Mrs. Higgins' suggestions have been taken up by Canadian writers. Prime ministers need not have passed from the scene before the hatchet is out, and the public learns more than it wants to know of the seamy side of politics. Explorers and statesmen, churchmen and medical men nowadays get a going-over rather than the non-informative eulogies of half a century ago.)

When it came to a discussion on poetry, John Murray Gibbon gave a short talk, advocating free verse as a proper method for Canadian writers (in opposition to the vigorous denunciation of the form expressed by English poet Alfred Noyes on his sweep through Canada not long before, "laying down the law that Free Verse is not musical, that the only musical verse is rhymed.")

Said Gibbon,

> Most writers of Free Verse have had knowledge of music, far more so than writers of rhymed verse. If you look into the lives of English poets you will find a surprising indifference to music, and some were tone-deaf.

Dr. Gibbon gave a most interesting recital accompanied by gramophone records, demonstrating the musical qualities of verse. The accentuation of the rhythms emphasized the musical reality and this was enhanced by the presence of his lively delivery throughout the poems recited.

Miss Ermatinger Fraser (Vancouver), leader of the poetry group, gave a lengthy paper on influences and tendencies in modern Canadian poetry. She touched on the racial origins of Canadian poets as having unavoidable influence. To trace distinctive Canadianism one looks to those writers sprung from families of several generations back, such as that poetic brotherhood born in the eighteen-sixties — Campbell, Roberts, Carman, Lampman and Scott.

> We are on the whole, a robust and energetic people, as are the Australians, but Canadian poetry in the main of the same era is not swinging strident ballads of action, but was rather refined and delicate in rhythm probably because the United Empire Loyalists had had more education than was possible in the Australian colonies, and culture continued to flow north from the United States. Waves of Trancendentalism and reverberations of the conflict between the New Science (evolution of species) and the Old Creeds entered Canada through poetry-

loving Canadians, without the storm which greeted them elsewhere.

The melancholy of end-of-the-century English poets had little influence in this land where poets expressed a strong spiritual confidence, and many of its writers belonged to the clergy or were children of the manse. As Dr. MacMechan wrote, "There is no lapsed Canadian West."

Victor Morin, president of the French Section (Montreal) and member of *L'Academie Canadienne* sent an excellent paper on *La Littérature Canadienne-Française*, read in French by Gustave Dutaud, K.C. (Montreal). Unhappily, only a few could follow the speech closely.

But straying attention was focussed again when Lee Martin of the Canadian National Railway Radio Department spoke on copyright as it affected broadcasting. The audience viewed this new medium with some apprehension, and showed more enthusiasm for a discussion on copyright as it appeared to editors of US periodicals. They were demanding North American serial rights, instead of just US rights, and thus injuring Canadian magazines by seriously restricting Canadian writers who seek both markets. Since the exercise of those rights would affect even more American writers seeking to sell second serial rights to Canadian periodicals, the CAA members authorized the executive to confer with the Authors League of America to work out harmonious cooperation.

That was the end of the business session. Thankfully, all adjourned to a reception given by the Canadian Women's Press Club of Calgary.

Post-conference events began early Saturday July 7, with a ninety-mile drive to Banff. En route, the cavalcade paused at the Sarcee Reserve, where with due ceremony, National President Dr. Charles G.D. Roberts was made a chief of the Sarcee tribe by Chief Joe Big Plume. Roberts' new name was Na-Kee-Tle-See-Ah-Kih-Tcha, "the Writer Chief."

The final session of the convention was the annual banquet in the great dining hall of the baronial Banff Springs Hotel with all the guests in evening dress. The head table parade chaired by Dr. Roberts in tuxedo, ribboned pince-nez instead of eagle feather bonnet. The music was under the direction of Harold Eustace Key (Montreal), one section being specially adapted from Canadian sources, such as: "Duna," by Marjorie Pickthall; songs from *Sappho*, by Bliss Carman; *Canadian Song Cycle* (Free Verse), by J. Murray

Gibbon; "O Canada, Mon Pays, Mes Amours," by George-Etienne Cartier.

A dance (the third that week!) concluded the evening.

But all was not over even yet. Some members had struck up durable friendships and were able to accept the hospitality extended for visits in the West, notably in Vancouver. A very special post-conference junket was extended to members returning via Edmonton. Howard Angus Kennedy, president of the Montreal (English) branch, donned his other hat, that of a prairie home-steader. His farm lay at Lacombe, en route to Edmonton, and his farm family would welcome any who cared to break the journey there for refreshment. Thus on the following Monday, eight or so members headed north by train, and were greeted by a rather large party at Lacombe Station.

Juanita O'Connor (Halifax) recalled:

> We had been highly impressed with the informality of the West, and felt we knew exactly how to behave, so stepping down from the train, we shook hands, said a hearty, unadorned "Hello" before we realized we were being given an address of welcome. We felt embarrassed, but important. One of the reception committee was Mr. Reed, superintendent of the government Experimental Station who suggested a drive around the Station first. He spoke so enthusiastically of the plants they had established and of the fine cattle and poultry, he almost persuaded one Haligonian to move West.

> On to the Kennedy place with its thousands of sheep in charge of a Norwegian farm family. Mr. Kennedy gave a brief history of the farm, and the whole party was hosted at what might well be described as a banquet. Toasts were drunk to the success of the farm, the owner, the farmer and his family. The departing guests boarded the train to Edmonton in the late twilight, our only regret that Mr. Kennedy had farm business to attend to, and thus unable to accompany us.

113

Chapter 8
In the Shadow of a Slump

In fact, the business that detained H.A. Kennedy was the sale of the farm, long rented to the Norwegian family. During the convention in Calgary, Kennedy had been persuaded to take on the position of permanent secretary of the Canadian Authors Association. He would accept half-pay of $600 a year, and continue freelancing in his spare time. The farm family was happy to purchase the land on easy terms.

A veteran journalist of sixty-eight, Kennedy was author of nine books and innumerable articles. (His *The New World Fairy Book* went through at least twelve editions.) Now he plunged into the office work of the CAA and gave it almost full-time for the next nine years until his heart gave out. He operated out of Montreal. The original plan of shifting head office every two years was smothered under the sheer bulk of files. Only with incorporation in 1947 was headquarters fixed in Toronto, home of a large vigorous branch and the publishing centre of the country.

In addition to the routine office work, the national secretary gathered information about new Canadian books, edited branch news for publication, made up the program for conventions and called executive meetings with a prepared agenda. He was devoted to the CAA and went far beyond any job specification or time-table, making full use of his energy and imagination to further the cause. His life was in the service of words and action.

London-born of Scots parentage (his father was a well-known clergyman), Kennedy thought of himself as Scotch-Canadian, with the emphasis on the latter. He came to Canada first as a young man of twenty, in 1881, planning to learn farming, but paused to work on the *Montreal Witness*. Four years of that, and he was reporting on the Riel Rebellion for the *Witness* and the *New York Herald*. Then he became city editor of the *Witness* for five years, when he was offered the editorship of the weekly edition of the London *Times*. No boomer, he stayed with it for nineteen years, until in protest over policy, he resigned and returned to Canada for the life of a freelance writer. He produced books, innumerable articles and pamphlets, and tried short stories, less successfully. He now had his first novel *Unsought Adventure*, a thriller about the theft of a Gutenberg Bible in New York. It was published in Montreal by Carrier.

Because he spoke French fluently he was sympathetic to *La Section Française*, and made sure that the "French fact" was represented on the programs of the convention in Halifax in 1929, in Ottawa in 1930, and in Toronto in 1931.

Kennedy, as executive secretary, though he never used the term, was in a position to steer convention programs, and give them some continuity. For the Halifax convention of 1929, the national officers determined to keep three things in mind: 1) to begin the story of the regional contribution to our national literature 2) the craftsmanship side of the author's work, through discussion from magazine editors and publishers 3) discussion of the possibilities of Canadian history as a field for the Canadian writer.

The year 1929 saw the first CAA convention to be held in the Maritimes. When Prof. Kirkconnell had raised the possibility to the president of the Halifax branch, Dr. MacMechan wrote back whimsically:

> I must confess it touches my conscience. I have long felt that a meeting of the CAA in Halifax was due either this year or next. As the curate said, "I have a feeling that I feel we all feel" and I ought to respond to it.

Which he did, not without some apprehension, since hosting a convention is a heavy responsibility for a small group. It requires a lot of willing hands.

The convention was held in the Lord Nelson Hotel where Dr. C.G.D. Roberts presided over a large turnout, no doubt buoyed by the fervour of the previous Calgary convention. Dr. Roberts could report the branches in good shape, and the revival of the London branch under Dr. Sherwood Fox, of the University of Western Ontario. Association membership now stood at 856, having lost twenty, gained sixty. The budget for the year ran to just over four thousand dollars.

The National President paid tribute to recently deceased members: Isabel Ecclestone Mackay, charter president of Vancouver & Mainland branch; Dr. W.S. Wade, historian, of Kamloops, and Bliss Carman. Roberts' voice trembled, then steadied as he spoke of his cousin:

> No one else can have known Bliss Carman, this great and greatly beloved poet as I did. Close kinsman, he was closer still to me in spirit, in the kinship of aspiration and dream. We were schoolmates, collegemates, travel-mates, room-mates through long and significant periods of our lives . . . Thanks to his unfailing gentleness and tolerant humour, ever patient with my impatient self-assertive egotism, no rivalry ever arose to cloud our lifelong comradeship. It is my considered judgment that Carman is not only incontestably the greatest poet Canada has produced, but that in the final estimate he will rank as at least the peer of the greatest now writing in our language.

Dr. Roberts then turned to the rest of the program,

> I would urge that a special effort be made to enlarge the representation and increase the influence of French-Canadian authors in our councils. This Canada of ours is a bi-lingual nation. Our literature and our history are bi-lingual. This Association is peculiarly fitted to the vitally important work of developing a closer understanding, sympathy and cooperation between the two great branches of our people, each of which has so much to give the other. French Canadian literature should be abundantly presented in all French courses in our English-speaking schools, and vice versa.

> I now call for the address on French Canada's regional literature, by Louis Dantin of our French Section. Since M. Dantin cannot be present, he has asked poet Mlle. Alice Lemieux to read his critical review of French-Canadian literature "Après Cent Ans."

(It was in French, but was translated for the next issue of the *Authors' Bulletin*.)

Dantin wrote,

> Exactly a century had passed since the publication of the first book of French-Canadian verse, and new-fledged lawyer François-Xavier Garneau had started work on his celebrated *Histoire du Canada*.

A hundred years ago, education was restricted, books were rare. Relations with France were cut. It is a wonder that our culture survived at all. Yet the rhymes and pale prose of our writers saved our French language. Our literature is now in full tide of energy and progress.

Our historical writings have grown into an important and remarkable collection. Our scientific writings in every branch display both imposing erudition and excellence in the literary art. Our fiction has made less progress. Strangely enough, our best magazines do not encourage native works, but are filled with insipidities from overseas. Our most neglected field is the dramatic, in spite of Louvigny de Montigny and others.

Literary criticism, the guide most urgently needed by a literature in its youth, has lately widened its borders ... The biting criticism of Asselin and Turc, if hardly encouraging, at least discourages decadence. Above all, it is in poetry that we have marched forward and affirmed our French mentality. After the lively blooming of Crémazie and Fréchette, these last years have seen young talent injecting a bold personal note into our song. To name only a few, we have Paul Morin, Albert Ferland, Ernest and Jules Tremblay, and in the other sex, even more. Seeing Marguerite Taschereau enter the philosophical field with such mature and striking work as *Les Pierres de mon Champ*, masculine monopolies are in peril!

Let us avoid the fatal error of being satisfied with ourselves. Let us hope that our successors a hundred years hence will have advanced far beyond us, as we have advanced beyond our ancestors of a century ago.

A.M. Pound (Vancouver) gave a paper on the contribution of the Pacific Coast.

Literature that is too obviously national is mere propaganda ... There is nonetheless, a wealth of outlandish and picturesque material in the past of British Columbia, a rich ore for literary prospectors. British Columbia writers are doing some of the best Canadian literary work, as the late Lord Shaughnessy discovered when he presented the nucleus of a Canadian library to the Canadian Club of New York. It would be out of place for me to give here a list of the many books written in British Columbia.

But he couldn't resist the temptation of a rather impressive roll call.

117

Dr. Archibald MacMechan, author of *Headwaters of Canadian Literature*, dealt with the Maritimes contribution to Canadian literature, beginning with Thomas Chandler Haliburton's *Clockmaker*, going on to Marshall Saunders who grew up in Nova Scotia. ("Her *Beautiful Joe* has sold more than a million copies, and has been translated into a dozen foreign languages.") Prince Edward Island had produced Basil King, author of many novels, Sir Andrew Macphail, essayist (Montreal) and Lucy Maud Montgomery, author of the "Anne" books.

Archdeacon H.A. Cody, Saint John spoke on the literary field offered by the history of the Maritime provinces. He himself had dipped into the lore of the past in his *The King's Arrow* and other stirring historical adventures. It was an inspiring talk and the archdeacon might well be gratified if he could see the plethora of books that have since emerged from the history of the Maritimes.

He brought a vision of the great shipbuilding period, of long lean clippers manned by our Bluenose breed. He depicted the Indians' grand sagamore Membertou, a hundred years old yet leading his Micmac warriors to avenge the death of a clansman. And what about Indian folk lore, those tales of Glooscap and his titanic feats? What material for some Canadian Homer!

Cody touched on source material, the *Jesuit Relations*, histories of the provinces, not least MacMechan's *Old Province Tales*, a veritable storehouse of noble deeds. He regretted that the Loyalists had no Boswell to record their life day to day, no Scott to portray in glowing words their acts of heroism.

> And many other scenes such as the old lumber days, the stirring days of Confederation, the explusion of the Acadians, the abortive Chignecto ship-railway. Why, there is no end to the subjects which might be mentioned. And it is all our own, right near at hand. Material, spirit, vision, we need them all. But we need something else as well — labour. Pegasus needed the wings to uplift him but the wings needed the old cart-horse Pegasus as well.

The delegates were entertained at luncheon by the Government of Nova Scotia, with Premier Rhodes as speaker. In the afternoon, came the first of three papers on "Canadian History as a Field for Canadian Writers." Dr. F.O. Call (Montreal), author of *The Spell of French Canada*, could not leave his duties at Bishop's College, Lennoxville, and entrusted the reading to B.K. Sandwell.

The poet, essayist and novelist have already been demonstrated. I propose to deal only with fields that lie within the province of Quebec. It seems to me that the historical novel is again coming into prominence. We need only a few bare historical facts touched by genius and illumined by imagination to produce a work of art as Thornton Wilder did in *The Bridge of San Luis Rey*.

Although the city of Quebec has frequently been used, the material for romantic or even realistic writing contained within its grim walls is not by any means exhausted. A work of fiction dealing with the early struggles of the teaching sisters would require special knowledge and tact, but I believe it could be done.

(The American author Willa Cather was not present, but it was she who shortly wrote the haunting *Shadows on the Rock*, and American Agnes Repplier who wrote *Mère Marie of the Ursulines*. There is no guarantee that these same works from a Canadian pen would have achieved any more success than did Ralph Connor's *The Rock and the River*.)

It was the heroic Marguerite Bourgeoys, in her efforts to bring education and religion to French and Indian girls who travelled from on foot over the ice of the St. Lawrence from Ville Marie (Montreal) to Quebec in April to gain concessions for her school from the Bishop. Her story has never been adequately used.

But my mind turns to the Richelieu, one of the most beautiful rivers in the province, and almost unexplored territory for writers.

Dr. Call wrote of the historic forts along its banks, that had defended Quebec from Indian and American attack, and referred to the orchard-clad slopes of Mont Ste. Hilaire, where the fairies are reputed to have made a last stand against approaching civilization.

Who but a college professor could say where history breaks off and legend begins? It is in her legends, folklore and folk songs that Quebec offers material to future writers, richer even than her history.

The Association's convention meetings did not stretch as long as revivalists' camp meetings, but they were equally fervid. All present enjoyed the stimulation of the addresses, were involved in

119

the business of the Association, but relished the social offerings as well. After the dose of history, they welcomed a tour of Halifax, where history was not only aural but visual. This day's hospitality culminated in a reception and dance given by Lieutenant Governor Tory at Government House.

The subject of Canadian regional contributions and regional history as a springboard for literature was too broad to cover at one convention and still leave space for the third specification — practical help in the craft of writing.

Robert Watson (Winnipeg) began:

> To any who are tempted to investigate the historical field — I would disillusionize them of the idea that there is money in it in light reading. But if the writer has something greater in mind, the field is well worth looking over. The average fiction writer like me will be entirely forgotten in a few years, while he who produces something new and definite in Canadian history is likely to live for generations. . . .

> On the subject of financial returns, I might say that I never travel without a camera. . . . Most of our magazines are open for articles, particularly when they are well illustrated. And my training in accountancy has been all to the good in writing factual stuff or fiction. I was schooled in accuracy.

> My experience in fiction writing was a help in historical work because it had taught me to make my writing attractive to the average reader; it gave a sense of literary values, an eye for highlights, for the dramatic. If a little of the life and vigor of our fiction writers were injected into our histories without departing from the truth, our students would get to know and remember more history and geography than from dry-as-dust textbooks.

> Many important Canadian historical documents are still to be discovered in the trunks and cupboards of old-timers all over the Dominion. A definite crusade should be made to uncover all such historical material, have it copied and safely housed. Much material of the explorer and fur trader Chief Factor Robert Campbell, after lying hidden for years is now coming to light. Just two weeks ago I managed to obtain from his granddaughter a number of Campbell's unpublished record books and diaries for the purpose of copying them.

(Watson did not write about Campbell, but his point was made when, a generation later, Clifford Wilson, another editor of *Beaver* came upon these records and produced *Campbell of the Yukon.*)

More fascinating to the younger members was a paper by H. Napier Moore, editor of *Maclean's Magazine.* Here was "the straight dope from the horse's mouth." Moore's paper, read by John Elson (Toronto), began with the right things. In the past year, all the articles and 89 of the 101 short stories and all the serials used in Maclean's had been written by resident Canadians. (Applause) The company's new magazines — *Chatelaine, Mayfair, Canadian Homes and Gardens* had widened the market and the outlook was even more promising.

Still *Maclean's* had higher costs than American magazines, and nothing like their revenues from advertising. The main problem facing authors and magazine publishers was a question of serial rights. Most US magazines would not agree that when they bought US rights in a Canadian story, a Canadian magazine could purchase the Canadian rights for simultaneous publication. And *Maclean's* would never agree to the inferior position involved in a later publication date of the same story; in other words no "first *Canadian* serial rights" were good enough for Canada's Number One periodical. But the higher US rates were irresistible to some writers. The US editors could not legally, under our Copyright Act, buy Canadian rights. But they could reject the work of any writer who held out for them. They seemed to consider Canada as an extra state of the Union. Napier Moore's written lecture went on to scold:

A very large percentage of manuscripts submitted are badly written. Poor form, phrasing and punctuation, and in some cases, amazingly weak grammar, make rejection inevitable. The author who sells consistently is the author who takes time to polish his writing and correct obvious errors, and gives thought to the appearance of his manuscript.

Non-fiction articles which have a time element must possess a news angle at least eight weeks after the ms. is mailed. The personality sketches submitted are too much like a succession of paragraphs from *Who's Who.* They lack colour and life. The vast majority of stories received are grim and grey, dealing, for instance, with some tragedy on a farm. No magazine can fill its pages with grey material. Another reason for rejecting is slenderness of plot or theme. This can only be overlooked when the writing is extraordinarily fine.

Another editor-publisher took up the theme of unsatisfactory manuscripts — Louis Carrier of Montreal. He was devastating. About ninety-five percent of the manuscripts received by an editor should never have been sent out by the writer. "Too many books are being published — six or seven thousand titles a year in the US alone." (It now exceeds forty thousand.)

After that, M. Carrier got back to his subject, on the selling of books geared to the public taste — novels, biography, travel and popular history, in French and English.

> We are on the threshold of great developments in mass marketing, certainly within the next twenty years.
>
> The employment of ignorant and non-bookish clerks has a very bad effect. The average reader doesn't go into a bookstore to buy a particular book, but is influenced by the displays and the clerk's recommendations.

"What do you think of rental libraries?" someone asked.

> *Comme ci, comme ça!* They have spread reader interest, but they cut down sales of individual books. A work formerly selling 18,000 copies in Canada cannot expect more than 12,000 now. The average bookseller gets half his income from stationery and other articles, at much less risk.

"Why are books so expensive?" queried another delegate. "You would sell more if they didn't cost so much."

The publisher had his figures handy.

> A book costing 38¢ to manufacture retails at $2.50. Half of that goes to the retailer. The publisher pays 10% to the author, 15% to manufacture, 20% to sell the book, leaving only from 12¢ to 18¢ for himself."

Alas for M. Carrier's rosy dreams of the future — he was teetering on the edge of bankruptcy, and toppled that autumn of 1929. While few CAA members who were affronted by his pompous address could muster up much sympathy for him, they did feel a pang for the unlucky authors caught in the Carrier debacle.

Among them was Howard Angus Kennedy. His novel *Unsought Adventure* had been taken up as Book-of-the-Month by the Carillon Book Club of Montreal, which ended its short life before it paid the publisher, and Carrier himself went broke before he could pay anything appreciable to the author. Kennedy was, of course, not the only victim.

The CAA national secretary took steps to safeguard the copyrights of the authors involved. They could not hope for royalties, for no one wanted to buy the firm with its liabilities. When the trustee of the bankrupt estate wanted to dump the entire stock of books on the market, Kennedy managed to persuade him to auction them off, at which he and other authors could buy back their books for personal distribution.

The auction was held only after Kennedy convinced the trustee that the estate did not own the copyrights, which must be returned to the author, since the publisher had failed to keep the books in print, or pay royalties.

The auction brought giveaway prices, and buyers could "take the lot" but not less than twenty-five copies. The best price was obtained for Prof. Waugh's *James Wolfe*, two dollars for the special and a dollar and thirty cents for the ordinary edition. Of other finely illustrated books, *La Paroisse* went for thirty-five cents and *Horatio Walker* for a dollar, Connor's *Archibald Lampman* for twelve cents, ten cents for Madge Macbeth's *Great Fright*, Robert Watson's *High Hazard*, and Louis Arthur Cunningham's *This Thing Called Love*. Blodwen Davies' *Storied Streets of Quebec* did only slightly better at eleven cents. Jessie Sime's charming booklet on Thomas Hardy sold for a cent apiece. Purchasers used them for Christmas greetings.

Howard Angus Kennedy bought up six hundred copies of his own book, and sold all but fifty in the next ten years.

Graphic Press of Ottawa was another optimistic publishing concern, full of ambition and experimentation. It began about 1926 by offering an annual prize of $1,000 for a new novel. The 1931 award went to Ella Bell Wallis (Calgary) for *The Exquisite Gift*. An advertisement in the *Canadian Bookman* in 1927 proclaimed "Canadian Literature is Enriched by Graphic Books — Every Graphic Book is a Canadian Book." The list included: *A Search for America*, by Frederick Philip Grove; *Only This — a War Retrospect* by James Pedley; *Yvon Tremblay*, by Louis Arthur Cunningham; *The Shadow of Tradition*, by C. Holmes MacGillivray; *Scottie*, by E. Benson Walker; *Boobs in the Woods*, by Merrill Denison. And to come: *Four Jameses*, by William Arthur Deacon; *Kinsmen at War*, by J.N. McIlwraith; *How to write*, by Robert Watson.

But Graphic was over-extended and under-financed, and never got around to publishing Mrs. Wallis' book. By May, 1932, the company went into bankruptcy. National Secretary Kennedy, drawing on his experience with Carrier, hastened to interview the

trustee, and alert the authors, some of whom had only contracts.
By September Kennedy reported in the *Authors' Bulletin*:

> The Graphic Press failure at Ottawa has been a severe blow to
> many of our authors. The Association's executive took prompt
> steps to protect their interests as far as the anemic condition of
> the estate allowed. This involved long and difficult negotiations,
> which are still proceeding.
>
> However, the Trustee realizes that royalties due to authors con-
> stitute a preferred claim on the estate. He says that manuscripts
> demanded have been found and returned.
>
> If the Company's books have to be put up for sale, either by
> tender or by auction, the prices obtained will probably be very
> low. To prevent these books from being dumped on a market
> already depressed, and retailed at prices far below the figure
> their sale would fetch if spread over a normal period, authors
> may themselves wish to buy the stock of their books. The
> National Secretary offers to negotiate for any writer who sends
> him the necessary information and authority, including con-
> tracts.
>
> As no other publisher was prepared to take over and continue
> the normal process of selling the books by degrees, the Trustee
> planned to sell them in one lot — a matter of 55,000 volumes —
> an awful avalanche of books to be dumped on a market already
> in a flattened state. Our suggestion that authors should at least
> be allowed to buy the stock of their own books, and save them
> from the price-crashing effect of the general dump, was dis-
> regarded at this stage.
>
> It was only when the national secretary appeared before the
> Registrar in the Court House at Toronto, to ask that in any set-
> tlement of the estate that authors' rights to royalties should be
> provided for, that the Trustee offered to pay them 10% of what
> the sale might realize. As there seemed no probability, in a
> lump sale, of the books fetching more than a nominal price of 5
> or 6 cents apiece, or maybe 8¢ for the bound books alone, the
> offer amounted to an uncertain fraction of 1¢, instead of the 20¢
> provided for in the average contract (on a $2.00 book).

But the thing dragged on and on, and in March 1934 came the
last word on the subject:

> The prospect of an almost immediate settlement with the cred-
> itors of the Graphic Publishers, long ago held out to us by the

Trustee, has not even yet been fulfilled. To our latest communication, the Trustee answers that he will be in a position to wind up the affair as soon as he has disposed of the estate's interest, "if any," in a certain property. He expects the negotiations will be completed shortly, but over this he has no control.

It will be remembered that the Association obtained an agreement that the authors holding contracts with the firm should definitely receive ten percent of the price obtained for their books on the stock being sold by the Trustee, and that, pending such sale, the authors would be able to buy in such quantities as they required of their own books at a similar price. That was done to a considerable extent.

In addition to the completed volumes, the Eaton Company acquired a quantity unbound, in sheets, and some of these dressed in paper covers have appeared on the bargain counters @ "6 for 25¢."

The authors appreciated the efforts of H.A. Kennedy, not only for the slender returns, but for the way in which he handled the negotiations. "I had given the whole thing up as a bad job, when your letter came," wrote one. "I must congratulate you as well as thank you."

In his role as guardian of the flock, Howard Angus Kennedy was aware of an unprecedented number of rackets in the writing game. Writers were plagued with the seductions of vanity publishers, whose siren songs enticed beginning novelists and poets in all stages into "cooperative publishing." (You pay, we print.) The slick contracts would deceive even the wary — and in fact, the vanity publishers did fulfill their contracts after a fashion. Hack musicians set their poems to music of some kind, regardless of plagiarism or quality. Then it was up to the author to hawk his wares. The songwriter beat his way to musicians and studios in the futile hope of a large commercial success, or even a once-over-lightly at a concert. The *Canadian Author* sounded the tocsin with no uncertain sound.

A much more ominous sound came in the autumn of 1929 with the crash of the stock market on Wall Street. Canada appeared to be immune at first. That year, Prime Minister R.B. Bennett declared, "Canada as a whole is on the verge of a great era of prosperity." And opposition leader W.L.M. Mackenzie King insisted that Canada had never been so prosperous. Everyone was eager to believe them. Anything else was unthinkable.

Chapter 9
The Literary Life

The 1930s began hopefully with attention to literary memorials. The CAA Halifax branch nagged the Nova Scotia government to rescue the home of Judge Thomas Chandler Haliburton from its current low state as a rooming house and make it into an Historic site. The CAA would furnish the library of the museum. This was done, though not immediately, and the old house is a shrine in the town of Windsor. In the West, CAA members watched with critical eyes the plaques on the monuments set up by the Historic Sites Board. Having found one error they observed them all, lynx-eyed.

The memorial to poet Archibald Lampman was unveiled on a sunny autumn day, September 13, 1930, largely through the urging and good example of Arthur Stringer. Although domiciled in New York, he maintained a keen interest in the area of his boyhood, and donated fifty dollars to the monument, and Toronto branch contributed another twenty-five dollars. Other groups and private contributions brought up the total.

The cairn of grey fieldstone at Trinity Church, just west of Morpeth village near London, bore two bronze plaques; one facing the highway bore the poet's name, dates 1861-99, place of interment (Beechwood Cemetery, Ottawa, marked by a boulder bearing the name Lampman in large letters); the other plaque inscribed with the closing lines of Lampman's poem "Outlook":

> Yet patience — there shall come
> Many great voices from life's outer sea,
> Hours of strange triumph, and when few men heed
> Murmurs and glimpses of eternity.

A copy of Lampman's collected works in leather binding, the gift of the publisher (Musson), a manuscript copy of "The Song Sparrow," a list of subscribers to the memorial, all encased in a copper box hermetically sealed, were placed within the cairn at the close of the ceremony. After the singing of "O Canada," speeches were made by Dr. Sherwood Fox, president of the Western Ontario branch, and chairman of the Memorial Committee; followed by General E.A. Cruikshank, chairman of the Historic Sites Board, and by J.H. Cameron, who craved more recognition of Canadian poets in schools.

Arthur Stringer, big good-natured Ontario Irishman, spoke of "The Poet in Everyday Life," insisting that the pioneer of plough and axe was not more essential than the sodbreaker of the soul. Dr. Duncan Campbell Scott, a close friend in Ottawa, sketched Lampman's short life "whose golden voice was silenced all too soon." The Archbishop of Huron read Nat Benson's dedication poem, said a prayer, and the service closed with the "Last Post" and "God Save the King."

Members of the committee and visiting delegates (from Montreal to Windsor) were then entertained at tea by Mrs. F.C. Sifton at her residence in the vicinity. They did things up in style those days. The timing was right, however, for soon afterwards the grey shadows of the Depression blotted out generous impulses toward literary affairs.

Near the end of June, the Association had returned after nine years to its natal city. Owing to a shortage of space — or rather the growth of the CAA — the Association was not able to carry out its original plan of meeting in the Old Medical Building. All sessions were held in the ballroom of the Mount Royal Hotel.

It seems impertinent to abridge the speeches that were made, grave, admonishing, inspiring as they were. But necessary.

National President, Dr. William Douw Lighthall K.C., a charter member, welcomed the delegates, and quoted the memorable words of visitor Samuel Butler's famous skit "O God! O Montreal!" which was printed in *Punch*. Later Butler recanted, and Dr. Lighthall was happy to quote the repentant journalist, "I think Montreal is one of the most beautiful places in the world."

The President spoke solemnly,

> While guarding our heritage of history, let us all, as Canadians and thinkers recognize that still more splendid attraction — the future. If we, the artisans of ideas give it a false, a trivial or cor-

rupt service, who can correct our default? Unless we can soundly construct a new patriotism, we are in danger of losing our souls, and our national existence by sectionalism, by dissension, by sordid accident, even by drab dissatisfaction. . . . We have been saved from the brink of dissolution at several junctures. We are now at another juncture. We are again beginning to hear the old voices of money, greed, material bigness, sectional rivalry . . . Is there not a duty and privilege here for the writers of Canada to hold up the heroic in our history, to strive for kindly harmony, to battle against private and public meanness?

Audiences then were not ashamed of patriotism, but rather uplifted by such emotional language. But the report of National Secretary Howard Angus Kennedy brought inspiration of a different order.

The secretary of a body spread over 3,000 miles and working through a baker's dozen of branch centres, must realize he is but one of fourteen secretaries. Of course, neither a national officer nor any single member must ever forget that the tree comes before the branches — the branches have grown out of the tree, and exist to promote its national objectives . . .

The fact that Head Office is located by the present arrangement at one or other of four different central points does not influence relations with or regard for any branch. The interests of all branches are identical.

The National Executive has never desired to curtail the full liberty of every branch to carry out whatever programs it may judge best fitted for local conditions, and which show a clear vision of the Association's objects — to defend the professional interests of writers and other creative artists, and by raising the quality of our work to make it more worthy of defence. Both need constant vigilance.

Now about the proposed establishment of a permanent office and secretariat, it cannot be done without increased resources. Some have suggested lowering the annual fee. The present income is too small. It has been proposed that the Association incorporate (to be able to receive donations) and build up a capital endowment. Your executive, if it is your pleasure to retain them, will relax no effort to make a little go a long way.

National Treasurer Leslie Gordon Barnard presented his statement of expenditures totalling $4,631 — up from the previous year by the $620 paid to the national secretary, down by the small sum allotted to convention costs. The bank balance showed $1,383, an improvement of nearly $400, due undoubtedly to Kennedy's re-organization of the membership roll.

Major H.G. Christie, president of the New Brunswick branch proposed that the fee for an Associate member be reduced from five to three dollars. "That should not occasion much reduction overall," he thought.

Former treasurer John Elson (Toronto) pointed out that 179 Associate members contributed nearly $900 and reducing their dues meant a loss of $358.

"Should we have Associates at all?" someone asked. "Aren't we supposed to be a company of professional writers?"

"No, the Association never aimed at being strictly professional, and certainly not exclusive to writers. Some of our most valued members — apart from their dues — are Associates," Murray Gibbon explained for the nth time.

(These questions continued to cause heartburn to members of the Association until resolved by the organization of numerous independent groups in the 1970s, specializing in playwriting, poetry, periodical and children's literature. The problem of an association of professional writers only was solved by formation of the Writers' Union of Canada in 1972.)

Dr. E.A. Hardy, Toronto branch president returned to an earlier suggestion of groups within the Association specializing in different disciplines, such as existed in British and American authors' societies, and indeed in some CAA branches.

After luncheon, members gathered for the afternoon session, a continuation of regional contributions to Canadian literature, as begun in Halifax. Now it was the turn of Ontario and Manitoba.

Walter McRaye of Brockville had been slated to deal with the Ontario contribution, and the audience was all set to sit back and enjoy his drolleries. He was well-known to Canadian audiences because he and the late E. Pauline Johnson had together toured the country and abroad with their recitals, as McRaye recounted in his book *Town Hall Tonight*. McRaye made a specialty of reciting W.H. Drummond's *habitant* verse and amused the crowd with the humour of "The Wreck of the *Julie Plante*" and melted hearts with the sentimental "Leetle Bateese," while Pauline stirred consciences with her poems of Indian attitudes such as "Half-breed," as clad in white buckskin, bearclaw necklace and feathered headband, she declaimed with all the studied arts of elocution. It never occurred to either poet or performer that their efforts to rouse sympathy and understanding might someday be regarded as racial slurs.

Now the delegates were disappointed to learn that McRaye had been called to Northern Ontario for an election. But he had sent his paper in advance. For a start, he admitted that it was hard to determine who was an Ontario writer, since westerly migration brought to Ontario writers from the Maritimes, and Ontarians had shunted farther west. But he cast a wide net, of which we give only excerpts.

For instance, the first novel written by a Canadian, he claimed, was *St Ursula's Convent,* written at Kingston in 1824, by Julia Beckwith who came from New Brunswick. The first real Ontario novelist was Major John Richardson, born at Queenston, Niagara, in 1796, where his father was assistant surgeon in Governor Simcoe's Queen's Rangers. Of his many books, *Wacousta* was our prime historical novel, and Ontario gave Canada its first published poem "A Day at Niagara in the Year 1825" by J.E. Alexander. John Strachan, headmaster of Cornwall Grammar School, first high school in Upper Canada (before Strachan became a bishop and founded Trinity College) produced the first educational textbook in Canada. It was an arithmetic: "If 234 bales of cloth, containing 84 16/27 yards each, cost £678 26s 8¼d, what costs it for 48 bales containing 39 13/29 yards at the same rate?"

McRaye referred in passing to William Kirby, customs collector at Niagara, who wrote the Quebec "Gothic" romance, *The Golden Dog.* Sir Gilbert Parker born in Camden East, a hamlet in eastern Ontario would be remembered for his early writings, all with Canadian settings: *The Seats of the Mighty,* and that gem of construction *When Valmond Came to Pontiac.*

He referred to Grant Allen who wrote nearly three dozen novels, forgotten even in 1931, one being a best-seller considered very risque in its day. *"The Woman Who Did"* might almost find inclusion in a Sunday school library today. Robert Barr, author of half a dozen romances, flounced out of Canada asserting that Canadians were an unappreciative lot who preferred booze to books. Sara Jeannette Duncan of Brantford, first woman journalist in Canada (known as Garth Grafton of the *Globe*) wrote charming stories that were popular in England and elsewhere. *The Imperialist* is the best-known.

McRaye ignored E.J. Pratt's Newfoundland birth by claiming "dear old Ned" as an Ontarian by residence, having done most of his work in Toronto

> where he is the leader of the younger group of Canadian poets. His poems of the sea have fine colouring and are full of dramatic force.

The writer had less warmth for Wilson MacDonald,

> at times dissatisfied with us. There are critics who boldly say that MacDonald's opinion of himself is almost justified by his poetry ...

> The Hon. Frank Oliver, that royal old editor of other days, once wrote me that he considered the humour of Canada is cynical but kindly, as distinguished from the extravagance of statement which is humour in the United States, or grotesque situations which is humour in England.

Dr. W.T. Allison, a past-president of the Association gave an account of Manitoba's contribution to Canadian literature:

> It was not until the gay nineties that any work of imagination was composed in the Red River Settlement. Our western writers had devoted themselves almost entirely to local history. R.M. Ballantyne, a young Scot, spent only seven years in Canada, and his *Hudson's Bay* was but the first of eighty volumes of adventures for young folks.

> The first writer in Manitoba to stand clear of local history was Ernest Thompson Seton. Born in England in 1860, he came to Canada five years later, lived in Toronto, and in 1882 was appointed naturalist by the Manitoba government. After his official works on the birds and mammals of Manitoba, he became famous in 1898 with his *Wild Animals I have Known*.

> But history soon re-exerted its appeal to Manitoba writers. Agnes Laut came west in early childhood and was educated at Manitoba University, taught school in Winnipeg, and for several years was on the staff of the *Manitoba Free Press*. In 1904, her best-known book, *Pathfinders of the West* firmly established her growing reputation. Like Seton, she has long been an exile in the United States.

> In the main, Manitoba history has been written by those who helped shape events. One of the most voluminous is the Rev.

Dr. George Bryce, now in his 85th year. No busier man ever lived than this gentle ecclesiastic. History is with him a passion. A son of old Kildonan stock, Rev. R.G. MacBeth, is a graduate of the college Dr. Bryce founded. His first book, *Selkirk Settlers in Real Life* (1897) was followed by a number of volumes, chief being the official history of the North West Mounted Police, and a history of the Canadian Pacific Railway.

Dr. Allison went on to fiction writers, instancing the Rev. C.W. Gordon (Ralph Connor) and Nellie McClung, whose first book, *Sowing Seeds in Danny* was inspired by Dickens' *Martin Chuzzlewit* when she was reading it to her pupils in a little schoolhouse in southern Manitoba. Robert J.C. Stead was author of half a dozen novels, all descriptive of prairie life, of which *The Cow Puncher* had sold over 100,000 copies. Laura Goodman Salverson heard her father tell of the coming of his people from Iceland, and wrote *Viking Heart*, a most distinctive novel.

Four years ago, Martha Ostenso, who taught school in rural Manitoba, wove her impressions into the story entitled *Wild Geese*. This won a prize of $13,500 in a competition held by an American publishing house and an American magazine. Her three later novels show great skill in portrayal of character.

These ethnic writers led to Frederick Philip Grove, whose sombre *Settlers of the Marsh* also appeared in 1925, and which Dr. Allison regarded as the most powerful piece of realistic fiction yet written in Canada. He gave only a nod in the direction of several lesser novelists.

After two such lectures, the delegates were glad to divide into two parties, one to walk around historic Montreal, the other for an excursion on the river, as guests of the Harbour Commissioners. At the evening reception, the two chief features were contributions by Helen Creighton and Gilbert Hart, both of the Nova Scotia branch. Miss Creighton related her discoveries of old sea songs and ballads among the fishing folk, and Mr. Hart sang many of them. This was followed by a performance of T.M. Morrow's play *The Blue Pitcher*, arranged by the Drama Group of the Montreal branch, of which author and director were members. Music for the subsequent dance was provided by Miss Wynne's orchestra.

Next morning's session was devoted to editors. Napier Moore repeated some of his remarks at the previous convention, and added:

Every week I get about 250 manuscripts, and can only accept one in fifty. The vast majority should never have been submitted. Their writers, for one thing didn't study the market. Every magazine has certain taboos. My readers cannot accept women smoking or drinking. I also have to be blind to certain biological facts. Babies have to be brought by the stork or in the doctor's bag. Writers who appear often avoid the taboos, write constantly, are not disheartened when rejected, and are paid pretty much the same as a newcomer.

Hugh Eayrs, president of Macmillan of Canada, regretted his absence in England, but wrote that he regarded two-fifty as too high for the average novel, and two dollars for "a lot of the bilge that is published," while one dollar was far too low for publisher or author.

In 1931, I expect that prices will drop. As for suggestions to authors, I will only say they should know what they are writing about, and write honestly. They need to polish their work to the utmost of their capacity. Above all, they should learn not to write anything which is not a real contribution to their subject.

Dr. Lyman Beecher Stowe, the fraternal delegate from the Authors League of America, apologized for the absence of the League's secretary, Louise Sillcox, who was in Washington involved in the struggle for

a civilized copyright law in the United States, a country which shares with Russia and Siam the distinction of being ineligible for the Berne International Convention. The American copyright law is the most antiquated in existence. For instance, a drama based on my grandmother's story, *Uncle Tom's Cabin* has been produced oftener than any other play in the world — about eight million times before Grandmother died. And on the six million times it had been performed outside the United States, she received nothing — for lack of international copyright. American writers are asking that literature be regarded as property, intellectual property, with or without registration.

In closing, he said,

The Canadian Authors Association, with its 800 members, is very much larger in proportion to population than the Authors League of America with its 2,000 members. I am sure you will find an immense advantage in a permanent office and staff, as the League did — even if you have to raise your dues to $25 like

133

the League, instead of your present $5.

After lunch as guests of the City of Montreal, at which Dr. Stowe was heard to murmur,

> If an authors' convention was held in New York, Mayor Jimmy Walker and his cabinet would never have heard of us. If they did, the last thing they would dream of doing would be to ask us to luncheon.

"Literature and National Life," by a professor from Winnipeg, anesthetized the members that afternoon with a ponderous address from which they were awakened by Dr. Salem Bland (Toronto) who was mercifully brief.

> Canada came into existence in an extraordinarily unplanned way, and the difficulties in the way of national unity seem here to reach their height. Yet Canada unitedly had a mission on this continent. Canadians have certainly shown a gift for tackling hard jobs. We must aim to develop an international mind, if we are not to go to pieces in the next fifty years. We must be broad-minded. At present many Easterners think Westerners a selfish lot, caring only for their own interests, while many Westerners have thought the East only concerned with making money out of the West. The very difficulties we have to face should stimulate us to conquer them.

The conventioneers did not pause for discussion, but happily took to automobiles provided by the Montreal Tourist Bureau for a trip to Ste. Anne de Bellevue for tea, and a drive back over the mountain. Nor was the day done yet. In the evening, through the hospitality of the Cunard Line, two saloons aboard the *Ascania* in harbor were given over to two meetings: The Short Story and Drama groups in one, Poets in the other.

The session on Canadian fiction next day was lively, chaired by Montreal branch president, Leslie Gordon Barnard, himself a noted short story writer along with his wife, Margaret. They were a devoted couple, collaborators in all ways. Barnard was also national treasurer that year. Jean Steele Foley, short story writer (Montreal), claimed that the form of fiction was more important than marshalling factual detail — if that conception had passed through the imaginative experience of the author. She hoped that Canadian fictioneers would experiment in writing about space-time, as novelists were now doing.

Frank Packard of New York, at home in Lachine for the summer, a founding father of the Association (a mild little man in rimless glasses) contributed a craft talk based on twenty-five years of writing thrillers.

It's emphatically not true that anyone can write," he began. "But anyone can write who really gives anything that is in him, and gives it eagerly. A very few — the geniuses — reach editorial acceptance as on a magic carpet, but the rest of us can only reach the goal by persistent study and effort. The competition in literature is fierce. Many who might have won success allowed themselves to be discouraged by rejections. I myself wrote for four years before I ever earned any money from it.

Don't hang around waiting for inspiration, and don't take the first plot or idea that occurs to you. Strive for a better one. Don't write about scenes you know nothing about. If a story is set in the Rockies, don't have your characters frisking about among coconut palms. It is the author's job to check and cross-check his work.

You can write a highly improbable story purely for entertainment, but it must have the illusion of reality. My own efforts to be accurate in detail brought me a compliment I treasure. After I had written a certain prison story, I had a letter from a convict in a penitentiary, saying he was dead sure I had done time, and was I still in stir? As a matter of fact, I had spent considerable time in St. Vincent de Paul Penitentiary, by kind permission of Ottawa, not enforced.

Dr. Newton MacTavish (Ottawa) thought that in Canada we were too prone to be our own judges. Not until we could arrest the attention of critics abroad could we really claim any great distinction.

No considerable volume of first-rate art can be expected from Canada, as ours is a new country. We are given to patting ourselves on the back and believing we are doing great things, while we are doing on the whole very meagre things.

William Arthur Deacon (Toronto), literary editor of *Saturday Night* rose up in wrath.

You sit there and endure this because it has been said so long that you are willing to think the worst of yourselves. I wish you were not so patient, so pathetically humble.

The so-called fact of your fundamental artistic inferiority is a
fallacy. Canadians have shown that their brains are as good as
anybody's in engineering, in finance, in medicine, though if the
handicap of "a new country" operated in anything, it would be
in building of railways, bridges and in vast commercial
enterprises which we have in plenty . . .

Some loose ends of business were cleared up early in the afternoon of the final day. A report on the current music copyright
situation from Lawrence Burpee. An alarm on possible government
monopoly of radio broadcasting by J. Murray Gibbon. A proposal
for revision of the constitution. Nominations. Last year's executive
agreed to continue for a second term. Future conventions. (Toronto
in 1931, Quebec City and/or London, England in 1932.)

A three-man panel on pictorial art in Canada held forth in the
Tudor Hall of Ogilvy's department store, followed by a talk on Canadian music, illustrated by voice and instrument. It was brief, for
"the atmosphere of Canada is not favourable today to musical composition."

A unique exhibit had been arranged in an adjacent gallery by
Aegidius Fauteux (Montreal, French Section) the librarian of St.
Sulpice. It included the first books published in Canada. Delegates
were reminded that under the old regime the king of France did
not allow books to be printed in Canada. In 1764, immediately after
the fall of New France, two printers came to Quebec on horseback
from New England, and the year following produced the first Canadian book, a French catechism. The first English book was
printed two years later, an account of a trial.

The convention reached a brilliant climax that night in the
annual banquet. The tables were graced with flowers donated by
Lady Roddick (Montreal), and the speakers proved urbane and
witty, though today's diners might consider there were too many
"talking heads."

Dr. Beecher Stowe led off:

You in Canada have a great opportunity, blending three
cultures — British, French and American. From this blend you
have already obtained great results and will in future obtain
greater. After thirteen years of editing, I can say that to be even
a third-rate author requires more brains than the average
citizen possesses. Though you wonder about some; such as a
lady who listed twelve reasons why I should publish her
manuscript, one being that it was typed by an eminent lawyer!

Dr. Victor Morin, president of *La Section Française*, spoke next, briefly and in French.

> My hope is for closer union in the efforts of English and French Sections. You know your literature. We know ours. But we don't know enough of each other's. The country owes profound gratitude to the founders of this Association, Murray Gibbon in particular, and on the French side to such active members as Louvigny de Montigny ...

In thanking Dr. Morin, Marshall Saunders (Toronto) declared she had never attended such a distracting convention — the people she met were so fascinating. She lamented not being able to speak French, and thought it should be taught in every Canadian school. Only one drawback had she found in Montreal. The books of a Montreal member were completly sold out. "Why doesn't the Association start a book store of its own?"

B.K. Sandwell in closing, referred to the projected tour of Britain, and hoped that the Association would go on to Paris. Toronto members left for home wondering how they could possibly match Montreal's program when their turn came next year.

The 1931 convention in Toronto, in friendly competition with Montreal, scored by reducing diversions, and jam-packing the program with interesting talks. Branch reports were circulated as broadsides, not read aloud. Never again was any convention so thoroughly documented.

Out of 756 members including 38 in the French Section, 171 attended. The budget of $6,126, raised entirely from members' fees, showed improvement enough to justify a Newsletter to sustain interest.

"Nature and the Writer" was a theme for much of the program, with addresses by W.A. Fraser, author of *Mooswa*; by Martha Black, M.P. from Yukon on wildflowers of the far north; and Wallace Havelock Robb, poet-naturalist of Abbey Dawn Sanctuary near Kingston. (Out of more than a hundred thousand birds to which he played host, only one had bitten the hand that fed it — a bittern.) E. Wyly Grier the artist, spoke on "Nature in Pictures."

The Annual Dinner was hosted by Ontario Premier G.S. Henry himself, in Hart House, University of Toronto. Unhappily, a squabble developed after Wilson MacDonald delivered his diatribe on "The Stigma of Colonialism," at which B.K. Sandwell took umbrage. Arthur Guiterman, representing the Authors League of

America, said it reminded him of the days fifty years ago when American critics sneered, "Who reads American books?"

MacDonald attributed slurs and rejections of Canadian writing strictly to the fact that they emanated from a former colony. (He was not surprised when later, Robert Choquette (Montreal French Section) agreed that Quebec writers got that same reception from France.) MacDonald told of his address to a club of American authors, and of chiding them for their indifference to Canadian poetry. One listener replied forcefully that Canada had to believe in herself first, and quoted a Canadian critic writing in the *American Mercury*, who had assured its readers that "nothing worthy of comment had ever been produced in Canada."

Dr. Lionel Stevenson, an expatriate member from Duke University spoke at considerable length on Canadian writers living in the States, astonishing many with the names he dredged up.

> Residence in the States is not necessary for the acceptance of Canadian writing, though the difficulty of finding first publication there may be greater. Canadian settings are not necessarily unpopular, as proved by Stewart Edward White, James Oliver Curwood and Willa Cather.

Mgr. Camille Roy of Laval University and of the Quebec branch (French Section) spoke briefly in English and longer in French. He began by admitting that French-Canadian literature had not reached that degree of perfection it should have in a community three centuries old, though it had, during the last thirty years produced works worthy of praise. In that literature there were two chief schools — the *nationaliste* (French of France) and *Canadienne* (Canadian French.)

He himself had advocated the nationalization of French-Canadian literature, which thirty years ago suffered from too servile an imitation of France. But the *Canadienne* school went to the extreme, setting aside as useless works inspired by other than Canadian themes. That school had even encouraged the use of the popular language in works of the imagination, especially in fiction. The popular diction had a savour that writers might well utilize, but overloading with popular words produced a vulgarity incompatible with art. As for the patois attributed by Dr. Drummond to the *habitant*, it never existed in the province of Quebec, even among lumberjacks.

(Dr. W.H. Drummond of Montreal had worked among *habi-*

138

tants both as a young telegrapher and later as a physician. He had no intention of belittling French-speaking Canadians and indeed died among them fighting a smallpox epidemic in Cobalt, Ontario.)

Robert Choquette spoke in English of the younger poets of Quebec province and touched on the few novelists. Why so few? Because of a lack of market for their wares.

> Our authors work practically for nothing. Our only public up to now has been a reading public extracted from the limited population of French Canada, a minority of a minority. Our authors therefore cannot live on their writings, alloting to their literary efforts their spare time only. They remain hardly more than amateurs ... It is not surprising therefore if some of our writers have established themselves in Paris and will not come back; if some others have their work published abroad. We need firstly, more publishing houses.

> But the point we also want to develop is penetration of the English-speaking market. Our best works could be offered to English readers. It is my belief that good translations in Canada would help towards a closer friendship. It would be a practical step towards pulling down the wall that has always kept our two cultures in hermetic chambers. Our English compatriots would be helped to understand us better, to see the other side of the medal.

On Thursday morning, Nellie McClung (Calgary) continued the series of talks on literature of the various regions of Canada, by discussing the writers of Alberta. At least that was the subject assigned to her. The effervescent Nellie wandered down interesting bypaths of anecdote and reminiscence:

> No writer is impoversihed by the activities of another, but rather helped and encouraged. For instance when the late Isabel Ecclestone Mackay looked at a huddle of immigrants in Calgary station, she saw a new nation, tired of old wars and old hatreds, ready to begin life in a new world. Canada, in the days gone by was the most hospitable country in the world. We wanted people to do the rough work, and they came to us in swarms. But now the pinch has come, and some Canadians are saying that all those people we no longer need, should be sent home. They have no homes. They gave them up to come to us. Here is a theme for the writer. They came in sheepskin coats, and went to the rougher parts of Alberta that no one else wanted. You should see them now!

When Nellie McClung spoke, no one cared whether she stuck to the assigned subject or not. Anything she said with her native wit and forthrightness went down well with most audiences, even politicians. She gave examples of dramatic material in the West, instancing Laura Goodman Salverson's *The Viking Heart,* and various slices of life such as the Methodist minister who brought lighted candles to the bedside of a dying Catholic Polish woman, and recited for her the prayers of the dying.

Nellie's vigour proved a hard act to follow, but George Palmer of Regina spoke well on Saskatchewan's contribution to Canadian literature, admitting it was somewhat limited as yet. He had great hope for the work of playwrights, and the demand for stage presentations was difficult to keep up with.

"Bravo!" cried M. Luchkovich, M.P. for Winnipeg, who followed with "New Canadian Readers," of which there were many more than before the war, the third largest ethnic group in Canada being Ukrainian. "All of these people have read Ralph Connor's *The Foreigner.* Write more books like that."

To business. Who would be the next national president? No problem. Dr. Duncan Campbell Scott was voted in by acclamation, with Lawrence Burpee as national treasurer. (He had a marvellously efficient private secretary.) H.A. Kennedy continued as permanent secretary.

The locale of the next convention presented more difficulty. The 1932 convention could be held in Quebec — if the proposed Overseas Tour came off. If not, Vancouver was willing, but too far for most, now that the Depression was making itself felt in Canada. Somewhere central then, and since the President was located in Ottawa, better hold it there. This decision was reinforced when Vancouver counted the cost and realized its treasury was too bare.

So the 1932 convention was held in Ottawa, with a good sound program, abbreviated to three days. Frills were reduced to a minimum — the City laid on a luncheon, the Mayor presiding. Meetings were held in the Chateau Laurier. In addition to the business sessions and the plenary sessions, an innovation was introduced, that of the delegates dividing up into interest groups. This grew naturally out of so many branches developing the Group system, for discussion of craft questions among writers working predominantly in fiction, poetry, drama, the essay or the feature Article. *La Section Française* simultaneously held a business meeting under the presidency of Jean Bruchési (Montreal).

140

The final segment of the regional contributions to Canadian Literature came from Arthur Woollacott, president of the Vancouver branch, with an uncritical sketch of the field of history and biography, of which he listed many examples. Current writers in this field included Dr. W.N. Sage and Judge F.W. Howay (both of Vancouver). Mrs. W. Garland Foster's *The Mohawk Princess*, a life of Pauline Johnson, included several unpublished stories and a critical estimate of her poetry. *By Shore and Trail in Stanley Park* by Robert Allison Hood included the story of her monument near Siwash Rock.

The fiction list was shorter, even including juveniles. But poetry abounded, rising to genius in Audrey Alexandra Brown (Victoria) and Annie Charlotte Dalton (Vancouver).

Delegates to the Ottawa convention were informed of a notable exhibit of Canadian books that filled two shop windows at the time of the Imperial Conference. Over 1,000 current books in French and English were displayed along with portraits of their best-known authors. Each visitor, official and unofficial, received a card of greeting from the Association, soliciting their attention, for few of them knew anything of Canadian literature, though well aware of Canada's other natural resources.

Quebec City hosted the 1933 convention, largely because it was the point of departure for seventy-five members and friends who were making the Overseas Tour to Britain and possibly France. By now the Depression had struck home, and the Board of Railway Commissioners had tightened its definition of who was eligible for press passes on the railways. These were restricted to journalists regularly employed on newspapers and magazines, which left freelance writers out in the cold, no matter how prolific they might be as contributors. It certainly cut down the attendance at CAA conventions, especially of those from distant points.

Still, special convention rates were offered by the Chateau Frontenac, no doubt due to Murray Gibbon's influence, and all facilities were laid on. Civic and provincial authorities proved hospitable, as did the members of *La Section Française*, and a great deal of harmony prevailed. The dates, June 29-July 1 was set to coincide with the sailing of the *Empress of Britain* on Saturday, Dominion Day.

National President Dr. Duncan Campbell Scott (Ottawa) presided, along with Prof. Jean Bruchési President of the French Section. Speeches were in English or French, or sometimes both, strongly supporting the ideal of national unity. Bruchési began by saying there were certain peevish folk who still asked if we had a Canadian literature: *"croquemitaines qui gaspillent encore leur temps à se demander si nous avons une littérature canadienne."*

National Secretary Howard Angus Kennedy reviewed the past year, noting that membership had dropped slightly to 809 and National Treasurer Lawrence Burpee noted that the budget had similarly dropped to $4,242.

Burpee also sent a paper on "Early Literature of the Canadian West," which related almost entirely to the fur trade and exploration . . . La Vérendrye, Kelsey, Thompson, Hearne and Mackenzie left splendid narratives of their journeys, as did more modern explorers and men of the Hudson's Bay Company.

Katherine Hale, Mrs. John Garvin (Toronto) was already off on one of her many lecture tours, this time in England, but her paper on "Some Women Writers of Canada" was read by the new Toronto branch president, Margaret Howard. "We know the names and histories of the few who matter. If scant in number, they are a distinctive company."

She began gracefully with Mère Marie de l'Incarnation and Frances Brooke, whose *History of Emily Montague* was written a stone's throw from the Chateau Frontenac, a witty chronicle of the social life of Quebec City; went on to Anna Jamieson's uncomplimentary "rambles" through backwoods Ontario, and the valuable records of the Strickland sisters, Susanna Moodie and Catherine Parr Trail.

She cited the poets Isabella Valancy Crawford, and "Seranus," (Frances Harrison), Marjorie Pickthall and Pauline Johnson; the journalists "Kit" Coleman and "Janey Canuck" (Emily Murphy) and Nellie McClung; the novelists Marshall Saunders and L.M. Montgomery. "Nor can we forget an historian of such colour, vigour and freshness as Agnes C. Laut. In two important novel competitions in the United States, laurels came to Canadian women — to Martha Ostenso for *Wild Geese* and to Mazo de la Roche for *Jalna*.

> When it comes to short story writers and contemporary poets, the catalogue cannot be complete. There are so many. Clearly, women writers in Canada stand alongside of men in those branches of literature which they have essayed, and moreover this has been in spite of inadequate support. There has been no log-rolling — quite the reverse, indeed!

After a short speech on "Quebec, the Cradle of Canadian History," by Alphonse Desilets, the national executive and the convention committee were luncheon guests of the Kiwanis Club. The Annual Dinner brought together a company of nearly three hundred. Toasts and speeches were bilingual and brief, for all wanted to view the displays of new Canadian books — French in the Palais Montcalm, English in the Angus Book Shop.

The following morning the delegates broke up into groups — Drama and Poetry under Dr. Scott, Fiction under Leslie Gordon Barnard, French under Jean Bruchési. The afternoon was agreeably devoted to a drive around the city and environs, a visit to the provincial archives, and had its climax in a garden party by the Lieutenant Governor at Spencerwood. Many of the members were afterwards entertained at a "Poets' Dinner" at Kerhulu's.

On Saturday morning, compliments flew, and appreciation was expressed right, left and centre for various services performed, and then it was "Bon Voyage" for members boarding the *Empress of Britain* for three weeks in England and Scotland. Those left behind consoled themselves with a visit to artist Horatio Walker on Ile d'Orléans, and waved as the great ship slipped down the St. Lawrence.

Chapter 10
The Canucks are Coming

The record does not say whose idea it was to lead a group of Canadian authors on a three-week literary pilgrimage to Great Britain in the summer of 1933. Undoubtedly, the credit should go to National Secretary Howard Angus Kennedy's innovative and fertile mind. And from the amenities offered by the CPR's London office and its fraternal link with British railroads, it is obvious that John Murray Gibbon had a large hand in the planning.

Arrangements for the Overseas Tour began in 1930, when CAA members were first queried. Would they like to make such a trip, at a cost of $400? Nearly a hundred eager acceptances came in, but then doubts arose, with the increasing pressure of the Depression. Would enough members be able to afford the tour? Would the hosts in Great Britain really welcome a horde at a time when many Britons were on the dole?

Kennedy decided to visit his married daughter, Helen Barrett in England in 1931, for a reconnaissance. This energetic pair came up with a staggering program of places, people and events, to be laid on for 1932 or possibly 1933.

Kennedy admitted modestly,

> While personal acquaintance with leaders in literary and journalistic circles doubtless brought a speedier opening of doors, giving access to more sources of information and influence than would otherwise have been possible in the two weeks at my disposal; yet the heartiness of the welcome promised was due to the immediate realization of the importance of the projected event — a collective visit of the representatives of literature in

the premier Dominion to the literary centre of the Empire.

Perhaps a letter from Archibald MacMechan spurred the Association. He wrote from England that autumn:

> Nothing has brought Australia so favourably to the notice of London as the exhibition of Australian literature at Australia House. The papers were enthusiastic and gave it long notices. . . . Canada House would provide excellent showrooms for Canadian literature. The federal government could be brought to see reason in the way of assistance, and our publishers would be glad to cooperate for the sake of the advertising.

Kennedy explored that avenue in Canada, and got the green light from both bodies. When the *Empress of Britain* left the port of Montreal, over six hundred Canadian titles and illustrations by Canadian artists were packed in the hold. These were exhibited first at the High Commissioner's office in the Strand. The collection was then loaned to Bumpus, the well-known Oxford Street booksellers, for their exhibition of books representing the whole British Empire. The collection was planned to form the nucleus of a permanent Canadian library at Canada House, and to receive fresh material from each year's literary harvest in the Dominion.

In the canvassing of entertainment possibilities, Kennedy began, logically with the Society of Authors, which assured him of cooperation. Its president, J.M. Barrie, invited him home to tea, and determined to provide a reception. Rudyard Kipling couldn't have been more cordial, though he rarely appeared in public these days. Perhaps he remembered his tour of Canada, for he wrote, "It will give me great pleasure to meet the authors of Canada." Kipling was Fellow-Stationer to the Lord Mayor elect, who took a good-humoured interest in the project. "You shall have an afternoon reception at Mansion House," (his official palace) and promptly made a note for his secretary's information — "Tea and music."

Kennedy had planned that the CAA members would hold three official meetings in London, a sort of continuation of the truncated convention in Quebec. He hoped they would take place in historic settings such as the Stationers' Hall, "not only ancient and impressive in itself, but has the closest historical connection with the rise of English literature."

The Lord Mayor's genial smile broke out, "I am Master of the Stationers' Company, and I say you shall have the hall."

145

Thus encouraged, Kennedy went on to invite the Prince of Wales, who telegraphed the message that he would be glad to meet the Association delegates, if he were available. Both Prime Minister Ramsay MacDonald and Opposition leader Stanley Baldwin, sent cordial messages, that since Parliament would be sitting, they would meet the Canadian authors for tea on the Terrace.

A smattering of members of the Society of Authors professed themselves willing, even eager, to meet their colonial counterparts. A distinguished list it was, too, even by today's standards, for instance John Galsworthy, Compton Mackenzie, Rose Macaulay, John Masefield, G.K. Chesterton, A.A. Milne, J.B. Priestley, George Bernard Shaw, A.P. Herbert, Francis Brett Young, Edith Sitwell — all expressed approval of the program, and most would join us at one or other of our gatherings.

Howard Angus Kennedy must have had a remarkable felicity for winning and keeping friends. The chief proprietor of *The Times* welcomed him very cordially in Printing House Square, where Kennedy for two decades had edited the weekly edition, before homesteading in Alberta, or joining the Montreal *Witness*. Sir Campbell Stuart, a leading member of the Empire Press Union — and a life member of the Canadian Authors Association promised all possible cooperation.

Oh, it was heady stuff for Canadians whose loyalty to Britain and the Empire was not weakened by events and doubts. Mr. Kennedy's report to the national executive left members drooling, and some borrowing money to make the trip. "I really can't afford to go," said one, "but equally I can't afford *not* to go."

Friends and relatives felt the same. Non-members were allowed to join on the recommendation of two members, and as the time approached the fare was whittled to $310. That figure included tourist class on the *Empress of Britain* outward bound, and return on any of the four "Duchess" steamers, at your own date. It included overseas rail and motor-coach fares, hotel rooms and all meals, entrance fees, baggage transfers, even tips.

By March 1933, the *Authors' Bulletin* could announce a firm timetable, and fifty-six members had signed for the expedition. They would sail from Quebec on Saturday July 1, land at Southampton on Thursday July 6, spend a week in the south of England, some days in the Lake District, and a week or so in Scotland, departing from Greenock on July 22. By June the program was fleshed out:

The need of assembling such a party as would adequately and honourably represent the membership was a chief concern. . . . Even before all names had been secured, our hosts were expressing satisfaction. They were equally prepared to welcome the rank and file, who must naturally form the majority. They perfectly realized that with us — as with themselves to a lesser degree — the rank and file of authors were not exclusive professionals who could devote their whole time to writing.

Every mail brings new indications of the warmth and the extent of the welcome, and also of the thoroughness with which all the details of travel have been worked out by Sir Archibald Weigall's committee, through the agency of the Pickford Company for the southern part, and the London, Midland and Scottish Railway for the northern part of the tour, with the constant assistance of the Canadian Pacific Railway's London staff.

Space cannot be afforded here for the complete time-table, but as the whole membership has from the beginning taken a keen interest in this enterprise, we give here a summary, subject to minor alterations. In many of the places mentioned, the visitors will be privileged to see parts not open to the general public.

Thursday, July 6. Dock at Southampton. Evening motor drive to Romsey Abbey, of Saxon foundation.

Friday, July 7. Drive through the most beautiful parts of the New Forest, pause at the Rufus Stone, by Wimbourne Minster, and Bere Regis (the Kingsbere of *Tess of the D'Urbervilles*) to Dorchester (Hardy's *Casterbridge*). Received by Mrs. Hardy at Thomas Hardy's home. Drive. Tea with the Mayor and Corporation. Drive to Salisbury.

Saturday, July 8. Received at Salisbury by the Dean. Drive by Stonehenge and Stockbridge to Winchester (King Alfred's capital), met by Dean at the Cathedral. Afternoon, drive by Farnham and Guilford to Box Hill (George Meredith's home). Tea at Burford Bridge Hotel (where Keats wrote *Ode to the Nightingale*). Continue by Epsom and Leatherhead to London.

Sunday, July 9. Westminster Abbey and Cathedral services. Drive through parks. Afternoon, time for art galleries and museums if desired. Drive through northern heights, Hampstead (tea with Lady Pentland, daughter of Lord and Lady Aberdeen) and Highgate. Evening, Zoological Gardens.

Monday, July 10. Drive through the City to St. Paul's Cathedral and Tower of London, etc. Afternoon drive by Record Office

Museum (Magna Carta) Dr. Samuel Johnson's house etc. to the Mansion House, official residence of the Lord Mayor of London. There the Lord Mayor's reception; with Sir James Barrie, Rudyard Kipling, and Viscount Cecil. Evening, Lyceum Club reception.

Tuesday, July 11. Drive by Chalfont (Milton's Cottage) Jordans (Wm. Penn) Beaconsfield (Disraeli) Wycombe (Burke) to Oxford. Received by John Buchan, John Masefield (Poet Laureate) and Sir Gilbert Murray. Lunch at Rhodes House with the Warden. Visits to Colleges and Bodleian Library. Tea at Colleges. Drive by Henley-on-Thames and Maidenhead to London along Chelsea Embankment in London to Kingsley Hotel for a week.

Wednesday, July 12. Received at Westminster Abbey by the Dean; drive to Temple Church and Lincoln's Inn. Lunch at Claridge's given in our honour by the Royal Society of Literature, Marquess of Crewe presiding; Rudyard Kipling and Sir Henry Newbolt to speak. Afternoon, Lambeth Palace, where the Archbishop of Canterbury hopes to meet us. Houses of Parliament: tea on the Terrace with Members. Evening, meeting in the Middle Temple Hall (Shakespeare), Lord Gorell presiding; J.B. Priestley and John Drinkwater to speak; G. Bernard Shaw also, if in London.

Thursday, July 13. Drive, out by Hampton Court Palace and Runnymede to Windsor Palace: received by Canon Deane and O.F. Morshead, Royal Librarian; luncheon in Castle Hotel. Return by Eton and Stoke Poges (Gray's country churchyard). Evening, Forum Club reception.

Friday, July 14. Drive by Southwark Cathedral, the George Inn (Sam Weller), out by Farningham, Maidstone, through northern Kent on the trail of Chaucer's pilgrims to Canterbury; received at Cathedral by Dean. Lunch in Queen Elizabeth's Guest Chamber. Return home by Rochester Castle, Gad's Hill (Dickens' home) and Cobham. (Tea at Mr. Tupman's "Leather Bottle.") Evening, Royal Empire Society's reception.

Saturday, July 15. Drive to Houses of Parliament, Zoological Gardens or Galleries, as desired.

So far all travel is by road, with special courier.

Afternoon, train by Harrow (Byron), Tring (Mrs. Humphrey Ward) Rugby (Arnold and Tom Brown) and Coventry, to Leamington. Drive by Warwick Castle to Stratford-on-Avon.

148

Evening, Shakespeare Theatre, performance of *Macbeth*.

Sunday, July 16. Stratford Church service. Afternoon, Shakespeare's birthplace Anne Hathaway's Cottage, etc. Drive by Kenilworth Castle to Rugby or Coventry, train by Nuneaton (George Eliot), Lichfield (Samuel Johnson) and Stafford (Izaak Walton) to Chester.

Monday, July 17. Drive: City walls, castle etc; received by the Dean at Cathedral. Afternoon, train to Windermere. Drive to Ruskin's house at Coniston; received by owner, Mr. Whithouse, President, Ruskin Society.

Tuesday, July 18. Drive from Windermere by Ambleside (Harriet Martineau) to Rydal Mount (Wordsworth's home); received by Gordon Wordsworth. Train from Keswick to Carlyle, cross border into Scotland. Drive to Sir Walter Scott's home at Abbotsford, Melrose and Dryborough Abbeys. Train to Edinburgh.

Wednesday, July 19. Edinburgh; drive to Castle, Holyrood Palace, St. Giles Cathedral, etc. Luncheon with the Lord Provost and Corporation in the City Chambers. Drive through Stevenson country. Evening, entertained by the Overseas League.

Thursday, July 20. Train to Callander; drive by Loch Katrine to Loch Lomond; steamer to Ballach, train to Glasgow.

Friday, July 21. Drive to Ayr (Robert Burns) and Blantyre (David Livingstone). Evening, reception by Glasgow Literary Society and Overseas League.

Saturday, July 22 — Greenock. Sail for home in Canadian Pacific liner *Duchess of York*.

Who could resist the allure of such a program, dazzling with names of the great and the honoured? Only those already victims of the Depression.

As it was, seventy-five Canadians joined forces in London, and the program fulfilled its promise. It was the opportunity of a lifetime to meet the literati of Britain under ideal circumstances, to visit scenes familiar through books, to gain stimulation to write books more worthy of our hosts, and to gain memories for a lifetime.

For the program was almost perfect, with minor changes. John Murray Gibbon's responsibilities caught up with him at Father Point, and so he missed the tour on which he had laboured. John

Galsworthy died before he could express his kindly welcome. Many were the speeches of welcome, pat phrases rolled off the tongues of members of Parliament, mayors and councillors, and every single one had to have a seconder and/or a reply.

> May we not hope that on a future occasion another over-seas pilgrimage can be organized with France as chief objective? Special arrangements would be made for any member of the French Section or others who would prefer to spend the first few days before London, in a visit to Paris, or would desire a longer trip to the Continent after our departure. Meanwhile, we gather that the members of the French Section who intend to join the expedition of 1933 will probably not desire to miss any feature of the program, and that the English-speaking members may look forward to the pleasure of their company throughout the tour.

The Annual Meeting of the CAA for 1933, opened Friday, June 30 at Quebec, the trippers sailed the next day, and reached London on Saturday evening a week later. It was a happy week, a calm sailing, with photographs on deck of regional groups, of Sunday morning service conducted by Rev. Dr. Gordon, who shortly after retired to his cabin for most of the crossing. As "Ralph Connor," he was reaching the peak of his fame, with at least a million copies of his books already published, and he had a deadline to meet. The members saw little of their new President on board, but he set them an example of industry in the face of temptation to socialize. Again in London, he stuck to his writing even while the house guest of Prime Minister Ramsay MacDonald. Miss Ishbel MacDonald entertained the Canadians at tea one day.

Helen Creighton (Nova Scotia branch), at thirty-four was among the youngest of the passengers. Her first book *Songs and Ballads from Nova Scotia* had been published the previous year. Wide-eyed, she kept a diary of the tour, amazed at the royal treatment the Canadians received.

"Our first night on board, we put on the first of two plays, prepared for the occasion, written by Claire MacIntosh of our branch. The other, produced on the fourth was by George Palmer (Regina).

"We had five National Presidents with us: Dr. Lighthall (Montreal) Murray Gibbon (Montreal), Dr. W.T. Allison (Winnipeg) Dr. C.G.D. Roberts (Toronto), and of course Dr. C.W. Gordon (Winnipeg). B.K. Sandwell and Justice Fabre Surveyer were other eminent passengers.

"The trip was planned so that we toured England and part of Scotland, with our route passing through those places where great writers lived, or had lived. Our first experience of this was the Thomas Hardy country, and we visited his home, walked through his garden, and many of us for the first time saw the interior of an English residence.

"It was an era of large hats for women, and high-boned collars, both prominent in the Kingsley Hotel lounge. There were many highlights, such as the afternoon at the home of Lady Pentland, daughter of Lord and Lady Aberdeen. Lord Aberdeen had served as Governor-General of Canada, and Lady Aberdeen had among other services established the Victorian Order of Nurses. The Right Honourable R.B. Bennett, Prime Minister of Canada, received with Lady Pentland, and another guest was Howard Ferguson, High Commissioner of Canada. As the Canadians were about to leave, Lady Aberdeen arrived, full of years but still vigourous.

"The literary pilgrimage was not lost sight of. At Dorchester, the Mayor and Corporation gave us tea to which many English people had been invited. They couldn't have been more friendly. Here we met H.M. Tomlinson, very shy and unassuming. At Salisbury the next day, the Dean himself took us around the Cathedral, and pointed out the tomb of St. Swithin. We visited Stonehenge and Winchester (where Jane Austen died). We were reminded at Alresford of Mary Mitford (*Our Village*), at Farnham of Swift's Stella, at Guilford of C.L. Dodgson ("Lewis Carroll") and this was where he told Alice his immortal story. We spoke of Keats at Burford Bridge where he wrote his "Ode to the Nightingale."

"On Sunday morning we attended a service at Westminster Abbey and later drove out to Hampstead and stopped at the home of Keats where we saw the old house with its garden and museum. . . . Saw two houses where Dickens had lived.

"On Monday, we strolled through the Tower of London, and went on to Mansion House.

"After signing the visitors' book, we were received by a distinguished line ... including a little man who looked vaguely familiar. Rudyard Kipling, my favourite author, the one I most wanted to meet! There was music and speakers. Lord Dunsany seemed nervous at first, but probably wasn't, and he gave a humorous talk. He looked immensely tall to me, had a heavy brown moustache and enormous feet. He spoke with a slight lisp, and many people liked him best ... Ernest Raymond, popular

151

author of the day, spoke on the England he loved, and we loved this tanned man with his cheerful outlook. Ralph Connor spoke for Canada, and it was a good speech, but any speech at that time would have seemed long ... Other guests were Dean Inge, Rose Macaulay, Sean O'Casey, F. Brett Young and many more.

"As we left this room, I found myself beside Mr. and Mrs. Kipling, and heard him say, "Hurry, we're going to eat!" Mr. Kipling was distinguished by great bushy eyebrows that stuck out like brushes, and Mrs. Kipling chatted constantly. They seldom appeared at any public functions, yet we were to have them again on Wednesday.

"At a reception at the Lyceum Club, an exclusive club where more of England's great writers had been invited to meet and address us, Katherine Hale (Mrs. John Garvin) responded for us, and I expect we all wondered what we had done to deserve all this.

"The next day, Tuesday, we visited the house where Milton wrote *Paradise Lost* and *Paradise Regained*, and then to Oxford and lunch at Rhodes House. Here to meet with us were John Buchan, Poet Laureate John Masefield, and Sir Gilbert Murray. Rev. Father Knox, large, witty without a smile, blue of eye, felt he had a connection with Canada by virtue of being nephew to Miss Knox, first principal of Havergal School, Toronto. Dr. E.A. Hardy (Toronto) spoke well for us, and students took us to the various colleges and served tea.

"We were guests of the Royal Society of Literature for luncheon at Claridge's, a gala affair, and I was placed near the head table with members of the English press. Rudyard Kipling was dwarfed by much bigger men, and there being no microphone then, we had to strain to hear him. The portly G.K. Chesterton referred to himself as no newspaperman in the United States sense, for who could imagine him sliding through a skylight to get a story? Henry Newbolt was the final speaker, and Dr. Lighthall and Charles G.D. Roberts spoke for us.

"Perhaps our most memorable evening was spent at the Forum Club, the leading club in London for women interested in the arts. There we met Elinor Glyn, the first of the avant garde writers, a very daring person in those days. Her *Three Weeks* was the talk of two continents, and exploded in sales around the world. An orchestra played and London's literary elite made friendly conversation as we awaited the crowning moment, the speech by George Bernard Shaw. Time went on and the guest speaker failed to show up. Several impromptu speeches were made. Refreshments were served before rather than after Mr. Shaw's address. He arrived so late that some were already leaving, and he was very rude. At 10:45 the great man arrived, and I overheard him mutter, "Disgraceful hour to be going anywhere. I've been at a dinner party."

"Mr. Shaw was immaculately dressed in tails and white tie, and began by saying in a strident high-pitched voice, "Ladies and gentlemen, you have all come to see me this evening. Well, here I am; take a good look." He thrust his hands behind his coattails and pirouetted like a manikin with no apology for being late. We laughed and applauded. Then while smiling genially, he set out to abuse us like a naughty boy seeing how far he can go before being sent home."

The indispensable National Secretary, H.A. Kennedy, published his account of the belated speech in the September 1933 issue of the *Authors' Bulletin*.

> Mr. Shaw confessed ignorance of Canada. He had recently gone around the world in a ship full of Canadians and Americans, and saw no difference between them. 'No one in England could, because there isn't any. I missed the opportunity of crossing Canada, but another time I think I will go to Canada and make the trip across to Vancouver. . . . If I go to outlandish and savage places like Canada, I shall become the victim of intellectual starvation. I suppose I shall be mobbed all over the place, or else blindly idolized.

Helen Creighton fills in the dotted section above: "He'd never heard of a Canadian author. He didn't know there were any. Nobody in England ever read a Canadian book. (I'd enjoyed him up to this point, because it was so obviously an act.) He then asked if we had had enough, and when we clapped feebly, he said the applause wasn't loud enough so we clapped a little louder and he said, "There, that's better; now is the time an experienced speaker stops," and he sat down. The whole thing didn't take ten minutes if that long.

"The Canadians were too numbed to offer the usual thanks to the speaker. The chairwoman looked mortified and quickly asked, "Is there any Canadian in the audience capable of replying to Mr. Shaw?" Ralph Connor shook his head, so did Charles G.D. Roberts. The atmosphere was very tense when our beloved National Secretary made his way from the back of the hall and mounted the platform. In a well-modulated voice, Mr. Kennedy said, "The sword of

Damocles has been hanging over my head all day until I have no brains left. And I am sure that Mr. Shaw will agree with me that I have no brains left when I say that I enjoyed his speech." We all sat a little straighter. "I am sure we all agree with Mr. Shaw when he says he knows nothing whatever about Canadians or Canadian books. He says he has never been to Canada and he is afraid if he did come that he would be either mobbed or blindly idolized. Let me assure Mr. Shaw that nothing of the kind could possibly happen in Canada, but that he would be treated as a distinguished British citizen." As he stepped down there was tremendous applause from hosts and guests, and when he passed the speaker, Kennedy put out his hand and said, "We trust, Mr. Shaw, your foreshadowed trip may soon become a reality. G.B.S. threw back his head and laughed."

(Shaw had achieved much of his reputation by being outrageous, and the Canadians had no need to ask themselves what they had done to merit such behaviour. But the insult made a deeper impression than all the fine and noble phrases of the three weeks — just as Shaw intended. The Canadians felt that the *enfant terrible* had been given an urbane come-uppance. But the chairwoman was heard to grit her teeth and swear, "That Shaw will never be invited here again!")

However, Helen Creighton and her fellow tour members had a hectic schedule to keep to:

"From sheer exhaustion, I had to skip some items including a tour of Canterbury Cathedral where Dean Hewlett Johnson was our host, and a tour of Stratford-on-Avon. However I managed to see *The Merchant of Venice* and *Macbeth* when we were guests of the director, Sir Archibald, and Lady Flower. At tea in their garden the following day, we met Maurice Colbourne and many Shakespearean actors, and that year we all received Christmas cards from our host and hostess. This kept up until the war, probably to those that acknowledged them. Little did we think then that war would come and we would be the givers, for when food was rationed, many of us sent parcels to the Flowers.

"We saw Windermere and Ruskin's home; Rydal Mount, Wordsworth's home; and Abbotsford, Sir Walter Scott's home where the pipers played thrilling music in the valley. Later we paid a visit to Stevenson's home and that of Robert Burns in the town of Ayr.

"When we visited Edinburgh Castle, we Nova Scotians performed a little ceremony in memory of Charles I, who in 1625 had created the Baronets of Nova Scotia and had given us our flag. For the investiture, King Charles had a piece of ground in front of the castle declared Nova Scotian soil. Laura Carten (Halifax newspaperwoman) thought this link with Scotland should be made an historic occasion. She had brought along with her a staff and a silk flag measuring a yard by a yard and a half, not knowing the area had been paved over. Ten N.S. members stepped forward as it was presented to the Lord Provost at his luncheon. I believe it is still in Edinburgh Castle as a memento of our visit."

The National Secretary, wishing to carry as much as possible of the interest and pleasure of the Overseas Tour to members who had been unable to join, paused in Montreal only long enough to send the September issue of the *Authors' Bulletin* to press. Then he set out on a tour of all the Association's western branches, welcomed everywhere.

His story was told both orally and pictorially, thanks to the cooperation of fellow travellers and the railways, from whom he had collected nearly a hundred lantern slides. He was also able to screen a unique film, sent from England by the Royal Society of Literature, of Rudyard Kipling and G.K. Chesterton addressing their Canadian colleagues in Claridge's dining hall.

A very experienced speaker, Kennedy held not only CAA members enthralled, but also high school students in Regina. In Edmonton, branch president Don Thomson called a special meeting of members and friends — and borrowed the private theatre of the Moving Pictures Censors and their sound projectors. The stay-at-homes both saw and heard better than had members actually on the spot.

In Calgary, the International Harvester Company loaned its projector for the benefit of a large crowd in the Palliser Hotel. In Victoria, Kennedy showed the moving picture at the Dominion Theatre in advance of the matinee, and told the story at night to an enthusiastic hundred in the Empress Hotel.

Reaching Toronto in time for the launching of Book Week, the National Secretary told the story to an audience of a thousand in the Concert Hall of the Royal York Hotel, where the sound movie was screened by the Associated Screen News, who later obliged in the Tudor Room of Ogilvy's store in Montreal as the wind-up of Book Week.

"We enjoyed every minute of the trip," enthused Prof. Norris

Hodgins (Ottawa). "It could not have been better arranged. . . . A wonderful month, a perfectly delightful experience. We've never before spent money to such great advantage. . . . I hope the visit inspired us to write better. It certainly gave us a memory to cherish for the rest of our lives." "An amazing and unprecedented success," glowed Charles G.D. Roberts. "It could never happen again."

No, never. But it almost did. By April 1938, the indefatigable Kennedy again with the aid of his daughter in England, had arranged an extended time-table in answer to invitations from John Masefield, Walter de la Mare and others. Kipling had written, "I am more pleased than I can say that the trip was a success. The organizing and holding it together must have been the heaviest of work. For me personally it was a joy and a pleasure. I believe very greatly that your trip was of the utmost use in every relation as well as the literary, and I only hope it will become a habit."

Unhappily, a second heart attack caught up with the dedicated National Secretary, and Howard Angus Kennedy slipped from life in mid-February, the most severe loss the Association had sustained to date. He was literally irreplaceable.

His son, Roderick Stuart Kennedy, long editor of the *Family Herald & Weekly Star,* and Dr. E.A. Hardy, president of the Toronto branch, felt that the tour should go forward as planned, at a cost of $445 for twenty-three days, provided enough members and friends signed up.

But the long Depression had depleted savings and spirits, and war in Europe seemed unavoidable, so the plans were quietly dropped.

Chapter 11
"And It's Hard, Hard Times"

After the excitement of the Overseas Tour, members of the Association were brought down to earth by the enduring Depression and shrinking markets. Magazines dwindled and relied on reduced staff for everything but fiction. School boards had little money to spend so the demand for textbooks slackened off. Public libraries had their budgets slashed, and circulated books so shabby and torn that some parents tore up their children's library cards.

Publishers leaned on their backlist of published titles, and drew on their banks of manuscripts already accepted. Newspapers' circulation fell away. Writers accustomed to producing book-length manuscripts found themselves turning out fillers, hoping that the publishers would be buying again "next year," as they claimed. Those that did not merge, or collapse entirely.

In the early 1930s, it was astonishing what efforts people went to in order to 'make a buck'. Some were honest, most devious. Apart from a proliferation of vanity publishers' ads for book or song publication, some editors were forthright. "We can't pay," they admitted, "but we can act as a showcase for your talents." Too many writers fell for the unsubtle flattery.

Some publishers (printers, rather) advertised for material to get them launched. Some even charged for the privilege of appearing in projected anthologies with titles such as *Great Poets of the World*, and found plenty of takers among the ungreat and unknown.

The Writers' Club of Toronto in the mid-thirties, decided to publish a fiction magazine (no doubt desperate for markets for their own material). Just one issue, unless its reception warranted more. They informed the *Canadian Author*:

> The immediate object is to find and help short-story writers whose work, however excellent, is shut out of "the stereo-typed" popular magazines, but who, given this initial publicity, may be helped to establish a literary career. "We have no pre-dilections for any kind of story," says a member of the Club, and there are a great many divergent views among ourselves as to what a good story is; but there are enough of us engaged to guarantee a rational decision. Our endeavour is to comb Canada for short-story talent, and to publish a book of say, ten pieces of fiction by writers nobody ever heard of, both to prove the quality of unrecognized Canadian writing and get recognition for it. Even some who are commercially successful in the short-story field, may have unaccepted mss. of greater artistic value than those they have been able to sell. Anything halfway decent is assured of at least five readings before the discard, and work in the best grade will be read by twenty people before it gets into type. Contributions should be sent with return postage . . .

This blurb in the *Canadian Author* was much appreciated by The Writers' Club, which received hundreds of mss, in due course, in spite of nobody being paid anything. It never went beyond one issue, if that.

A Regina firm in 1934 proposed an even more blatant exploitation of writers' talents. For the first three issues of a proposed new magazine, there would be no payment for contributions, and the Saskatchewan branch of the CAA was asked to do the editorial work, in the hope that when the magazine was well on its feet it would provide a new paying market for western writers. The branch set up a special committee to communicate with other western branches, whose co-operation was desirable.

Howard Angus Kennedy, from long experience in various aspects of publishing, urged western members to explore the financial and other factors on which an estimate of probable success could be formed.

> The successful establishment of a new magazine, especially for a constituency scattered over a vast area, is notoriously difficult . . . It depends not only on expert editing and the generosity of such able writers as will give away what they could sell, but on the business management required to build up circulation and

advertising revenue, and on the amount of money the owners are willing to spend in the try-out period before the magazine begins to pay.

The Saskatchewan branch resisted the temptation.

During the lean days, *Elbert Hubbard's Scrapbook* enjoyed great popularity (and the flattery of imitation). Some amateur anthologists (*not* members of the Canadian Authors Association) got the notion that their personal scrapbooks containing poems cut from magazines and snippets of homespun philosophy must be every bit as good, likely better. Without further thought, they presented such clippings to publishers, and were horrified to learn about copyright regulations. It had not occurred to them that they query author or publisher for permission. Indeed in many cases, they could not trace either from a yellow clipping.

More than one such anthology was privately printed and distributed, sometimes for a price, with the collector's name emblazoned as a by-line. Sometimes copyright was infringed innocently, sometimes with full awareness that the material collected was not "in public domain," but taking the chance that the authors anthologized even if they were to chance upon the literary theft, would not take legal action. Usually they were right about that. Poets are notoriously impecunious.

Another cost-cutting development of the thirties, and beyond, was a proliferation of "digests" aping the highly successful *Readers' Digest*. Most did not imitate the notable leader very strictly with regard to copyright and payment. Many simply lifted material from various sources, hoping the author would not notice and demand compensation. Often enough the material was simply stolen, and the by-line changed.

Complaints reached the CAA National Secretary, who queried the digesters, starting with the bellwether, *Readers' Digest*. Back came the good word promptly. Not only did it require the author's permission to print his material, plus that of the original editor — but they paid both, liberally. Many magazines felt honoured to have their articles thus given a wider circulation. *Maclean's* routinely rejected requests from other digests.

The editor of *Health Digest* replied that the author's permission was obtained first. "This digest is an organ of service, without advertisements, and has been run four years at a loss. Therefore it does not pay for what it uses."

The editor of *Science Digest* dealt with publishers only, not authors. "We do not pay a definite amount for the right to reprint articles. In fact, most of our material emanates from technical sources, where professional writers are not involved."

"The *Consumers' Digest*, deals with the owner of the copyright, who sets his rates, often making no charge. We supplement reprinted articles with original material, and pay the author two cents a word or less."

Digest magazines flourished briefly, before most folded.

In some instances, an editor who had purchased "all serial rights" might re-sell to a digest, with or without the author's permission; and he might or might not split any resulting cheque with the author. Other editors seemed to regard publications as a daisy field where they picked at will, without any toil or expenditure on their part. Some authors were flattered by the selection, until disabused by the National Secretary in the *Canadian Author*. Said he: "One thing is certain — a digest editor does not reproduce the story or article to compliment or advertise the writer. He takes it because he considers it of value to his business and he should pay for it. The more free gifts he gets to fill his pages, the harder it is on all free-lance writers."

By 1934, the Depression was cutting into every aspect of living. People cut out luxuries first, of course, and many societies and clubs dwindled and vanished as members decided they could not afford dues and subscriptions. Nor could the Canadian Authors Association afford the luxury hotels, even though the CPR and probably also the CNR arranged for reduced rates. Railway passes had never officially been held out as an inducement to join the Association, but unquestionably the word got around unofficially. "It was swell while it lasted," the authors admitted privately, and started saving nickels and dimes for the next convention.

No doubt John Murray Gibbon had a hand in the unusual setting of the 1934 convention. It was a brief assembly, held at Devil's Gap Bungalow-Chalet Camp, south of Kenora, Ontario. The site was deliberately chosen as midway between oceans, and the time was prior to the well-heeled vacationer of midsummer. Most of the burden of arrangements devolved on the Winnipeg branch as being nearest, which meant that it fell on Watson Kirkconnell, president of the branch and regional vice-president. National President Dr. Gordon (Ralph Connor) was abroad much of his biennium, in Britain and Australia.

Prof. Jean Bruchési, President of *La Section Française* which that year numbered an unprecedented 97 out of a total membership of 837, sent a warm message from Cairo where he was attending an International Postal Conference. Mme. Turgeon (Quebec) read his address, in which he referred to the historic past of the Lake of the Woods area.

> Especially to the La Vérendrye family and those who followed them, who formed a brilliant epic. Writers in French and English are natural liaison officers to bring together two great races in generous cooperation. None are better fitted to destroy prejudice and misunderstanding. A still closer collaboration, with a larger knowledge of each other's works would bring about a state of mind essential to our country's progress.

The camp on the bank of the Winnipeg River which drains Lake of the Woods into Lake Winnipeg was a familiar route to explorers and fur traders of both races and to the original native people. All played a part in the convention program, the Indians with a near-pageant, a dance and a pow-wow, the French with dissertations, English with song and lecture. A fourth voice was heard — that of the third great minority, the Ukrainian voice of the New Canadian.

After luncheon hosted by the town and Board of Trade of Kenora, the mayor presiding, the delegates settled down to the afternoon session, resisting the lures of canoe and beach. Donatien Frémont of Winnipeg, read a paper on Archbishop Taché as author. M. Frémont, French by birth and Canadian by adoption, editor for the past ten years of *La Liberté*, the French weekly of Winnipeg, was author of a recently-published biography of Radisson. Archbishop Taché is best remembered for his intercession on behalf of Louis Riel, but he also left two important volumes, indispensable to any student of the early Canadian West.

Louis-Phillipe Gagnon also of Winnipeg spoke on "French Literature in the West," and deplored the fact that most of it was ephemeral, from La Vérendrye down. "French writings in the West reproduce much more the resounding call of the trumpet than the gentle voice of the muses." Professor Kirkconnell, in thanking *La Section Française* for its contribution to the program, spoke of his translations from the French, as did Dr. Charles G.D. Roberts. President Dr. Gordon, prophecied confidently that by cooperation between the French and English cultures we in Canada

161

would build up a truly indigenous culture finer and richer than either could have given us alone.

The company departed to the outer sunshine briefly to watch the arrival of the Indian canoes as promised by Capt. Edwards, superintendent of the Rat Portage Reserve. It was a moving sight, as canoe after canoe rounded the point, paddles dripping, paddlers in full dress, with their wives and children.

Shepherded back into the convention hall, members settled down to the second session of the afternoon, devoted to the foreign language literature of Canada. As Honoré Ewach remarked, "Canada has three civilizations being welded together at this time, the third and latest, the Foreign. His address on "Authorship among the Ukrainians" told of the pioneer period before the Great War, which was dominated by four writers — Kudrik, Krat, Fedik and Novak. The post-war period with the immigrants thinking of themselves as Canadians, was dominated by authors who like himself, were educated in Canada. Ewach was a graduate of the University of Saskatchewan, and associate editor of the *Ukrainian Voice*. He had also published two chapbooks of poetry.

> Our Ukrainian writers in Canada may lack historical tradition, and their cultural level may not be very high, but as they are very rich in artistic qualities and have an insatiable desire for knowledge, they may be expected to enrich Canadian literature with many valuable contributions.

Professor Watson Kirkconnell of Wesleyan College, Winnipeg, concluded the meeting with a speech notable for his impressive reading of many beautiful translations he had made of the work of foreign language poets in Canada. He had a gift for languages, which he put to full use, as his final bibliography shows. He read first a poem from a Greek, George Vlassos (Winnipeg), then one by a Hungarian Hamilton woman. Most important of the New Canadian literature was the Icelandic, he declared, because of the comparatively high cultural level, and their long poetic tradition. One of them, Stephan Stephanson was greatest. For forty years, he was a farmer in Alberta. On a visit to his native land, he was greeted with almost royal honours. Dying in 1927, he left almost 1,500 poems in five volumes.

Kirkconnell himself could not anticipate that he would receive a knighthood in Iceland in recognition of his translations. He touched on Italian and Swedish newcomers, then swung back to the Ukrainian songsters.

> Some 10,000 poems await disinterment from newspaper files by any student who will tackle such an enormous but valuable task. Showing that the Ukrainians do appreciate their literature, let me say that in sixteen years, 50,000 copies of Fedik's poems were sold. Our speaker, Honoré Ewach is becoming the most significant of the Ukrainian poets.

The afternoon startled some delegates who had never thought much beyond the Anglo-Canadian point of view, and had had little occasion to make contact with authors other than those writing in English. It was a salutary jolt, for in the years to come, many New Canadians contributed to Canadian literature and to authors' groups.

But it was solid fare, and the program moved on inexorably as the delegates and speakers tripped aboard the S.S. Argyll for a cruise on Lake of the Woods to the Rat Portage Indian Reserve. Some were too hungry to wait, and nibbled at their box suppers, while the Indian school band played on deck. The pow-wow began, and men, women and children took part in dances and rites around a campfire. As a climax, the Chief made a speech in Ojibway, presenting President Gordon with a stone pipe of peace. The non-smoking clergyman could not be persuaded to demonstrate its practical use, but he kept it as a valued memento. The pow-wow over, Association members and friends from Kenora returned to the Devil's Gap camp to stage a dance of their own, fox trots, waltz, two-step, and a bit of square dancing.

A craft session next day was an editors' panel on the magazine situation, in which L.E. Brownell (Winnipeg), editor of the *National Home Monthly* reminded listeners that an editor could not confine his acceptances to stories he himself liked, but must provide enjoyment to the subscribers. He had little interest in big names — rejected them by the bushel, he averred — and gave preference to Canadian writers, other things being equal.

Roderick Stuart Kennedy (Montreal), of the *Family Herald*, asked why the minority of readers who preferred artistic stories did not get their fair proportion of top material? But of course he knew the answer as well as any editor. The circulation manager and the accounts department carry weight in editorial decisions.

The nominations committee presented its slate — same as last year. The resolutions committee announced the 1935 convention would likely be held in Montreal. The most important resolution was to include in the *Canadian Author* not only news of *La Section Française*, but to list all the new French-Canadian titles in addition to the English. This listing began with the next issue.

The 1935 convention was held again in Montreal, at the Mount Royal Hotel. One of the chief topics was discussion of a poetry magazine, as urged by the Montreal Poetry Group. The most interesting speaker was Frank L. Packard on "Thrillers." However, the most valuable talk was probably given by Hector Charlesworth (Montreal) on "Writing for Radio," still a comparatively new medium. This meeting was also memorable for its strong recommendation that there should be a tightening-up of qualifications for Regular membership. Only those should be accepted for Active (voting) membership who had:

(a) one book at least, published on a royalty basis
(b) four short stories in a recognized magazine
(c) at least six poems, paid for
(d) an article of at least 1200 words, paid for
(e) a play, staged or on radio.

At the 1935 convention, Dr. Pelham Edgar (Toronto) became National President, and things began to happen.

First, the bad news. The ominous threat of independent French action came closer to realization, with additional boons for French writers. The slogan of the rising Union Nationale Party made a strong appeal, "Quebec for French-Canadians," and affected the long-time Liberal government. In 1927, Provincial Secretary Athanase David had established the annual David literary awards (still much honoured). In addition his office annually purchased and distributed 30,000 volumes of Quebec writings. At the 1935 annual dinner of *La Section* the same Provincial Secretary had promised an annual vote of $1,000 to make possible a permanent secretariat for a new organization of French-Canadian writers.

"What would such a secretariat accomplish?" a CAA member asked.

Professor Jean Bruchési admitted, "Well, it would be an address and telephone, and some typing services, I suppose." He deplored the narrow individualism which was largely the reason for *La Section's* weakness.

The Canadian Authors Association has helped to build co-operation between French and English-writing Canadians. The

Canadian Author keeps subscribers informed of the literary production of the French colleagues. Many French-Canadian
works merit translation into English and distribution among
Anglophones. None of our writers know enough of each
others' writings. Could we not establish on solid ground an
exchange of French- and English-Canadian books? *Les oeuvres
de nos confrères de langue anglaise nous sont à peine connues. Que
savez-vous des notres?*

While heartily approving the idea of more translations, the Canadian Authors Association could do little to implement the suggestion. Its budget for the year had fallen to $2,000. Lacking outside
funding, it could only continue to list French publications, as well
as urge translation and publication. French-reading members had
thus accomplished production of the classic *Maria Chapdelaine*,
(translated on his own initiative by member Louis Blake Duff), of
Ringuet's *Trente Arpents* (which won a Governor General's medal)
and Mme. Guèvremont's Le Survenant (a commercial success in
English, as The Outlander). What more could the Association alone
do? Today, most translation is done under grants from the Canada
Council, more works travelling from French into English, however,
than vice versa.

Albert Levesque, secretary of *La Section* was more outspoken
than his affable president.

Only about one-fourth of some 250 French writers and artists
belong to the Canadian Authors Association. Some give infan-
tile reasons for not joining, such as so-and-so does not like
such-and-such an officer of *La Section*. Others, equally childish
hold aloof because they want independence of their Anglo-Canadian colleagues. No society of writers in the French language
can enjoy more liberty and autonomy than we do. Our freedom
of action has never been hampered by our English colleagues,
who are practical people and adapt themselves marvellously to
circumstances. We do the same and all goes well. Such an
excuse cannot be taken seriously.

Still, a committee was set up to discover whether a majority of
French writers in Canada, as they did not support *La Section*, would
support an independent society with the same objects. Otherwise a
change from the present form of organization would be useless.

The emotional racial appeal swept the Liberals out of office in
1936, but the Union Nationale Party fulfilled the promise of sup-

port to writers, including $500 per annum to the English-speaking Montreal branch.

In 1936, at the Vancouver/Victoria convention, Prof. Jean Bruchési had the sorrowful obligation to announce formation of *La Société des Écrivains Canadiens*, under charter of the Quebec government.

He assured the Association of the most cordial cooperation from *La Société*, and wished for affiliation with the parent body. The CAA granted the latter, grieved that all its efforts towards welding the two cultures had failed to maintain that ideal. A resolution was passed, thanking Prof. Bruchési, a valued colleague, and asking him to assure the new society of our fraternal desire for its complete success.

The link is tenuous, of course, but the two groups have shared conventions in Montreal more than once, to mutual enjoyment. Proof of the collaboration came in Centennial Year, 1967, when both groups compiled together an anthology of French and English writings of the past hundred years. *A Century of Canadian Literature/ Un Siècle de Littérature Canadienne* was edited by H. Gordon Green (Montreal) and Guy Sylvestre of Ottawa, with Cdr. C.H. Little (Ottawa) acting as liaison.

The elan of the 1936 convention thus subdued was further diminished by an acrimonious debate over new styles of poetry, between Dorothy Livesay and Mary Elizabeth Colman (Vancouver). Stimulating — but unsettling to the non-poets who couldn't see what the fuss was all about, and who wouldn't recognize an iambic pentameter outside a dictionary. A.M. Stephen, author of much traditional poetry spread oil on the troubled waters.

The economic slump wounded young and old, penniless students as well as professors on shrunken salaries. Dr. Pelham Edgar, entering his sixties, was well aware of the despondency on the University of Toronto campus as a busy and beloved professor of English at Victoria College. He also had observed the frayed cuffs of Dr. Charles G.D. Roberts and his tendency to cadge meals. A compassionate man, Edgar went into action in 1931, when president of the Arts & Letters Club.

E.K. Brown could write of him, "No academic figure has done more to foster Canadian literature than Pelham Edgar." The tall gaunt professor of English was a perceptive inspired teacher who "discovered" novelist Raymond Knister, E.J. Pratt and later Northrop Frye.

Edgar launched his project, a new humanitarian scheme to which he knew the men of the Arts & Letters Club would be sympathetic:

> In the absence of a Civil List in Canada, there is no established means (except by private charity) of providing financial assistance to an individual who has rendered distinguished service to his country and faces perhaps an old age of penury or actual destitution. I would like to propose that we establish a permanent Trust Fund to be administered by a Board of Governors in the interest primarily of creative literature and ultimately of all the creative arts. Writers who have brought distinction to their country should not be compelled to face an old age embarassed by financial distress.
>
> Members of the artist class have few opportunities for material gain, in fact they rarely provide more provender than suffices for a meagre annual budget. Their failure to accumulate a surplus for their declining years can't be imputed to improvidence.

The members of the Arts & Letters Club knew many an artist in such a predicament. They formed the Canadian Authors Foundation, whose Board of governors included Sir Robert Falconer, president of the University of Toronto, Duncan Campbell Scott (Ottawa) and R.C. Wallace, principal of Queen's University. Edgar was secretary. A fund-raising campaign conducted by Edgar, started in Ottawa. Governor General Lord Bessborough agreed to act as patron "convinced that the movement is very necessary to the literary life of Canada."

Edgar next solicited backing from Prime Minister R.B. Bennett and Opposition leader W.L. Mackenzie King. They agreed that Dr. Charles G.D. Roberts especially was a deserving case, and Parliament voted $2,500 annually to be paid to Roberts through the Foundation, for the rest of his life. Roberts could therefore taper off his scrounging on friends who welcomed his visits, (but who also welcomed his departure after two months, a Nova Scotia hostess confessed).

Roberts (who received a knighthood in 1935) after slight demur allowed his name to be used in fund-raising because it would help others as well as himself. People were appalled to learn that this renowned author of so many popular books lived in straitened circumstances. If he was hard up, what must be the conditions of other authors? His name did cause people to open their wallets as wide as they dared. In the western provinces, the name had somewhat less appeal, and there Dr. Edgar informed listeners of the plight of a distinguished B.C. poet who was disabled. (The Foundation observed confidentiality with names of the living, though it always emphasized the funds were meant as a tribute, not a charity.)

In fact, Prime Minister Bennett was so moved that in October, he attended a large public meeting in Convocation Hall, Toronto, chaired by Sir Robert Falconer. Other speakers included Hon. Athanase David, provincial secretary of Quebec, Judge Emily Murphy (Edmonton) and Rev. Robert Norwood, Canadian poet and preacher to a fashionable congregation in New York City. Some hundreds of dollars were raised.

This launching of the Canadian Authors' Foundation evoked wide and usually favourable comment in the press. "... A landmark in Canadian cultural history," commented the *Mail and Empire* of Toronto. *The Montreal Gazette* opined, "Unfortunately the arts seem remote to the average mind. Yet the writer, the poet, the man who holds the chisel or brush cannot very well live on lotus leaves." J.V. McAree saw the Fund as a patriotic device that might keep Canadian artists in Canada "where they are so much needed and so slimly rewarded."

At the 1932 convention in Ottawa, Dr. Edgar addressed the CAA delegates on the matter, since they would be the beneficiaries of such a Foundation. Dr. Edgar could report that local advisory committees had been set up in large cities of the west, where the name of Roberts had less appeal than the plight of a disabled B.C. poet of proven talent.

Edgar reminded the delegates of the purpose of the Fund.

> Not to bonus the young writer but for the benefit of any man or woman of distinction in Canadian letters, or their dependants, French or English. If sufficient funds can be accumulated, young writers of promise might be helped. I would like to see every branch devote a meeting or entertainment for the purpose of augmenting the Fund.

(In his gentle way, Edgar was also flexible, rather like a steel rapier.)

A member from Brantford wondered, "Isn't there any Dominion fund for recognizing such artists? The government spends a good deal of money on historic sites and monuments. It should have more consideration for living authors than dead ones."

M.O. Hammond (Toronto), author of *Canadian Footprints*, which commemorated distinguished Canadians of the past, pointed out that the Foundation now had a skeleton organization throughout the country, including wealthy businessmen. Surely it should exhaust its own resources before troubling the government.

Hammond therefore moved, seconded by Dr. Douglas Leechman (Ottawa) "that the Association warmly supports the aims and objectives of the Foundation, and urges upon its branches the desirability of practical cooperation with the local committees that now exist." Carried.

But there the matter remained through two more years of Depression.

Edgar was stricken later that summer by an agonizing letter from Raymond Knister, a sometime student who had shown great promise in poetry and novel writing. His *White Narcissus* was touted as being in worthy of Thomas Hardy, but the collapse of Graphic Publishers had reduced him to despair. His life and talent ended in suspected suicide. Edgar's compassionate heart never forgot. For the Fund's slender resources were committed to others in small amounts of one hundred dollars a month.

Some members failed to differentiate between the Canadian Authors Association and the Canadian Authors' Foundation. National Treasurer Lawrence Burpee was stung into indignant retort, when it was rumored that the Association funds went to the Foundation. Burpee reminded the convention of 1935 that the accounts were clearly audited, and available for study in the *Canadian Author*. It was not true that the Association paid a pension to a certain eminent author; nor had the Association paid any part of the participation of certain members in the authors' overseas tour.

> Not one dollar of the Association's hard-earned and jealously-guarded money is, or ever has been, used for such purposes. Nor have they even been considered. In short, the rumors are sheer invention.

Still, the liaison was close enough to confuse, and the Foundation soon became known as the Canadian Writers' Foundation/La Fondation des Écrivains Canadiens.

Several French-Canadian writers were helped over a rough patch, as well as English-speaking Frederick Philip Grove, whose long illness left not even enough for funeral expenses. No one informed the Foundation until too late of the dire straits of C.W. Lloyd, a noted Winnipeg essayist who lost his wife, his home, his vision, and his dog, and then took his own life.

A small stipend, in honour not charity, eased the latter days of Dr. E.J. Pratt when he became crippled with arthritis; and those of Leslie Gordon Barnard, as fiction markets dried up; Marshall Saunders (Toronto) was found in straightened circumstances, not due to sloth (she had twenty-six books published) nor sumptuous living (she spent any excess money on relieving birds and animals in distress). Blind writers were aided in practical ways.

With the death of Roberts in late 1943, the Parliamentary grant ceased, and Edgar had to go on the campaign trail once more. He began with the Governor General, and the Earl of Athlone not only agreed to serve as Honorary Chairman, but gave Edgar a personal cheque "to set the movement in action." Edgar went on to a one-man siege of Parliament, which eventually restored the small grant, which, after the Canada Council was formed, rose to $6,000 annually, to be matched by the Foundation. The Edgar Memorial Fund became the most effective means of building up an endowment.

In 1945, there was only $500 in the kitty, and the need was great. Parliament was not easily won over, though probably Edgar's earnest appeals had some indirect effect in bringing about the various pensions put through by the government in the 1940s. The reinstatement of the $2,500 brought down the wrath of two watchdogs of the Treasury. One suggested that writers of distinction didn't need charity, while the other had never heard of the Foundation and suspected it was a Communist front, "For the name hints at all kinds of sinister intrigue." Fortunately wiser counsel prevailed and the vote went through.

The *Calgary Herald* was displeased. "Why should authors be singled out and regarded as a privileged class? The money involved is trivial, and the beneficiaries doubtless deserving. But the principle is wrong. The honest writer cannot compromise himself by accepting state bounty."

The *Globe and Mail* thought otherwise:

> This belated and pitifully small act of charity and justice will not corrupt the writers of Canada and turn them into political agents. The beneficiaries have passed the time when they would be effective propagandists. Their political favor would

not be worth a two dollar bill to any party. The Writers' Foundation is most obviously a public responsibility.

Sir Charles G.D. Roberts, the first beneficiary, published more than sixty books that took Canada's name to many countries and furnished material for our school readers at home. In his early and middle years of heavy production, he followed the usual custom of outright sales to his publishers.

Though some of those books are still selling, he was legally entitled to nothing from them in his old age.

He visited schools in many parts of Canada where his mere presence was regarded as educational. He simply could not live on what he could earn. Many felt the public disgrace of Canada's foremost man of letters being a pauper — as he would not have been in many another country.

Dr. Pelham Edgar, by now chairman of the board, told the CAA delegates to the 1945 convention in Montreal,

Our government grant ended with the death of Sir Charles. Yet our minimum annual outlay approximates $10,000. At present our bank balance is $500. We are dependent on smaller subscriptions which are applied directly to Revenue Account. We have made application to the government for a parliamentary grant. If it fails, we will try again — and again.

CWF Honorary president Lorne Pierce, asked earnestly

Cannot the CAA set aside fifty cents a year from each membership fee, as a guarantee that someone who has brought honour to this Association and Canada, shall not lack the commonest necessities?

(The proposed levy was rejected by the membership, but each convention remembers, and individuals and branches continue to make their contributions, in amounts far larger than a levy would produce.)

In fact, Dr. Edgar declared,

There is a natural link between these two groups, a mutual service, and I hope it will continue on a voluntary basis rather than an arbitrary tax. The Foundation is an insurance resource for some of the Association's members, but most of you, I trust, will not be confronted with sore financial difficulties towards the evening of your lives.

The following year, finances still low, the Foundation hoped to

171

appoint a campaign director who might secure a hundred Founders, who would each subscribe $1,000, and a hundred Benefactors, who would each subscribe half that amount.

"We are determined that writers (and later artists when we have become firmly established) shall not lack help in their great need," said Dr. Lorne Pierce at the CAA Silver Jubilee convention in Toronto. "All Canada is in debt to these writers who have fallen on lean days. There comes a time when every artist's wares have no buyers. Fashions change and bread fails."

And now the good news.

The Foundation couldn't bring itself to squander much-needed cash on the services of a professional fund raiser. Wilfrid Eggleston (Ottawa) suggested Mrs. Don Thomson, the former Theresa Meeres (Edmonton) as office help. Terry had been literary secretary to Madge Macbeth and later to Duncan Campbell Scott. With her boundless sympathy, Terry Thomson became the one-woman staff of the Foundation at ten dollars a month. She worked under Dr. Edgar for his final five years. She set up good bookkeeping, her files ready for inspection at any time.

Upon Dr. Edgar's death, Terry became chief fund-raiser, bearding industrial tycoons and government mandarins and occasional Scrooges, strong in the worth of her mission. "Use my name any time you wish," Dr. Pierce told her, and she found it opened doors, so that he could say with conviction, "Terry Thomson has been and is, the feet and hands and the heart of the Canadian Writers' Foundation."

It was a little easier once the Foundation was incorporated in 1946, and received its "charitable donations" number. In the thirty years she served in this capacity, Terry was able to gather for the Foundation nearly $200,000, thus placing the CWF on a firm financial footing. The Pelham Edgar Memorial Fund is today the endowment he yearned for, and can pay its beneficiaries substantially out of the interest.

Is the Foundation really necessary any more, in these days of old age pensions, disability pensions, Canada pensions and the like?

Yes, in its original sense. There is no Civil List yet in Canada, and honour is still to be paid to distinguished writers.

True, there is no more "destitution among Canadian authors" as the charter puts it. Pensions alone can keep the senior author alive, but little more in a period of high inflation. Today CWF grants provide a fiscal cushion of freedom from economic anxiety and stress.

Terry Thomson served as executive secretary until her retirement in 1971, when she was named honorary president for the remaining few years of her life. Her husband, Dr. Don Thomson continues his deep interest in the CWF.

Chapter 12
Angling for the "Unreading"

All was not gloom and despair during the Depression years. Indeed, there was rarely a time of more expressed optimism (with little foundation), of hope that prospects were brightening, that prosperity was "just around the corner."

Three members of the Canadian Authors Association were singled out in "the birthday list" of honours dealt out by King George V in June 1934, though not for literary contribution. Duncan Campbell Scott (Ottawa) for his long and notable service as Superintendent of Indian Affairs was made a Companion of the Order of St. Michael and St. George; Marshall Saunders (Toronto) and Mary Waagen Allan (Calgary) became Commanders of the British Empire, the former for her services to animals, the latter in the cause of crippled children.

The arts in Canada were recognized for the first time the following year, when knighthood came to four members of the Association: to Dr. Charles G.D. Roberts in literature, to E. Wyly Grier in painting, to Ernest Macmillan in music, to the Hon. Thomas Chapais (Quebec) in historical writing. It was well that it happened when it did, for shortly afterwards, the Canadian government passed a ban on Canadians accepting titles, as being undemocratic.

In 1932, National President Pelham Edgar had established the Canadian Authors' Foundation. In 1936, he launched the *Canadian Poetry Magazine*, and the Governor General's Awards. Each of these merits a chapter on its own.

Something of greater immediate impact grew in the alert and compassionate mind of Dr. Edgar. He was eager to prove to the current Governor General Lord Tweedsmuir (John Buchan), honorary president of the Canadian Authors Association, that he was patron to an energetic outgoing organization. Edgar set about revitalizing the Association of Canadian Bookmen which had preceded the birth of the Association, and re-surfaced for a few years in Toronto as a booksellers' association. The new version would be less commercial-minded, would embrace all phases of the book trade — authors, publishers, booksellers, librarians and readers. It would reach out to the "unreading."

The notion of running their own bookshop appealed to some members, or better, why not a travelling bookshop? Was the idea inspired by Christopher Morley's delightful *Parnassus on Wheels*? or vice versa? It had been tried out in the United States, with some success. Then why not in Canada? Members were intrigued by the idea, knowing how poorly served were our rural areas. The obliging National Secretary instituted an enquiry, and discovered the project more romantic than practicable.

> "On the whole, book caravans have not been a great success," wrote the New York editor of the *Publishers' Weekly* in 1935. "I know only one dealer in the middle West who is now running a travelling bookshop — and she sells only to libraries.
>
> The great difficulty is to get enough sales per day to carry the overhead expenses. When customers come to a bookshop they have selected their own time for buying. When you go to them, they are likely to postpone, or to be out of the house, and therefore the number of effective calls per day is lessened."
>
> "Far more of a deterrent," noted a Halifax librarian, "is the imposition of license fees, which differ greatly in different localities. In some larger centres where there are bookstores, a heavy license fee is charged the 'transient trader'. The peddler's license costs only eight dollars in Halifax, but each district imposes its own fee."

Provincial libraries were sending out boxes of books to remote communities and making deposits in village libraries. In the USA publicly financed bookmobiles were beginning to make calls at schools and other appointed rendezvous, which would cut sales possibilities. So the matter was finally abandoned.

If only libraries showed more appreciation of Canadian books, more patriotism, in fact, surely all would be well with the book business, was the thought of some CAA members. "Why not ask the libraries themselves about their attitude to Canadian literature — why they don't support it better?" Questionnaires were a relatively new technique, and the ever alert Kennedy expected total response. He got eighty-three percent, a very high return.

> Nora Bateson, director of libraries for Prince Edward Island, reported that the public there read Canadian books gladly, just because they were Canadian — the exact opposite of what she had found in her Toronto Libraries career. Miss Vaughan of the Saint John public library wrote, "We do all in our power to bring to the attention of our readers Canadian books that come up to our standards. We always observe Canadian Book Week."

> F.C. Jennings, Ontario Inspector of Public Libraries, believed that many librarians attempted to guide readers to Canadian books. "But that guidance is very limited. Some people resent it. I think too little attention has been given to the choice of books for young readers."

Chief librarian at Regina, J.R.C. Honeyman was wary about guiding the taste of individual readers, "and besides, librarians have little time to do intensive work of this kind."

> "We try to have on our shelves at least one copy of every worthwhile Canadian title," replied Mrs. Lyle, head of Hamilton Public Library. "Canadian librarians are more than ready to stimulate the reading of Canadian books by means of lists and displays and book-talks."

> Calgary librarian Alexander Calhoun answered: "In our library, Canadian books sell themselves and are very extensively used. We buy all Canadian books of importance, and also, a lot of slight importance. Canadian librarians, and those in other countries as well, would, I am sure, like to have a selected list of Canadian books, especially if the list were annotated. This would be particularly helpful to librarians in smaller places who cannot afford to purchase many books."

"Amen" said L.F. Barnaby of Halifax Citizens' Free Library.

Dr. George Locke, Toronto's Chief Librarian, had his reservations, perhaps fearing an overdose of partisan enthusiasm, but his librarians turned out booklists much-sought by other libraries, and his annual *Canadian Catalogue of Books*, inaugurated in 1935, was so valued that the National Library in Ottawa took over the task some years later.

Edgar S. Robinson, Chief Librarian of Vancouver, was more encouraging: "Any list of books prepared by your Association would be helpful and appreciated. In our library we do pay particular attention to writings by Canadian authors, and occasionally buy a book because it is Canadian when we would not otherwise buy it."

Eleanor Barteaux of Windsor, Ontario, went overboard: "We buy practically every Canadian book published. We recognize the reading tastes of our public, and cater to them, even if we feel personally that it is a waste of money to stock westerns and mysteries. We try to purchase titles recommended by borrowers, and make it a point to take into our confidence teachers, study club leaders, clergy etc. before buying in quantity books in which they are authoritative."

Evalyn Srigley (Edmonton) was more specific: "Books seem to be taken out on merit regardless of nationality. Among popular Canadian books, Nellie McClung, L.M. Montgomery and Marian Keith are always in demand. Ethel Grayson's *Apples of the Moon* is a prime favourite. Frank Packard and Mazo de la Roche are asked for continually. Canadian historical stories and straight history meet with approval. Leacock's and McArthur's humor is appreciated. Very little poetry is asked for except that of Drummond or Robert Service. Lampman and Carman read by students only, or an occasional studious-minded person. Children read Charles G.D. Roberts' animal stories. Indian tales and legends are popular."

"Every good library 'sells' books," according to Mr. Calhoun. We are constantly giving people the details of publisher and price. The cultivation of the book market in the small town and farm in western Canda is deplorably inefficient — except for the peddler of subscription sets."

"Perhaps we could cultivate the book market by prodding the newspapers to carry more news of authors, more reviews — make a survey of just what is going on," the national executive suggested, and Kennedy quickly lined up another questionnaire. Out of eighty-two mailed, fifty-two brought replies. (Editors got more such forms to fill out than did librarians, and so were less concerned.)

They were asked if they were running a regular literary or book review section? If not, what sort of material would they print if it were made available? For instance:

1. Would you like to receive personality sketches of Canadian authors?
2. Would you like to receive "newsy" items about forthcoming, or published books?
3. Would you review good Canadian books if they were sent to you?
4. Would you like to receive, with any book sent to you, a competently prepared review, provided it was exclusive to your paper in your city?

"First," Kennedy reported, "It should be said that out of fifty-two replying, twenty-three run a book section regularly, eight occasionally, and only twenty-one never. As the great majority of Canadian dailies are small, this seems a gratifying figure. The Yeas far outweighed the Nays. Only three were entirely negative. Why, then did they not run such column?"

They told the national secretary:
1) It was hard to find such features;
2) Lack of space — other material was more important to the clientele;
3) Publishers don't spend advertising money on newspapers. "They're parasites, expecting us to use their free material to sell their commercial products. Well, we do — so long as it's news of interest to our readers. Books get more free publicity than most products, though not maybe as much as authors think they should get."

"We have not given a great deal of space to new books," wrote a Nova Scotian editor, "but we do make it a point to review any that are sent to us."

But what publisher can afford to send free copies (on which the author receives no royalty!) to every newspaper?

An Ontario big-city editor wrote that he would be glad to receive newsy items of writers and their books, "but they must be short and crisp, not a puff."

The editor of a small Ontario daily expressed the general attitude: "This is a small paper with limited space and mechanical equipment. Will be glad to help in any way possible."

Among the fifty-two replies was a single editor — evidently suffering from indigestion — who answered the question, "Would you review good Canadian books if they were sent to you?" with a curt scrawl: "There are none."

As a tailpiece, let us quote a well-known writer who has had many years of experience as the sieve through which publicity material passes on one important paper. He says: "Even when sending material for free publicity, book publishers and authors often do the job in a crude and irritating fashion. When one asks a favour, one should at least make it as easy as possible to grant it."

Convinced that the "unreading habit" is formed early in life, the national secretary was instructed to survey the provincial Departments of Education. A love of books has to be implanted early. The two-part questionnaire went out early in 1935:

    (a) What is your Department doing, and what more can it do to instill a love of reading?
    (b) What is being done to enable them to realize the value and interest of Canadian books?

The answers, as might be expected, came back full of complacency and self-righteousness, though the answer to the second segment showed a heavy reliance on school readers which contained smatterings of Canadian poetry and watered-down prose. A listing of Canadian titles showed not only a shortage of Canadian books for children, but lack of knowledge of those that did exist. Clearly, there was need for missionary work. Ontario spoke of school libraries which would be augmented in more prosperous times. New Brunswick praised the work of the IODE in placing libraries in many schools. In Prince Edward Island, the Women's Institutes were being encouraged to form reading groups, through the formation of travelling libraries, established through a Carnegie grant from the USA. L.M. Montgomery's books were widely read, and doubtless other Canadian authors would be sought after.

During the desperate thirties, there were more than usual cries of "Where can I find an agent to market my books/stories?" In June 1936, the first Canadian agent appeared on the scene — Kathleen McDowell, wife of CNR publicity director, Franklin Davy McDowell (Toronto) himself the successful author of historical themes, such as *The Champlain Road*. Kathleen had writing experience, a keen critical faculty, taught writing courses, and would also advise on manuscripts for a small fee. Her Authors' Agency of Canada arranged for local representatives in New York and London agencies which were generally too occupied in handling the work of established authors to afford the persistent flogging necessary to take on the work of untried authors. Some agencies flatly refused to handle new authors, especially those outside the country.

179

So there was some action going on. What brought it to a head was the near collapse of the Association of Canadian Bookmen. It produced a news publication, not a magazine. This became eventually the annual *Books for Everybody*, a combined publishers' catalogue carrying advertising for all member publishers (and still going strong). Posters, banners and stickers were provided to member firms, for use in book displays, as at the convention of the Ontario Library Association, and again when the American Library Association convened in Toronto in 1927 with George H. Locke as president.

But the dues and levies brought the Association of Canadian Bookmen to its knees financially. By December 1927, chairman S.B. Watson had to announce a severe retrenchment program:

> It was decided that in view of the impossibility of making any effective impression on the Canadian public and influencing their purchases of books with the limited amount it is possible to raise by assessments and subscriptions, that suggestions should be considered for a re-organization of the Association to carry on this most important work, and maintain the goodwill of the retail trade, at greatly reduced overhead expense.

The ACB did not entirely disband, but went dormant until in March 1934, a motion was presented to voluntarily wind up the affairs of the Association. It was defeated, because Dr. Pelham Edgar wouldn't let it die. He took the matter to the Canadian Authors Association and in the December 1935 issue of the *Canadian Author*, he made his pitch at considerable length:

> He reminded members of how the CAA had laboured during the Twenties to remedy the public's ignorance and neglect of admirable Canadian books. "Through evil report and good report — for some in the early days thought we should suffer in silence — we have persisted in calling our fellow-countrymen's attention to certain facts. Our work has brought about a distinctly wider appreciation of Canadian literature; but a mountain of apathy has still to be cleared away."

> To sell books is not our business, but to write them. Unfortunately, the publishers and booksellers whose business it is to sell them, have not achieved anything like the success that might be expected, neither Canadian nor others. It has been suggested more than once therefore that Canadian authors should establish a publishing and book-circulating business of their own. Such an enterprise — given moderate capital and

better-than-moderate management, might surprise the pessimists by its success. Rejuvenation and reform of the existing publishing system, however, with authors, librarians and booksellers all joining in aggressive alliance and pooling their brains seems more likely to succeed. Our National Executive determined to try. Our initiative was welcomed, and the new Association of Canadian Bookmen is the result. The Canadian Authors Association far from giving up one atom of its independence will gain greatly by the four-fold strength of the new body to back it up.

The author's and publisher's interests are identical in their primary aim — to see the Canadian people become a reading people.... Beyond that high point, publishers' interests are not identical with authors'. The great majority of books they list come from England, the United States and France, whether or not the name on the title-page is Canadian. These men know that a great national campaign to popularize book-reading will demand not routine salesmanship but the dynamic force of enthusiasm, with all the campaigning experience already gained by the organized authors of Canada. On both national and commercial grounds, therefore, the publishers and booksellers forming the trade wing of the alliance have agreed that the advancement of Canadian literature must be a prominent feature of the new association's program.

A list of twelve proposals mentioned by the energetic committee for its missionary work:

a) Distribution to all members of thoroughly reliable information about books in the form of frequent and carefully organized lists and bulletins.
b) Information on special topics to reading groups and individual members.
c) Written lectures to be available for local delivery.
d) Radio broadcasting.
e) An enlargement and improvement of book-review columns.
f) Organization of ACB branches in every centre where membership warrants.
g) Organization of a book token system, such as in England.
h) Free admission to exhibitions sponsored by ACB
i) Lectures from author members and other distinguished speakers.
j) Establishment of junior groups.
k) Co-operation with educational organizations, public li-

181

braries, schools, churches etc.

l)   Free presentation to members of an important contemporary book to be chosen from a submitted list.

All this for membership dues of two dollars annually. Small wonder that the membership grew apace, including many members of the CAA.

Dr. Edgar was not only National President of the Canadian Authors Association, and a professor at the University of Toronto, but an enthusiast. Having launched his idea for a re-vitalized ACB, he travelled at his own expense all across Canada, promoting interest. Some members of the CAA were dismayed lest their President should overstrain himself, to their detriment. To say nothing of the fact that demands might be made upon the Association's limited resources, especially financial.

That same month, Toronto Branch president, the artist Albert H. Robson calmed fears by describing ACB's planned projects.

Its first public meeting would be held on January 21, 1936 in the Concert Hall of the Royal York, Toronto, and would be addressed by the Governor General, Lord Tweedsmuir. Following the address, a reception would be held for His Excellency hosted by the Toronto branch of the CAA.

That visit, like one to address the CAA Montreal branch, was unavoidably delayed by the funeral of King George. It took place a month later, when members of the new ACB jammed the Concert Hall.

The Association of Canadian Bookmen established "centres" first in Toronto, then Montreal, Winnipeg, Regina and Edmonton, and also in smaller communities. Its avowed purpose was "to increase the habit of reading throughout the country."

Their fears allayed, at the conclusion of the 1936 convention in Vancouver, John Murray Gibbon moved:

> that we welcome the new alliance, formed on this Association's initiative, of the Association of Canadian Bookmen, to increase the use of books in this country. . . We particularly commend to the new alliance the need for prompt adoption of new and aggressive methods to reach and influence the deplorably large class of the Unreading.

The resolution was adopted unanimously, even to the extent of making a grant of one hundred dollars, and carrying ACB news and promotion free in the *Canadian Author*.

H.A. Kennedy explained that the Association of Canadian Bookmen would find it necessary to make experiments, especially in rural or semi-rural regions where no bookstores were available. The experiment of travelling bookshops or caravans had been suggested; but this was practically impossible in provinces where the bookseller had to pay a new license fee every time he passed from one municipal district to the next.

With a large membership assured and a few dollars the ACB established its executive, and Dr. Edgar, a man who made his actions fit his speech, was persuaded to stand for president.

Officers and executive members included the literati of the day:

President, Dr. Pelham Edgar, Victoria College, U of T; vice-presidents: H. Burton, bookseller, Montreal; C.R. Sanderson; deputy-chief librarian, Toronto Public Libraries (Dr. Locke was ailing) S.B. Watson, manager, Thos. Nelson, Toronto; hon. treasurer, H.S. Eayrs, Macmillan Co. of Canada; hon. secretary, W.A. Deacon, literary editor, *Mail & Empire*; J.M. Gibbon, Montreal, founder; Wendell Holmes, bookseller, London, Ont; T.F. Pike, Longmans manager, president of publishers' section, Toronto Board of Trade; B.K. Sandwell, editor *Saturday Night*; F.C. Jennings, Ontario Inspector of Public Libraries; Thos Allen, Toronto publisher; Wm. Tyrrel, Toronto bookseller; A.H. Robson, artist, president Toronto branch C.A.A.; Miss Marjorie Jarvis, president, Ontario Library Association; John McClelland, publisher; Roy Britnell, Toronto bookseller. Anson Bailey Cutts, executive secretary, worked from a Toronto office.

Borrowing an idea from British and American experiments, the Bookmen planned Canada's first National Book Fair in the fall of 1936. It would be held in Montreal during Canadian Book Week, and space in the Mount Royal Hotel was booked for the Canadian Authors Association, and many Montreal members would be involved. However, Montreal ACB chapter found itself unready, and the project defaulted to the Toronto chapter which reserved a large space in the King Edward Hotel.

Since the original plan for a Book Fair had fallen through, the Montreal branch of the CAA reverted to its former practice of a display of Canadian books in the five-day "National Produced in Canada Exhibition" in the Sun Life Building to celebrate Canadian Book Week. Space was granted free, and publishers lent books, and photographs of authors. The booth was eye-catching to attract visiting non-readers,

> who are the majority, and who have a magnificently developed
> inferiority complex as far as Canadian literature is concerned.
> The enlarged portrait of Frank L. Packard evoked snorts of
> unbelief from some who did not know he had a home in
> Lachine, but who did know that he couldn't possibly be a Cana-
> dian author — until practically throttled into belief.

Keeping their fingers crossed, the Toronto chapter of the ACB
arranged a book exhibit, and hoped for maybe 5,000 visitors. After
all, New York with ten times Toronto's population had drawn
nearly 50,000 viewers. To everyone's surprise and delight, attendance tallied 15,000, of whom two-thirds paid the twenty-five cents
admission. Many joined the Bookmen, bringing ACB membership
up to 2,500, at two dollars per head in the midst of the Depression.

> The exhibition was more than a passive display of books. It was
> planned to include book-making and kindred processes in
> action, but time and cost did not permit. A picture-film called
> *Chapter and Verse* bought from an English producer, using the
> new sound-recording technique, told the story of books right
> up to the printed page.

The film was originally programmed for two showings a day, but
the crowds' enthusiasm made it necessary to screen it forty-four
times in the six days.

So successful both in prestige and pelf was the first Book Fair,
the Bookmen decided to repeat it the following year with minor
variations, such as a demonstration of the new process of micro-
filming rare books and making facsimiles.

Toronto's second National Book Fair was opened by the
Lieutenant Governor of Ontario, Herbert Bruce, after a dinner
addressed by President Edgar, Hugh Eayrs and Murray Gibbon.
The days following presented an extensive and varied program
including daily addresses by authors, performances of plays,
repeats of *Chapter and Verse*. Special entertainments were given to
school children who came in droves and enjoyed the visit.

On Canadian Night, following a dinner given by the Toronto
branch CAA, the new National President, Leslie Gordon Barnard
(Montreal) and Toronto Branch president William Arthur Deacon,
jointly chaired a large assembly in the Crystal Ballroom, where tall
Arthur Stringer and tiny Louis Blake Duff shared the podium with
petite Kathleen Strange (Winnipeg) and Dr. Fraser Smith.

Deacon wrote later:

The Canadian Authors Association never previously appeared to as great advantage before the public. I was personally gratified beyond measure at the friendly atmosphere created. Everyone says that the Canadian Show was the life of the Fair, thus proving that idealism can be coupled with efficiency.

In fact, there were speeches or lectures every afternoon and evening in the Crystal Ballroom. The program included British and American writers as well as Canadian: Grey Owl, Ralph Connor, Wilson MacDonald, E.J. Pratt, Marius Barbeau, Leslie Gordon Barnard, Ethel Chapman, John Gunther, Edgar Guest, John Spivak, Margaret Lawrence (N. B.) Carl Van Doran, Elizabeth Sprigge, and D'Arcy Marsh.

The numbers attending these lectures were astonishing. The ballroom was seated for 800, but the actual attendance on the opening night was over 1,700, and some 500 were turned away. That was when Grey Owl spoke, in picturesque Indian costume of buckskin and feather head-dress. And the crowd was at least as great on Saturday afternoon to hear poet Wilson MacDonald.

The committee had allotted the CAA without charge, the largest and most prominent space available, the Alexandra Room, with a stepped pyramid in the centre, adorned with portraits of Canadian authors, and squared-in with two-tier tables, holding hundreds of Canadian books on loan from publishers and owners. A glass display case borrowed from Eatons held rare Canadiana lent by A.H. O'Brien (CAA honorary counsel), Sir Ernest MacMillan, Dr. Sigmund Samuels, Dr. Lorne Pierce, Elsie Pomeroy and many others.

The Canadian exhibit was arranged by Evelyn Weller, indefatigable and experienced in organizing displays of Canadian literature for the Canadian National Exhibition. Co-ordination of the whole Fair was in the hands of Dorothy Stevens, ACRA who brought the nineteen publishers' stalls into harmony.

Members of the CAA had made out a list of the Canadian books of the past year, and while they smilingly refused to sell any of their display, directed buyers to the publishers' stalls, where about $1,000 worth of books were sold — to say nothing of the later Christmas sale of books. Veteran bookseller Wm. Tyrrel introduced the new idea of Book Tokens, which could be used in any bookstore in the country.

A week later the scene shifted to Montreal and the National Book Fair occupied almost the entire top floor of the Mount Royal Hotel. The exhibits were the same as in Toronto, with the addition of valuable volumes from McGill University. The CAA display was not positioned so advantageously, but did have more space to lay the books open rather than standing them side by side, with only their spines showing. Again the T. Eaton Company loaned a glass case, this time with electric illumination, to contain memorabilia and treasures from the collection of Charles Gordonsmith, editor of the *Family Herald & Weekly Star*.

The Fair was formally opened by the Mayor of Montreal at a preview dinner, at which Christopher Morley spoke for fellow-writers in the States, and Elizabeth Sprigge for those of England. Nellie McClung MLA (Calgary), Arthur Stringer and Pelham Edgar spoke briefly for the Canadian Authors Association.

During the week, Louise Morey Bowman, president of the Montreal branch held two oral book reviewing sessions of representative Canadian books, and a Sunday reception at the Ritz Carlton Hotel for visiting publishers and authors. The films were shown daily, and the ever ready Howard Angus Kennedy also showed them to more than 600 high school students.

The Montreal Book Fair closed with a dinner address by the Governor General, Lord Tweedsmuir.

> If we are to read good books with a full understanding, if we attempt to produce literature ourselves, we must preserve a clean and fastidious palate. Our sense of values must be at once austere and catholic. We should be able to appreciate good writing of every kind — P.G. Wodehouse, as well as Dean Inge, Professor Whitehead not less than James Thurber . . .

He referred to literary fashions and fads such as the Spasmodics and the Dellacruscans and the shapeless "novels" dredged up from the subconscious — Virginia Woolf excepted.

> The mere digging out is not art, but the raw stuff of art. We must demand form, and shape an integrated structure. And what must be the canon to guide us? There is only one — knowledge of the best books, the study of the greater minds.

While gratified by the success of the two Book Fairs, Hugh Eayrs, president of Macmillan of Canada, pointed out,

> The Book Fair must be repeated next year, not only in Toronto

and Montreal, but in such centres as Winnipeg and Vancouver. I suggest to every bookman, wholesaler and retailer, that he begin to survey the Fair in retrospect, and put down on paper his ideas for betterment, so that Canada's next Book Fair will outdistance the past.

An unusual idea was tried out by the ACB in May, 1937: a "Talking Tea" at Simpson's store, Toronto. Nearly 400 members and guests listened to addresses on current literature from Lady Marjorie Willison, Charles R. Sanderson, and W.A. Deacon. Sydney B. Watson presided, and Dr. Pelham Edgar announced the winners of "Undergraduate Library Prizes" of twenty dollars and fifty dollars given for student essays showing the best appreciation of the books they had collected. (Dr. Edgar was a great believer in prizes for stimulation of effort.)

"Congratulations! However, you are preaching to the converted," complained a letter to the *Canadian Author*. "It's not the city people who need Book Fairs, but people in rural areas." It was true that not all provincial libraries catered to the reading desires of remote constituents. In Ontario, wooden boxes of books were shipped by rail or truck, sometimes even by canoe, to corners of the province off the beaten track.

National Secretary Kennedy knew from personal experience the isolation of farm life, particularly while homesteading in Alberta.

He asked editorially,

What new lines does Mr. Eayrs suggest to increase the reading and thus the book-buying in country districts beyond the city bookshops' range? What systematic surveys are being planned, to discover the needs and tastes of the people who never buy books? And then, what adventurous, ingratiating bookman is ready to set out in a caravan loaded with the very books that will supply those needs and tastes?

Now, Hugh Eayrs could point out that the ACB was invited to work with the Literature Committee of the Community Welfare Council of Ontario, which sponsored a wider distribution of good books through travelling libraries in rural districts. Through its auspices, ACB executive secretary A.B. Cutts gave two radio talks about books for readers outside the cities.

As a result, forays into the rural areas close to the publishing centres seemed indicated. The ACB had already received requests for smaller Book Fairs from Whitby and Pickering to the east of Toronto, from Goderich, St. Catharines and Guelph to the west in autumn. Other towns were pencilled in for next spring, when the snow was gone.

Ideas are contagious. The notion of spreading reading on the blown-out prairie lands was taken up by Major H.G.L. Strange, probably at the suggestion of his efficient wife, Kathleen. Major Strange, Honorary Secretary of the ACB at Winnipeg, appealed for quantities of suitable books to be circulated free by the grain companies at their elevators. "As a result, hundreds of little circulating libraries find a home in grain elevators. What a chance for East and West to get together!"

In December 1937, the *Canadian Author* could report another example of the CPR's good public relations, no doubt inspired by John Murray Gibbon. Sets of ten selected books, inexpensively produced and costing $4.50 were made available to employees at less than half price, the company paying the balance. "Over 130,000 volumes have already been purchased on this plan."

The plight of the book-hungry in the country was well-known to Dr. Edgar. Indeed it formed part of his inaugural address when he had ACB presidency thrust upon him. He told his fellow-members:

> You members are missionaries of a great idea. There is a vast semi-unlettered community in our country that is eager for the light, but does not see it because it is not there. If we can raise the cultural level by one inch in twenty years we shall have done something. We in centres where books exist may abuse our opportunities, but let us transport ourselves in imagination to regions where books are unattainable and more to be desired than gold . . . There is no object nearer our hearts than to benefit this vast constituency that needs our help, and which at present does not know we exist. We do not expect to pick up members there, but what, I ask you, does that matter?

Dr. Edgar certainly knew how to strike fire and compassion in his audience. The Toronto Bookmen agreed that they were casting bread on the waters when they displayed their wares before thousands of impressionable schoolchildren. Adults were chiefly of the reading class — though they hoped their interests were stimulated. The same might be said of any rural groups.

But the tensions created by Hitler in Europe were casting long shadows, and concern over reading paled under the threat of imminent war. The ACB found its attention distracted, and in 1939, President Dr. Lorne Pierce purchased the rights to the magazine *The Canadian Bookman,* and turned all over to the Canadian Authors Association, with only one proviso, that the title be incorporated with the *Canadian Author.* The first issue of the *Canadian Author & Bookman* rolled off the press in April 1940.

Chapter 13
Coping with the Late Thirties

Another marked development during the 1930s was the rise of craft groups within the CAA branches. This had begun in a small way in the 1920s, and proved popular. But many branches viewed it with alarm, fearing that the fracturing would detract from the general meeting, and perhaps end in splinter groups, who might forget they were part of the trunk tree. In fact, in some instances, notably Toronto, the poetry group showed more energy than the branch, and this resulted in a loss of outside esteem.

Montreal had two short story groups, a drama group, and one for poetry. They met in smaller units, (as does Sarnia today) frequently in homes, where host or hostess often found themselves distracted by making coffee, or surreptitiously flicking dust, rather than giving close attention to the criticism (sometimes too kindly) of a manuscript.

Nonetheless, an impressive number of sales were racked up, and plays produced as a result. In a decade of shrunken markets, poetry yearbooks were produced to sell for thirty-five or fifty cents. Some branches, notably Victoria formed a radio-writing group.

All through the thirties there was demand for one-act plays used as curtain-raisers for vaudeville shows, and by amateur players in schools and by the Little Theatre movement. With the rise of radio drama in the latter half of the decade, a new market opened up — the half-hour dramas aimed at both adults and children, not least school broadcasts. One-act plays proved easy to adapt or revise. Though the going rate was fifty dollars, some achieved double that for the excellence of their work. Newcomers too broke into this field with its wide variety of needs and huge appetite. Some plays formed part of a series, while others were "unit" dramas.

Radio had made its apperance in a tentative way in the 1920s, a small linkup of eight local stations. There was only the human voice, no music at first, certainly no sound effects. But a tide of American programs such as the "Lone Ranger" and "Amos n' Andy" flooded across the border to headphones in Canada.

The first recorded use of radio by the Canadian Authors Association was a series of talks on Canadian literature given by National President Lawrence J. Burpee from Ottawa during Canadian Book Week.

Dr. W.T. Allison (Winnipeg), head of the English Department, University of Manitoba, had syndicated a weekly literary column in Canadian newspapers from coast to coast, his primary interest being Canadian writing. The advent of network radio opened a new field for his special talents. Again the pioneer, he organized and aired the first series of university lectures ever broadcast in Canada. And his radio book reviews reached an immense audience, one of the most popular features on the western air until his death in 1941.

After the Dominion Broadcast Commission (now the Canadian Broadcast Corporation) was established in 1932, producers actively sought out Canadian writers. CAA conventions and branch meetings were given excellent instruction in writing for the new medium. Hector Charlesworth (Toronto), head of the Dominion Radio Commission led off in 1935. Horace Brown (Toronto) of the CBC Script Department, said in his talk to the Halifax convention of 1939, "There is no royal road to radio. Three things enter consideration — talent, perseverance and 'the breaks' — and the greatest of these is the last. The first step in learning to write for radio is the same as learning to write for any medium. *Study your market!* In radio, that means LISTEN." Ira Dilworth (Victoria), Regional Director, told the Vancouver branch much the same thing, and threw out a challenge to members to perfect their technique, for the CBC was largely experimental as yet.

Clearly, the members took the instructions to heart, as indicated by these random snippets from branch news:

> Margaret and Leslie Gordon Barnard (Montreal) broadcast every Sunday morning over CBM a stirring series of conversations entitled "This Belongs to You."

191

Gladstone Murray, General Manager of the CBC gave the Ottawa branch a comprehensive and interesting review of radio programs from the author's point of view.

The Drama Group (Victoria) is much interested in the broadcasts sponsored by the UBC "Drama School of the Air." These form the second half of the weekly meetings.

At Toronto's February meeting, Murison Dunn, script editor of CBC offered timely and practical hints as to the type of drama wanted, the timing of manuscripts, importance of sound effects, and proper use of historic background.

Rupert Lucas, drama supervisor of CBC addressed a joint meeting of the Saskatchewan branch and the Canadian Women's Press Club. He said that in 1939, the CBC had produced 456 half-hour plays, the majority of them written by persons living west of Regina "We like Canadian scenes, but it seems difficult for writers to transmute them into high drama. We're going in for adaptations of books, such as the *Jalna* series."

"Last of the Buffalo Hunters," by Mary Weekes (Regina) was broadcast weekly on a Dominion hookup.

Montreal's March meeting (Music and Drama) included a practical demonstration of radio broadcasting: presentation of a short play, and excerpts from an original opera; a selection from Murray Gibbon's *New World Ballads,* all realistically directed by a CBM producer, even to the "pause for station identification."

The CBC recently broadcast two plays by Fred Jacobson (Montreal).

Della Foss (Edmonton) sold ten radio plays in Alberta, and resold some into the States.

Doris Ferne (Victoria) has a weekly poetry program on the local station.

Marion Angus (Vancouver) had six dramas produced in 1935.

Three Nova Scotia members went on the air for the National Council of Education.

Madge Macbeth (Ottawa) recently sold a series of ten plays to CBC.

Myrtle Lane (Victoria) wrote a radio play on Sir James Douglas which was sponsored by the Parent-Teacher Association for a Victoria Centenary broadcast.

Joy Tranter (Winnipeg) has a long-running series entitled "Bridget and Pat."

The long poem "Brébeuf" by E.J. Pratt set to music by Healy Willan was successfully broadcast over CBC.

Dorothy Sproule (Montreal) has had poems used on the "Sweet Hour of Prayer" program originating in Montreal.

Dorothy Dumbrille (Alexandria) had poems read on the Australian Broadcasting Commission, with a request for more. Her poems *Thoughts for Canada* were read on a CBC Dominion Day program.

The Hamilton branch in 1943 carried out a unique radio broadcast. President Phyllis Pettit, Eric Johnson and Wynn Rutty, with the assistance of a member of the Hamilton Players Guild, gave a recital over CHML of the work of various members of the Jamaica Poetry League. The half hour on the air was by courtesy of the station, the musical arrangement being the work of the director. The program was to reciprocate the recent broadcast in Jamaica of the work of Marjorie Freeman Campbell. The international nature of these two events should be a lead to other CAA branches and to other organizations.

"Canadian Mosaic" is the title of a series of radio broadcasts consisting of new song lyrics written by John Murray Gibbon to familiar tunes representing the many nationalities that make up Canada's population. Mr. Gibbon himself acts as commentator at these Sunday evening broadcasts.

The end of an era in 1938 was marked by the death of Howard Angus Kennedy, the beloved and energetic National Secretary. Lord Tweedsmuir died suddenly. War clouds darkened over Europe.

Roderick Stuart Kennedy (Montreal) acted as stop-gap National Secretary after his father's death, but his duties on the *Family Herald* became too onerous for him to continue. A handsome young man, Eric Gaskell (Toronto) had just been elected president of the Canadian Literature Club in Toronto. Knowing that he would soon be uprooted by the military call-up, he obligingly took on the task and moved to Ottawa where the CAA files were now located. He had aided H.A. Kennedy at some conventions and knew more than most members of the office routines. Gaskell was introduced to the Association as one of our most promising younger writers, with the keenest possible interest in the Canadian literary scene and first-hand knowledge of the publication and marketing of books.

The new National Secretary plunged into the secretarial work, and editorship of the *Canadian Author*, bringing out an issue in April 1938, much of it a tribute to his predecessor, and carrying photographs for the first time. But soon wartime difficulties and shortages clamped down, and issues became irregular. In fact, the magazine suspended publication for fourteen months.

After Gaskell went into the Royal Canadian Navy Reserve on special duty, along came Charles Clay (Winnipeg) formerly literary editor of the *Winnipeg Free Press* and author of four books for young readers. If anyone could replace Kennedy, that man was Charles Clay. He showed the same involvement, was equally conscientious.

The seventeenth annual convention of the Association took place in Ottawa, a rather solemn affair to begin with, but ended in a kicking-up of heels. June 1938 was a time of uneasy peace — war had not yet been declared, but the thunderclouds were all around, steadily growing blacker and more ominous. Throughout the records of the convention were inspirational addresses, admonishments, references to the burning of books in Nazi Germany, to Duplessis' padlock law in Quebec, to censorship, to freedom of the press, and courage in the face of many problems looming, and as always to national unity.

Music publisher Gordon V. Thompson spoke long and earnestly on the rights of composers: two experts spoke of radio's future in Canada; craft groups met: Poetry under Leo Cox (Montreal), Drama chaired by Hugh Eayrs (Toronto) while Dr. Pelham Edgar presided over the Fiction group. Murray Gibbon, who had written three novels before he turned to more successful non-fiction, asserted that historical novels and those with biographical content were the only ones commercially profitable, though romantic novels afforded the author freer play for his talents. "Personally, I dislike romantic novels," he ended. "There is too much sex in them."

The irrepressible Madge Macbeth, got the last word, and drew a laugh. "In Canada, we writers aren't supposed to know anything about sex. We're far too superior — we might be criticized for using it in our books."

On their way up from Montreal by train, National President

Leslie Gordon Barnard and Roderick Kennedy put the finishing touches to a skit they prepared. This mock trial was the unique feature of the convention, as reported in the *Ottawa Evening Citizen*.

> "Prosecution by the Canadian Authors Association of Six Persons Accused of Non-Support of Canadian Books" read the headline. The hearing was held in the main convention hall of the Chateau Laurier, and for more than two hours the special conditions governing the writing, production, and sale of Canadian books in Canada were subjected to exhaustive investigation. Rod Kennedy, Acting National Secretary, was impressive in action as the chief prosecuting attorney. During the informative and humorous entertainment, there were frequent instances of lively repartee, eliciting unrestrained laughter from the floor, while the points brought out in the "evidence" and cross-examination of witnesses provided serious food for thought.

> Describing the trial *The Citizen* report named the defendants in order of examination and presented a résumé of evidence. Everything was done according to the best legal tradition, and judge and counsel were correctly attired in sombre robes of office.

> The presiding judge was Hon. George Herbert Sedgewick, C.M.G., K.C., Chairman of the Canadian Tariff Board, and counsel for the prosecution and defence respectively were Roderick S. Kennedy, and B.K. Sandwell, editor of the Toronto *Saturday Night*.

> The defendants were: all Canadian authors, or average author, in the person of Madge Macbeth; average publisher, Hugh Eayrs (Toronto), president of the Macmillan Company of Canada; average critic, William Arthur Deacon, *Globe & Mail*; average wholesale distributor, James Mahoney, American News Company, Montreal; average bookseller, Harry Burton, Montreal; average reader, R.L. Calder, K.C., Montreal.

> Leslie Gordon Barnard, opened the trial with a prologue. First in the dock was Madge Macbeth, representing the authors. Prosecuting counsel Kennedy elicited considerable information concerning the publication of, and attitude toward Canadian books. She maintained a defiant manner when charged with not writing masterpieces of fiction. She declared:

> "It's because of the unliterary attitude of the Canadian public to fiction, particularly Canadian fiction. Nothing can be done until

195

the average Canadian reader realizes that life in Canada is no better, no worse, than elsewhere, nor until he is educated to a point where he does not insist on his literature being glossed over with a false and sentimental attitude to life."

Hugh Eayrs, representing publishers, discussed the technicalities of publishing with the "prosecuting and defence attorneys" and said, "On the average, about $27,000 is spent yearly by publishers to push the sale of their books. London and New York publishers are well aware of what good books are written by Canadian authors. The best books written here are snapped up by outside publishing companies."

W.A. Deacon, representing literary critics, was accused of not supporting Canadian authors in his reviews. "That is not so, though I admit I have a different attitude to Canadian authors. I'm not sure why, but I believe I reflect the attitude of a simple and unsophisticated public, that of Canadians."

Booksellers Mahoney and Burton said they met the demand for Canadian books, which, however, was not large.

Mr. Calder, "the average reader" suggested that the fault lay with the publishers, reviewers and distributors, in that they did not sufficiently advertise their wares. "I'm not responsible for the results of their efforts, as an entirely innocent end to the means, being the public."

Hon. Mr. Sedgewick summed up the evidence and declared the accused guilty of the charge against them. He gave them a life sentence — to continue in their present employment.

Concluding a most humorous and interesting affair, Mr. Kennedy said that in reality all the accused had done a great deal for Canadian literature, and he thanked them and Mr. Sedgewick.

Much valuable and interesting information concerning the book trade, in all its phases, was disseminated in the course of examining the witnesses.

In a merry mood, the delegates left the convention hall, to return for the final banquet the next night, after which the seventeenth annual convention was brought to a unique and colourful close.

It was a glorious evening in mid-June, with the stately moonlit turrets of Chateau Laurier, the terrace illuminated by coloured floodlights, the brilliantly lighted Peace Tower across the canal,

196

and a distant prospect of dark Laurentian hills forming a perfect setting for the ballet presented by Gwendolyn Osborne's Dancers. The ballet was adapted from "Kermis Day," a story by Madge Macbeth — and the accompaniment was played by Percival Price, Dominion Carilloneur on the carillon. No wonder the delegates were reluctant to leave the terrace.

Not all sought their pillows. Perhaps keyed up by the stimulation of the convention, some forty poets took a notion to commemorate Archibald Lampman, dead lo, these forty years. It was said the poet had found inspiration for many of his poems in Brotherhood Wood, a lonely spot on the Aylmer Road several miles west of Ottawa. A nocturnal pilgrimage was arranged by Lloyd Roberts (son of Charles) and Wilson MacDonald.

The solemn ceremony of commemoration in the moonlit glades might have passed without dramatic incident, had not an irate farmer, armed with an ancient shotgun appeared, to disrupt the midnight reveries of our bards. What subsequently happened is a direct reflection on the Great Canadian Public. We respectfully draw the attention of constituted authority to the appalling fact that creative art is now persecuted in Canada. Christine Henderson (Montreal) (who lived to the age of 102) was one of the poets present, and immortalized the occasion in a hasty sonnet:

The Poet's Guerdon

We sought a Val Ombroso, where the shade
Of that sweet singer Lampman loved to dwell;
And eagerly we sought it, long and well,
O'er bridges field and fell — a cavalcade.

At length we gathered, matron, man and maid,
Where the full moonlight cast its wizard spell,
And solemnly recited (by a flashlight's aid)
Our own heart's poems, like a funeral knell . . .

Faint the dark pine trees wafted their perfume,
And nearby cowbells tinkled wan and drear,
When, from the forest's danksome nether gloom,
A raucous voice resounded harsh and near

"What are youse up to? What you doin' here?
I have a gun, so get youse out! Now, clear!"

197

Where would the 1939 convention be held? Vancouver invited hesitantly, Halifax the same. Since the railways were being commandeered for troop movements, long-distance travel was discouraging — and discouraged. William Arthur Deacon, Toronto president, plumped for Geneva Park on Lake Couchiching, near Orillia, Ontario. But finally the lot fell on Halifax, a shrunken, muted affair full of foreboding. Summer Tourist Fares by train to Halifax were quoted: from Victoria, $157; from Edmonton $134; Winnipeg $97. Rates at the Lord Nelson Hotel were equally low.

The most remarkable event at this convention was that the Association elected a woman as National President. Also unprecedented, Madge Macbeth served in that capacity for three terms. She had shown ability as president of the Ottawa branch, a dynamic leader — when not off on her world travels. Tall, slim, handsome, and crackling with wit, she could be a martinet to her private secretary, who mingled alarm with admiration. Wartime difficulties of many kinds did not ease Madge Macbeth's regime. And no doubt her "abrasive" manner grated on some wartime nerves.

Dr. Watson Kirkconnell, National Secretary for three years, and National President for four, commented in his autobiography, *A Slice of Canada*,

> A minor headache for a national president has always been the squabbles in the branches and even in the craft groups within the branches. The female of the species has always been more belligerent and deadly than the male, and these branch quarrels have almost always involved two or more women authors whose mutual hostility reminded me of "the baleful wrath of Achilles, son of Peleus" that brought such countless woes upon the Greeks at Troy. The *casus belli* might be as trifling as the use of a Minutes book in a branch's Short Story group, but both partners to the fight assailed me with long letters full of scratching, tearing words, demanding that I "avenge her of her enemy."

Undoubtedly such contretemps did occur, but the pages of the *Canadian Bookman*, the *Authors' Bulletin*, the *Canadian Author*, and the *Canadian Author & Bookman* successively exercised the censorship of discretion. There is no printed evidence concerning what Dr. Kirkconnell discovered when he succeeded Madge Macbeth as National President in 1942, and which he described as "a savage feud in progress between members in Ottawa and Toronto." No one now recalls the principal antagonists, much less the bone of contention.

Though Madge did make a half-apologia when she left office:

> Of course the Association is not administered perfectly. I know
> it is not administered as you yourself could administer it . . . but
> you must be aware of the physical problems that confront us.
> Keeping in touch with all sections of the country is difficult and
> arduous, requiring tremendous correspondence and often
> involving misunderstandings that arise from an interchange of
> letters. A disunity of this sort is geographical and relatively
> unimportant. Disunity of ideals, however, at this time is
> unthinkable. The aims and objects of the Association can and
> must be the same to everybody.

Chapter 14
Survival in the War Years

Two months after the Halifax convention, Canada declared war on Nazi Germany. Life in Canada changed drastically on September 10, 1939. Despite a small fighting force, an industry unready for war, and untrained manpower, by December, warriors were shipped to England, there to cool their heels during "the phoney war" when France fell. Unlike the 1914-18 war, this new conflict touched every life. Women as well as men volunteered for the armed services. Married women flocked into the war industries. Many thousands of men and women were building planes, ships, cannon, sewing uniforms and boots.

Many thousands of word-shapers went into government services to encourage thrift. "Make do. Make over." Paper, string and foil were re-cycled. Men and women became war correspondents, and young writers filled their shoes for the duration. CAA members were caught up in events like everybody else, and had no heart for full-time writing, or were too weary in their spare-time. Such openings in the literary marketplace spawned a host of new writers.

Gasoline, meat, liquor and butter were the most obvious items rationed. But so was paper for books and magazines. Even the small *Canadian Author & Bookman* was held to thirty-two pages. And travel. Railway station posters glared, "Is this trip necessary?" Even talk was curtailed. "Keep your telephone conversations short." Rationing of tires and gasoline curtailed movement, and attendance fell off in branches with far-flung membership, and meetings were reduced in number. Calgary, London and Saint John branches faltered and were re-organized. New branches were formed in Charlottetown, Hamilton and Windsor. It was branch custom to hold an annual dinner meeting in the spring, usually with an outside speaker (unpaid). Many branches abandoned the practice when travel became quicker by air, and members celebrated together at the annual convention banquet. With so much shifting of people, mail often went astray — manuscripts as well as contracts and cheques. Philip Godsell (Winnipeg) could complain of galley proofs bound for England lost when the ship was torpedoed, of publishing houses bombed out of existence, of book shipments sunk in sea battles, of skyrocketing taxation.

There was no assurance that there would be a convention in 1940 due to wartime restrictions. However, John Murray Gibbon who lived at Ste. Anne de Bellevue, was able to arrange accommodation at Macdonald College there.

This, "our wartime convention" (who guessed the war would go on for five years?), initiated the custom of using colleges rather than hotels for the Canadian Authors Association's annual convention. Most of the students were away, the facilities available at low cost. What began as a wartime measure when hotel space was at a premium with the whole country on the move, became a tradition in the interests of economy.

The 1940 convention opened with a message from Prime Minister Mackenzie King (no doubt prodded by the National President):

> I have been very much interested to learn of the determination of the Canadian Authors Association to carry forward its work, and it has been a source of gratification to my colleagues and myself to hear of its decision. At the present moment, it becomes increasingly clear that the struggle in which we are engaged is not only a military engagement, but a defence of the customs, culture and values of our people. Anything which the Canadian Authors Association can do to strengthen the regard for the literature and poetry of our nation is a great contribution to our defence and our victory.

With the curtailment of many forms of recreation, reading must come into its own. It was "a challenge, immediate and urgent for Canadian writers to keep alive spiritual aspirations, dreams of a larger democracy, to assist in battling defeatism, the insidious enemy within our gates, to demonstrate the value of a native literary tradition," ran the editorial in the *Canadian Author & Bookman*.

201

National President Madge Macbeth opened the sessions with characteristic verve, declaring that this particular convention came into being and developed with a sort of magic. "It built itself when I doubted that we could hold a convention at all. This has been a hard year, and next year will be harder." (This cryptic remark was never explained. Of course, she may have meant wartime difficulties.)

She went on to deliver a rousing presidential address that must have stirred the most sluggish patriot into action:

> We have a clear and definite duty to the heroic youth who are giving their all that we might be spared. As I see it, it is our duty to keep telling them and those who stay at home — what they are fighting for. There must be thousands of boys in the front line who don't know, who are giving themselves to this war with a sense of bewilderment and confusion. We can help.

Professor Watson Kirkconnell, now of McMaster University, Hamilton, Ontario, followed up with a talk on "A Writer's Tasks in Wartime," in which he pointed out that Nazi Germany had drafted science, archeology and every element in national life in the service of world conquest. "The writers of the Third Reich are among the most dynamic instruments in the hands of the Fuehrer. Against such weapons, the best brains and pens of the free world must be devoted."

He warned against disunity, an objective of the enemy who had infiltrated many organizations to foster anti-Semitism and disloyalty, especially among immigrants.

> In authorship as in any art, zeal is not enough. In these times especially, when we wish our words to move men's hearts and illuminate their minds to great issues, we must agonize as never before over the craftsmanship of our work. The Front Line runs through our writing-desks. Our typewriters are machines of attack in a great cause. We must consecrate ourselves — no less than does the munitions worker or the air gunner — to the most effective and devoted exercise of our skill. The issues are as broad as all mankind, and not for our generation alone.

William Arthur Deacon, literary editor of the Toronto *Globe and Mail* inspired the delegates to the nineteenth convention in another way — by comparing the present state of Canadian literature with the past. He called Canadian writing "the hopeful profession." He said:

Only exceptionally hopeful people would have become writers in Canada when we did; only optimists could have endured the disappointments. Oddly, though disillusioned we are glad to go on working on any terms obtainable. More and more am I sure that literature is as natural a product as grain, fish, minerals and trees that support our economy. Men must not only eat; they must think and feel also.

We are hopeful because fertilization precedes the crop by a long time. Our final fruits we shall not see. You writers have established writing as a profession between the wars. In 1918, Canadian literature consisted mainly of poetry. Roberts and Carman lived abroad; Duncan Campbell Scott remained a great amateur. In 1920 Canadian fiction was scarce and immature. Now the novel has won an honourable place with Grove, Callaghan, de la Roche and Salverson in a different class from any that went before. See the 80 pages of fine type listings in the University of Toronto Quarterly. It is impressive in the mass because it has all come about in twenty years.

Equally striking is the change in subject matter. Our fiction used to lack social significance and avoided the controversial sometimes shunning the contemporary scene altogether. Now there is Irene Baird's *Waste Heritage* on the Vancouver strike of the unemployed, Frank Taste's *Red Wilderness* on Ontario labour conditions, and Ethel Chapman's *With Flame of Freedom*, the dramatized social programme of the co-operatives ...

Canada is maturing. She has begun to think. This present war will bring the dramatists as surely as spring rain brings the dandelions. Our participation in this war is going to make a startling difference in our place in the world at and after the settlement ...

Provision should be made now for training our successors. The need for them will be intense. Encourage their hopes. They will whiz over the paved highway of Success where we had the thrill of pioneering. The sum total of positive achievement in the past twenty years fills me with pride, and I hope you are proud too. You would be if you would only read each others' books as now you seldom do, and you would more readily understand why I call writing in Canada, the Hopeful Profession.

Wilfrid Eggleston (Ottawa) joint Press Censor for Canada began his talk on censorship with the droll statement that,

A year ago I posed as an author. Now I have sunk so low as to become a censor. A censor is, of course the exact opposite of a writer. In algebraic terms, one author plus one censor equals zero. Censorship in wartime is inevitable. Successful campaigns require secrecy. Canadian writers have a more subtle task, that of waging a spiritual counter-offensive against Nazi propaganda. In so doing you will help to immunize Canadian morale against disintegrating influences. And the higher Canadian morale rises, the less we will have to interfere with the liberties of free speech.

Mr. Eggleston paid tribute to cooperation of the press, while sympathizing with their restraints. The people must be told what is happening, while military authorities preferred dead silence. One particular difficulty in his work was that US publications came freely into this country, and as America was not in the war, they were not under censorship. They frequently carried items that Canadian editors had been specifically requested not to mention.

The proximity of a great neutral country outside the bounds of censorship control adds considerably to the Canadian censorship problem. And we've had to deny entry to some 200 publications from the US that were unfriendly in intent, and deliberately aimed at breaking down Canadian morale.

(In fact, to conserve exchange (over six million dollars a year) some 250 US magazines were banned from Canada by the War Exchange Conservation Act. Some chauvinist editors retaliated by refusing to purchase Canadian manuscripts. Still, many of them were German-language publications which made relatively little difference to our writers.)

The 1941 convention, the twentieth, was held in Vancouver and Victoria, lasting an unprecedented six days. National Secretary Clay could announce formation of the new Hamilton and (Niagara) Peninsula branch, founded under the aegis of Prof. Kirkconnell who had moved to McMaster University. He was elected president, with Frederick Philip Grove as vice-president. Since the one was over-worked, and the other in poor health, the branch held few meetings that year.

The Vancouver/Victoria convention began with a telegram from the patron the Earl of Athlone, Governor General of Canada:

I send my warmest greetings to the Canadian Authors Association assembled on the Pacific Coast. It seems to me that in these days writers have a threefold responsibility toward the public. They have to illuminate the ever-changing facets of world events with the cold light of Truth so that the judgement of public opinion may be based on the proper presentation of facts.

Secondly they have to record these facts so that the historians of the future will have at their disposal a volume of material which is rich in quality and quantity for future generations to learn both of our greatness and of our weakness.

Thirdly, they have to give us the inspiration of the written word to carry us through the trials and tribulations that lie ahead. Only if our enthusiasms are tempered with a sense of perspective shall we be able to restore the world to an era of peace and happiness.

In his welcome to Vancouver, Robert Allison Hood, past president of the branch, reminisced about previous meetings, including the first.

None of us had known Murray Gibbon nor Arthur Stringer, and found their diverse personalities strikingly interesting. We started away to a good membership with Dr. R.G. MacBeth, historian, as president; the novelist Bertrand Sinclair was nominal secretary, although A.M. Pound did the work. I had the job of treasurer. Throughout Canada there were many applications to join, and there was a certain amount of sneering at the rather slight pretensions to authorship put forward by some aspiring to membership. However, the benefits seemed beyond question. Those interested in writing took new heart in their work, inspired by fellowship with others of kindred interests. That year more than fifty books were published, more than half fiction.

The program was of a decidedly serious nature, and craft meetings were particularly adapted to the needs of writers working under wartime conditions. Here is a rapid survey of salient points:

Ellen Elliott of Macmillans (Canada) spoke on Book Publishing in Wartime. A forum on Fiction was chaired by Ethel Kirk Grayson (Regina) and Arthur Phillips (Vancouver). J.E. LeRossignol (Montreal) Frederick Niven (Nelson) were panel members. McTavish of the *Vancouver Province* spoke on the Press in Wartime.

Kathleen Strange (Winnipeg) spoke amusingly about writing

205

her prize-winning autobiography *With the West in Her Eyes.* A.M. Stephen (Vancouver) urged poets to keep alive the flame of patriotism in wartime.

Michael Petrowsky (Winnipeg) spoke on Ukrainian Canadian literature. Audrey Alexandra Brown discussed Poetry and Life; dramatists Yvonne Firkins and Sarah Carsley (Vancouver) spoke of Canadian theatre; CBC representative Ira Dilworth (Victoria) told of opportunities in radio; Dr. Lorne Pierce of Ryerson Press (Toronto) sent an inspiring address *The Armoury in our Halls;* Irene Baird (Victoria) proposed and answered the question "Where do we go from here?"

On Monday delegates assembled in the Provincial Archives, Victoria, to hear Chief Justice Archer Martin speak on the "Spanish Settlements in Canada." Willard Ireland, provincial archivist, discussed "Searching for Historical Source Material." R.S. Kennedy (Montreal) editor of *Family Herald & Weekly Star* opened the next session on "The Crime of Silence." "New thoughts for Bookmen" was Prof. E.H. Morrow's contribution, and the Speaker of the Legislative Assembly talked on Adult Education. "The Public Library in War and Peace" became a symposium of several librarians.

Marjorie Freeman Campbell (Hamilton) jotted down thumb-nail observations about her new colleagues:

> Whoever will forget the war poems of Sir Charles G.D. Roberts, read with fervor by the author; well-loved words heard for the first time in a musical setting; the look on John Murray Gibbon's face when presented with the painting "Down Vancouver Way?" Whoever will forget President Madge Macbeth, dynamic, witty, keen, conducting brilliantly through its various phases a six-day convention? Jim Wright (Regina), author of *Slava Bohu* — broad-shouldered, strong, his weather-beaten face alive with restless masculine vitality? Professor Ellis H. Morrow, handsome, alert, business-like?

> Whoever will forget blonde Ethel Kirk Grayson (Regina), beautifully dressed, poised, aloof?; Kathleen Strange (Winnipeg), with her striking resemblance to Claudette Colbert; Irene Baird (Victoria) of features clear-cut like the figurehead on some ancient Greek ship; Ellen Elliott, of Macmillan (Canada), whose dainty feminine fairness conceals a most unfeminine knowledge of the publishing business; — impossible to describe them all . . . the irrepressible Professor J.E. LeRossignol "a Presbyterian in his wife's name" whose addresses wandered

determinedly and delightfully from their pre-ordained path. Who can forget them?

Forty years later, the events and personalities of that Vancouver/Victoria convention were fresh in the mind of Dorothy Dumbrille of Alexandria, Ontario, as she recorded them on tape.

"I wasn't used to CAA conventions, and Joy Tranter (Toronto) took me under her wing. She was an Irish beauty, and turned on the Irish brogue to wheedle small favours from the trainmen. She knew everybody, of course, and introduced me to Kathleen Strange, the cutest woman I ever met. And to Audrey Alexandra Brown, the crippled poet from Victoria. And to Nellie McClung. She was having heart problems then, and decided not to go on to Victoria. Would I take her place? Well, I'd never given a speech in my life, but I agreed, and told the audience about the writers in my own area, the county of Glengarry; you know, the pioneer writers, and the background of my own novels, *Deep Doorways* and *All This Difference*. Of course, I had done a lot of research for my non-fiction books, *Up and Down the Glens* and *Braggart in my Steps*. The audience seemed interested, and it went all right. Oh, it was a wonderful convention!"

For Eugenie M. Perry (Victoria) it was her eleventh convention, and as one of the hostesses she was keenly aware of small disasters.

> Delegates stumbling over cliffs in search of a supposedly easily-accessible sea beach; accidents to planes carrying publishers and award winners; a bus carrying a load of delegates that stalled in the middle of a long procession, while the benign CPR held its stately steamer in leash for three-quarters of an hour; rain pouring down where rain quite definitely was not supposed to fall.

Prof. Lionel Stevenson, making his annual return to Canada from the University of California, found naught for his comfort in the swelling lists of Canadian publication. His *Appraisals of Canadian Literature* had appeared in 1926, and since then he found little to please.

Speaking at the annual banquet in the Empress Hotel, Victoria, he declared,

> For the past seventeen years, Canadian literature has apparently suffered a steady and ominous decline. While mechanisms for recording and measuring Canadian literature have

steadily improved, the material itself has wilted and shrunk. Perhaps it is due to the 1914 war, perhaps to the economic Depression.

(The diners looked guiltily at one another. This sort of speech wasn't going to build morale!)

> I simply cannot believe that great achievements and yet greater potentialities of the national literature that existed when the Canadian Authors Association was founded do not still survive. I am looking forward eagerly to a rekindling of the flame. . . . One of the strongest causes for the black tide of confusion and fear has been an obstinate disregard for the past. Not only artists and authors and musicians, with their febrile pursuit of novelty, not only politicians and economists with their panaceas for all social maladies, but the whole mass of ordinary people have been seduced from the age-old habit of learning from the accumulated experience of the centuries; victims of rash educational experiments which cast tradition overboard and cast all its hopes upon a shallow philosophy of living for the present comfort and the present pleasure and the present self-expression; a generation that grew up without standards of spiritual value . . .

(The diners settled back. The speaker could not possibly be referring to them, a mature group of conservative Canadians. Poor Lionel must have got his notes mixed up, and brought along a lecture meant for his California students. Certainly he was not up to his usual form of expatriate patriotism!)

The year 1942 marked the depth of the war, a time of fear and anxiety. It also marked the twenty-first birthday of the Canadian Authors Association, attended by the Honorary Patron, Governor General, the Earl of Athlone. It seemed only fitting to hold the birthday convention in Montreal. National President Madge Macbeth instructed His Excellency in cutting the birthday cake. The Earl had never undertaken such a chore before.

Greetings came from John Masefield, president that year of the British Society of Authors:

> The authors of this country have asked me to send you a message of greeting for the opening of your Twenty-First Annual Convention. They feel, as I do, that Canada has again shown that the British Empire can at any time become an effective League of Nations for the defence of the Humanities. If the links between us may be drawn closer after the war, our League

may yet save the world. Full of gratitude to Canada for help in our trouble, we wish you a most happy gathering in Montreal, and hope that with returning peace we may soon welcome you to a gathering with ourselves in London.

On September 10, 1942, the CAA met in its twenty-first assembly. It was one of the briefest conventions in its history, only three days inclusive. Almost every branch was represented, and Victor Barbeau, president of *La Société des Ecrivains Canadiens* joined R.H. Mainer, president of the Montreal branch in welcoming delegates. Abbé Arthur Maheux (Quebec) declared to the delegates,

> We Canadians have too many quarrels between ourselves. Most of our difficulties come from a wrong interpretation of race, religion, language and national ideals. All Canadian authors have a duty in this matter. We have weapons — our pens. We can contribute to the war effort, and our first contribution consists in abating the quarrels that arise between our fellow countrymen. There are many excellent Canadian books that should be translated. Our Canadian public is deprived of really good reading because there are practically no translations.

Evelyn Eaton, author of *Quietly my Captain Waits* (and originally a Nova Scotian) spoke on "The Writer's Front"; Keith Rogers of CFCY (Charlottetown) addressed the audience on "The Future of Broadcasting"; followed by J.A. McNeill of the Canadian Press on "The Press in Wartime"; G. Carlyle Allison of the *Winnipeg Tribune* on "Topical Journalism"; and Dr. Franz Klein, editor of the *Voice of Austria* on "Dictatorship and Propaganda."

Perhaps the most important address, certainly the most far-reaching was given by Carl Carmer, president of the Authors' League of America, who spoke on the "Writers' War Board and its Work." This was an American body which organized the war activities of US authors. It had been set up immediately after the US entered the conflict, was very well-funded with $42,000 annually, had a free secretarial staff and free franking privileges for all its mail. Rex Stout, creator of the Nero Wolfe mysteries headed the Board. Its purpose was "To serve as liaison between the writers of America and government departments which want writing jobs done that will in any way whatever, directly or indirectly, help win the war; and to place with the proper government departments any ideas or pieces of writing collected from writers as a contribution to the war effort."

Delegates to the 1942 convention were fired by this report, and unanimously passed a resolution to establish a similar Writers' War Committee in Canada, chaired by Prof. Watson Kirkconnell. He had worked with the government's Office of Public Information, had written a forty-eight page booklet, *Canadians All*, which was distributed to every schoolchild in Canada and had done two radio series, "Let's Face the Facts" and "Canadians All."

No question about it, Watson Kirkconnell was a hard worker. He succeeded Madge Macbeth as national president at this convention and was president of the new Hamilton branch until he recognized that was unfair to both and resigned in favour of Phyllis Pettit. Now he took on the Writers' War Committee (WWC), which he knew must involve any amount of frustration.

In his autobiography, Kirkconnell recalled the aftermath of Carl Carmer's talk. He and five other Canadian authors (Gibbon, Clay, Sandwell, Alan Sullivan and Eric Gaskell) sat in a smoke-filled bedroom of the Mount Royal Hotel, holding a bull session with Carmer. Together they drafted the resolution which was ratified by the membership next morning: that the Canadian Authors Association set up a Writers' War Committee aimed at providing the War Information Board with a Dominion-wide reservoir of Canadian writing talent, the WWC to be autonomous within the Association.

The WWC boasted:

> Hon. Chairman Sir Charles G.D. Roberts (who proved one of its most active and valuable members)
> Chairman: Dr. Watson Kirkconnell, McMaster University, Hamilton
> Secretary: Nathaniel Benson, PR man with Young & Rubicam, Toronto
> Ass't Secretary: Verna Bentley, Toronto poet
> Plus a board drawn from across the country, not all CAA members, subdivided into committees.

The WWC met promptly. By November they had the government reply. Prime Minister King saw no reason for its existence, since he had already established the War Information Board, which he starved of both finances and cooperation. The WIB was hard pressed to allot $200 a month to the WWC, only enough to pay postage and a stipend to a typist.

Kirkconnell's closing speech at the 1942 convention bespoke

his sobriety of mind, his devotion to duty, and his Methodist background.

> On Setting Hand to the Plough: Authorship in this War should be a more real and vital thing than in any past epoch. When the whole of civilization is at stake in a conflict of spiritual principle, the writer, whose very phrases are weapons forged by the resolute mind, cannot afford to doze in his sentry-box or loiter on the line of march. For every member and branch of the Association I bespeak a year rich in achievement. May the words of our pens be worthy of our purposes, and may our purposes be worthy of our country in this floodtide of human history!

A literary event of international importance took place on November 10, 1942, when Rex Stout, the colourful and dynamic chairman of the Writers' War Board of America, spoke under the combined auspices of the newly-formed Canadian Writers' War Committee, the CAA national executive and the Toronto branch of the CAA. Mr. Stout's topic was "The World Fight for Freedom." All proceeds bought books for Canada's armed services. Later Kirkconnell wrote of the occasion:

> Stout had a vigorous business meeting with our WWC executive in the afternoon, and spoke to a public meeting in the evening in the auditorium at Eaton's uptown store. During the business meeting, Rex Stout told our executive that he had found the American Reds invading his Writers' War Board in such numbers that he had to throw them out en masse. In Canada, the War Information Board was comparatively free from Red infiltration, but the WWC was threatened from the start by a Communist-organized group whose ultimate loyalty was to our enemies.

He could report early in 1943 to the Canadian Authors Association:

> The WWC has been working diligently, although perhaps too quietly, for a year. This résumé should convey some impression of the service which it has already rendered to the Canadian nation, of the work which is in progress, and of the greater things which can be accomplished in the near future.

As a basis for an intelligent assignment of tasks in writing, he prepared a *National Service Register* of all Canadian authors and the fields in which they had published work. He had the National Secretary Charles Clay, send out a questionnaire. The response was feeble, and editor Clay, less patient than Kirkconnell, ripped into the membership with half a page of the *Canadian Author & Bookman*:

Calling All Members!

Last autumn, in a fit of patriotism, your National Office offered to undertake the compilation of a *Canadian Writers' National Service Register*. It therefore circularized the CAA membership and asked for information on the kind of writing done and the books and pamphlets published by each member. Over 650 of these circulars went out — but only a third of them came back. Despite this astounding indifference, the National Office went ahead trying to compile the Register.

The actual work has been done by our indefatigable National President. It has been a hard job — and now it cannot be completed until the information from the so-far uncooperative members comes in. Did you answer the first questionnaire? If not, please take a moment now to send the National Office the vital data concerning your work.

Do you write history, biography, criticism, drama, one-act plays, educational works, feature articles, fiction, juveniles, novels, serials, songs, short-stories, syndicated material, poetry, publicity, radio dramas, radio talks, religious work, reviews, travel works, technical articles.

We do not want the names of your fugitive pieces, nor the publications in which they appeared. WE JUST WANT THE KIND OF WORK YOU DO. We also want the titles and dates of your books and pamphlets. Include your address with your data. After this final attempt to get full information, the Register will be published, and if it contains nothing but your name and address (pretty useless to the Register by themselves), you will have only yourself to blame!

His raspy summons brought adequate response. Kirkconnell was able to present a fairly comprehensive list of practising Canadian writers to Charles Vining, general manager of the War Information Board.

La Société formed a French section of the WWC, which reported to Mr. Blais of the WIB. Its working nucleus consisted of Claude Melançon of Montreal, Séraphin Marion and Leopold Richter of Ottawa. Kirkconnell in Hamilton, and Gibbon in Montreal found Toronto the most convenient meeting place, and the Toronto members of the committee were there. With commendable speed the committee blocked out its objective — overall stimulation of war-time writing, especially by members of the CAA

Chairman Kirkconnell wrote, in his book *A Slice of Canada*:

"This work had three phases: (a) The appointment of regional directors; (b) the sending of detailed directives to the 650 members of the Canadian Authors Association and others. The WWC sends periodical "directives" to all members, suggesting subjects for morale-building material and giving sources where military data etc. can be obtained. One directive, on behalf of the War Finance Committee invited members to submit material that would stimulate war savings and promote the forthcoming Victory Loan. (In this system, writers were left to market their own work in the usual way, but three gigantic scrapbooks of the resulting clippings and radio scripts were prepared as evidence of our activity, and forwarded to Ottawa; (c) the inauguration of a syndicate to send gratis to a large number of daily and weekly newspapers, a series of brief specially written items in prose and verse.

"We also set up a number of sub-committees for specific phases of our work, such as a committee on songs, chairman John Murray Gibbon; radio, chairman, Nathaniel Benson; agriculture, Roderick Stuart Kennedy; drama, chairman, John Coulter.

"The song committee arranged for the actual preparation, publication and widespread public use of popular war-time songs such as "Back the Attack" (Gibbon and Murray Adaskin), the theme song of the fourth Victory Loan campaign and "Speed the Victory" (Gibbon and Dr. Healy Willan) for the fifth Victory Loan campaign; "Cross of Red on a Field of White (Gordon V. Thompson) theme-song of the Red Cross campaign; three popular Victory Loan campaign songs "I Want a Share in my Country" (Thompson and Freddy Grant); "Roll Along" (Gibbon and Abrahamson) the Navy Show song. In addition, John Murray Gibbon also prepared a radio series "Songs of Freedom," in which national songs of the Allies were broadcast over CBC.

"The radio committee undertook three main projects: an international broadcast in conjunction with the American Writers' War Board, a series of radio plays, and a series of Sunday evening talks under the general title "Inheritance of Freedom."

"Another important activity is the WWC Syndicate of morale-building activity, which went into operation in June, 1943. By September 120 contributions were received — mostly poems. Articles, stories and poems were sent out in groups of twenty to a hundred newspapers.

"Early in its work, the WWC selected a large number of capable writers in almost every section of the country, who were willing as part of their war effort, to submit special confidential fortnightly reports to the WIB, giving their impression of the trend of public opinion from week to week in their own districts. These reports covered every conceivable topic, especially those associated with the war. This constant taking of the public pulse was considered exceedingly valuable by Davidson Dunton's division of the WIB, and outlasted all other activities of the WWC."

By autumn 1943, Prime Minister King, still vacillating, cut the starveling budget of the War Information Board drastically and General Manager John Grierson resigned. Nathaniel Benson (Toronto), the energetic secretary of WWC was transferred to New York, and as Kirkconnell expressed it,

> Our bus was not only out of gas, but lacked a driver. No successor to Benson being available, we simply parked our vehicle for the duration.

Early in the renewed affiliation between the CAA and *La Société des Ecrivains Canadiens*, Dr. Victor Barbeau, the debonair president, addressed the CAA members in convention as follows:

> The French-speaking writers of Canada acknowledge with joy and pride the contribution of English-speaking writers to the greatness of Canada. No body of craftsmen have done more than they have to promote our country from the rank of an exporter of raw materials to that of a full-fledged nation.
>
> On our part with less success but no less endeavour, we are doing our best to create an impression of culture that derives its blood and spirit from the history and grandeur of our own land. Contrary to what is said and sometimes even written, we are devoted to Canada as a whole. We may be provincial by our habits and customs, of which we are far from ashamed; but this never meant and never will mean that we limit our vision and love to the frontiers of our own Province. We belong to Canada, and Canada remains our father land.
>
> We have unanimously agreed to cooperate with the Canadian Authors Association because we feel that in these times of suspicion and intolerance, it is the duty, especially of intellectuals to bring about an understanding amongst all nations.
>
> We in Canada have perhaps failed in that matter in the past —

our people of both racial origins. We shall not gain a thing by treating each other as foreigners.... We sincerely believe it is possible for us to be good Canadians, genuine Canadians without renouncing any of our racial characteristics. We dare to hope that our collaboration will be more efficient than those tried in many other fields before.

Finally, much later, Dr. Kirkconnell could reminisce with neither false modesty nor self-congratulation:

"My own share of the load went far beyond chairing the fortnightly meetings, paying an occasional visit to Ottawa, carrying on extensive routine correspondence and making occasional contributions to the syndicate. There were indeed six major projects that I undertook, four alone, two in partnership.

(i) The National Service Register of all Canadian authors.

(ii) As an aid to allied understanding, I prepared a series of *All People's Readers*, containing translated prose and verse from all the nations.

(iii) At the request of the WIB, I prepared a *Handbook of Canada* designed for young Americans.

(iv) At the request of the Canadian Legation at Rio de Janeiro, Brazil, and in consultation with Sir Charles Roberts, I prepared an anthology of Canadian poetry in English for distribution throughout South and Central America. A similar volume of Canadian poetry in French, edited by Jean Desy, had already been printed for this purpose of stimulating international good will.

(v) In the interests of national unity and in collaboration with Mr. Séraphin Marion, chairman of the French committee, I prepared a volume of French-Canadian prose and verse, *The Quebec Tradition* that would interpret the background, point of view and real spirit of French Canada. Mr. Marion selected the French extracts in prose and verse and these were printed on the left-hand pages, facing my translations in English prose and verse, on the right-hand pages.

(vi) In still another activity, I myself wrote a long series of biographies of great Canadians of all origins (Banting, Stefansson, Laurier, Macdonald etc.) which were mimeographed by the Citizenship Branch in Ottawa and supplied to some seventy foreign-language newspapers, regardless of their politics. I was likewise called in, on occasion, to advise the War Finance Publicity Committee on their releases to New Canadian communities.

"All six projects were completed but one or two of them remained unpublished because there were no funds to underwrite them. In the case of *the Anglo-Canadian Verse*, for example, the Department of External Affairs was unwilling to pay copyright fees, subsidize publication in any part, or even cover a small bill for typing. To my great satisfaction, however, La Faculté des Lettres, l'Université de Montréal, sponsored *The Quebec Tradition* in its *Collection Humanitas* and brought it out in both cloth and paperbound editions."

In these ways Watson Kirkconnell had served his country as truly as any rear-gunner or salaried general.

Chapter 15
Rod Kennedy's Cabinet

The war in Europe ended with jubilation on May 7, 1945, and a great wave of relief swept over Canadians. The war with Japan continued until August, mostly with American involvement, but Canada was engaged only peripherally at Hong Kong and through the United Nations Organization.

Women's role had changed radically, due to their war work, their participation in the armed services, and in jobs outside the home. They appeared increasingly in the publishing industry, in editorial offices and not just as typists. No longer relegated to the classroom themselves, they became compilers of anthologies (school readers) and designers of text books.

Postwar reconstruction plans were dusted off, and put into action. A sense of well-being and unity pervaded the country, not least in the publishing field. A huge backlog of unfilled orders from European countries whose presses had been crippled by bombing brought about a surge of publishing and reprinting. Hundreds of manuscripts which had been forced to wait the end of hostilities were now in print; the future looked rosier than it had in the past two decades.

The war years had robbed the Canadian Authors Association of more than rank-and-file membership. They had also removed by death some leading members who could not easily be replaced — notably Stephen Leacock, L.M. Montgomery, and Sir Charles G.D. Roberts.

National Secretary Charles Clay, who had served with devotion and made the CAA's cares his own for three years, to the undermining of his health and the detriment of his wallet, wished to embark on a publishing career of his own, publishing house organs and business magazines (in which he proved successful). The difficulty of finding someone of equal ability and enthusiasm delayed his departure for a year; and in that year, he cut his editorial teeth on his new version of the *Canadian Author & Bookman*.

To find a person of equal qualifications, at the low salary offered, proved not only difficult but impossible. A young man was hired, but did not last long. Without adequate supervision, which no one had time to give him, the new secretary did literally nothing. A blizzard of complaints over unanswered queries, receipts not issued, reached the harried National Executive.

National Treasurer Leo Cox and National President Roderick Stuart Kennedy travelled from Montreal to descend upon the Ottawa office and explore the situation. The hireling promptly resigned. Fortunately the office typist proved capable of carrying out the routine, not only keeping abreast of current affairs, but cleaning up the arrears of fees and application forms. The president handled queries and other matters outside her competence.

With the December 1945 issue, the *Canadian Author & Bookman* went on the newsstands, with a stiff cover, and contents geared to a writing community, a sixty-six page issue, with less than ten pages devoted to Association news, though all the contents were of interest to writers — and readers. "How do I Write?" by Hugh Mac-Lennan, author of best-selling *Two Solitudes*; "Bread, Art and Masterpieces," by Philip Child, author of *Village of Souls*; "Where are Canada's Literary Critics?" by Dana Doten; "The Writer and his Audience," by E.J. Pratt; "Profit in School Book Writing," by Claude E. Lewis, educational editor, were the major articles. "Looking over the Editor's Shoulder" was a new feature for correspondents. As well, the pages carried full-page ads, chiefly of Canadian books, and some institutional advertising.

Editor Charles Clay was justly proud of his product. He rounded up the advertising himself, as well as doing the editorial and makeup tasks. But since there was no space for the votes & proceedings of the Association, a *Supplement* had to be prepared as well, reverting to the custom of the 1920s, when the annual *Authors' Bulletin* supplemented the CAA news in the *Canadian Bookman*. From this first issue, the *Canadian Author & Bookman* has had an eye on the general reader, with Association news very much a sideline.

Any editor naturally prefers to put his product on public display, rather than a hole-in-the-corner drab record of proceedings. But the *Supplement* lasted only another year, and the strong clan feeling of the Association could not but dissipate, for lack of news. Instead of being familiar names, with bodies and personalities attached, the national executive became "They," disembodied shadows operating out of head office without adequate explanation. Ultimately the magazine carried only the Association's name in an obscure corner, not even the names of office holders, in an attempt to prove that the CA&B was not merely a house organ, but a cultural magazine worthy of government funding.

The 1945 convention in Montreal was originally planned for mid-summer, but partly due to the disruption at head office and partly because returning armed forces required hotel and train space the meeting was postponed until late November. It was still an austerity convention with few diversions, but an intense investigation into besetting problems.

Rod Kennedy had been instrumental in setting up a board to administer the Governor General's Literary Awards. Now he planned to extend this satisfactory arrangement to cope with other problems, both to ease the presidential load and make use of the talents of more members.

> The Awards board is a prototype of other standing committees we need, who will have to handle problems in an executive sense as well as studying them — committees for Copyright, Income Tax, Membership, Canadian publishing methods, beginners' problems and others as experience may direct.

He appointed Gwethalyn Graham (Montreal) as chairman of the Standard Contract committee, with D.M. LeBourdais and Marsh Jeanneret (both Toronto) committee members. Kennedy would chair the Income Tax committee himself, and one of his committee members was Hugh MacLennan (Montreal). All knew they would put in endless hours on these subjects, and not just for the benefit of CAA members, but also for those writers outside the ranks.

In the meantime, other reports must be heard. Charles Clay reported that the membership had regained its numbers — 916 as against the previous highwater mark of 915 in 1924, and National Treasurer Leo Cox could report a budget of $5,261. (By mailed ballot, the members had voted to raise the annual fee from five to seven dollars.) Of this total, the two magazines had cost $876; capitations to branches $619; secretarial services, an unprecedented $1,200, and $500 went into a government bond.

At the Annual Dinner, Msgr. Maurault, rector of the University of Montreal presented the Governor General's silver medals to the winners: Gwethalyn Graham for her novel *Earth and High Heaven*, and Dorothy Duncan (Mrs. Hugh MacLennan) for Creative Nonfiction as in *Partner in Three Worlds*, an autobiography tracing her American origins, her marriage to a Scots-Canadian, her life in a French-Canadian city.

> The writer's place is on the bookshelf. Writers are better unseen and unheard, unless they join the acting circuit. I beg young Canadian writers to first learn to know themselves with complete honesty, then to write with the same honesty. In no other way can true Canadian culture thrive.

In accepting her medal, Gwethalyn Graham, a tall handsome woman, admitted,

> I started cooking my book five years ago, but it was as always with me, a long job. Two years later, I had done three complete re-writes, as well as endless re-writing of bits along the way, and finally finished it a year later. Three years! One copy went to England with a returning British army officer and was accepted at once. Another copy went to my New York agent who didn't like it. But the second publisher I offered it to, accepted it. *Collier's Magazine* picked up first serial rights. The Lippincott ordinary edition was 300,000, the Doubleday Doran reprint for the Literary Guild was 500,000, and the Armed Forces edition was another 300,000. Contracts have been signed for translation into ten European languages. And the sale to Sam Goldwyn, of course. Now I'm worried to death about my next book — being so strongly identified with one title gives one an awful feeling at times.

Most of the audience gulped down the amazing statistics, and failed to grasp the hard work that went before success. Arthur Stringer, up from New York for the convention, chose to speak on "This So-Called Writing Game." He knew that success didn't come easily.

> Authorship is not a game, but one of the most arduous and competitive professions in the world. To the man in the street, the author's life may seem the life of Riley ... but success-

220

ful authors have made the grade by the grimmest kind of hard work, by going hungry, and ignoring rejection slips, and being the patient piper while the reading world danced to his tunes . . .

Then, with a broad grin, he went on,

> A new tribulation faces the male author — the lovely gynocracy that now seems to rule the book world. For it's women writers who are beginning to glow like a Mily Way. The disgruntled benedicts stand aside, feeling that the short-cut to getting published is to be female and photogenic.

(At seventy-one, Stringer was still good-looking.)

Gwethalyn Graham was more than just a talented camera subject. She turned a logical mind to the task of formulating a Standard Book Contract, in consultation with the British Society of Authors, the Authors League of America, and with the cooperative Canadian Book Publishers' Council, and no doubt in consultation with her own knowledgeable New York agent. For the need was great, as she said,

> Writers, especially new ones are so eager for publication they will sign any contract they are offered, sign it without understanding — and sometimes without reading — the various clauses. We need a Standard Contract that will be available to all Canadian writers, not just our own members. Most have no suspicion that clauses are flexible and can be negotiated.

Gwethalyn Graham and her committee worked hard — with her income, she could afford to donate time for the benefit of her colleagues. And by the 1946 convention held in Toronto, she had her facts marshalled. She gave a long and reasoned outline of contemporary practice which, she warned was flexible and changing:

> Book contracts throughout the world are in a state of flux. It is not so long ago that authors accepted a royalty rate which we would now regard as ludicrous — retaining no subsidiary rights for themselves, or worse, sold all rights for a few hundred dollars. Contracts have steadily become more complicated. With radio and now television in Britain, there are at least eighteen different outlets possible for a novel today, where a generation ago there was a single sale.

> In addition, the situation of the Canadian author is further complicated by the fact that since publication outside Canada is

almost essential if the Canadian author is to make a living by writing, he must be familiar with British and American publishing practices.

The British publisher will take 20% of the Canadian author's royalties on books he exports to Canada. The American publisher cuts your 10% to 5%, that is, he takes 50% of your royalties for books he sells in Canada.

The average Canadian publisher will take everything he can get in subsidiary rights such as 50% of your fee when your novel is serialized in a magazine or dramatized for stage or radio.

If this report and the Standard Contract we are now drawing up are accepted by the Canadian Authors Association, then for the first time, the Canadian author will have some basis for comparing the terms he is offered with the terms to which he is entitled. If he feels it advisable to sign a contract that does not come up to the minimum standards, at least he will no longer be ignorant of what he is doing.

The contract was still to be worked on for possible adoption at the next Annual Meeting, after every branch had had an opportunity to study and comment on it. Miss Graham then enlarged on specific points which had exercised her committee. Their conclusion was that Canadian publishers paid too little, and demanded too much of the subsidiary rights. Some contracts were better than others, but all contained clauses long since regarded as unfair to the author in Great Britian and the United States. No one could pretend that, from the sales standpoint, Canadian authors were as important as American and British. Still, the committee urged authors to try for a separate Canadian contract, though that would not be popular with the publisher.

Some Canadian contracts which we examined completely ignored the time element which to an author is often extremely important. Some even arrogate to the publisher the right to publish whenever he finds it convenient — even five years later — and the signing author has no redress. Should the publisher fail to publish the said work by such-and-such a date, all rights revert to the author. That's in our Clause Eight.

Clause Nine dealt with royalties. Its five subsections treated percentages, free copies, discount to jobbers and booksellers, sales of remainders, school editions and anthology rights. Clause Ten dealt with the publisher's commission when he acts as agent.

222

Clause Eleven covered the contingency that motion picture rights might be sold after publication.

> Clause Twelve touches on advance royalties to be paid when the contract is signed, no part of which shall in any event be returnable, nor chargeable against any other work by the author. Clause Thirteen deals with the rendering of royalty accounts, which should be semi-annual, and provide statistical details, not a naked annual cheque. Clause Fifteen deals with the question of book clubs. Sales to book clubs are a gamble — the low returns represent a terrific loss to both author and publisher should the book become a bestseller. There is only one other clause which requires explanation, Number Sixteen, dealing with reprints. Reprints are big business, almost the only aspect of book publishing that is big business. Clause Sixteen reads: "All reprint rights shall be controlled jointly by the Publisher and the Author, and no reprint arrangement of any kind may be made by the Publisher without the written consent of the Author and upon terms to be mutually arranged."

> Your committee has given this a great deal of thought. It is perhaps the most radical departure from current practice in all British, American and Canadian contracts, this safeguarding and delaying clause. The Authors' League of America is struggling to alter the royalty rates there where the author receives one to five percent of the list price, the original publisher taking the same amount. Since almost all professional writers in Canada have already benefitted, whether they realize it or not, from the work of the Authors' League, your committee is strongly of the opinion that members of the Canadian Authors Association should back the League for their mutual benefit.

Gwethalyn Graham produced figures that impressed the delegates sombrely. Sales of twenty-five cent paperbacks now amounted to $120-150 million in the United States alone — an income of thirty million or more. The *profit* to the publishers would be over six million, while the royalties accruing to all the authors under present rules would be only $6,000.

> As most of you probably know, the royalty on a twenty-five cent book is at present half a cent a copy, a two percent royalty. The Authors' League is asking ten percent. At the present rate, the sale of 50,000 Pocket Books would gross the author $250, which is indefensible. Additionally, the original publisher often does the reprinting, and takes fifty percent of all subsequent publication rights. Having taken his original profit, he takes half

the author's profit on the reprint as well. In other words, he pays himself twice. In conclusion, the committee on Book Contracts make the following recommendations:

1) That the principle of separate Canadian contracts be adopted wherever and whenever possible, by both Canadian and non-Canadian writers, and that this recommendation be forwarded to the Society of Authors and to the Authors' League of America.

2) That the standard book contract drawn up by your committee be adopted in principle, having regard to the inevitable variations between one contract and another.

This report on the Standard Book Contract was adopted with enthusiasm and deep appreciation of the committee's efforts.

Gwethalyn Graham had good reason to be aware of the intricacies of book contracts. Rarely had a Canadian author acquired so large an income as to impress the taxation authorities. Her *Earth and High Heaven* not only won her a second Governor General's medal, was published very widely, but was optioned by Metro-Goldwyn-Mayer in Hollywood for a sum of $148,000. It was a very impressive sum for a Canadian writer in 1945, and who could guess what further amounts would be amassed from distribution of the film? But the deal petered out, and the reason was not divulged until the late 1970s. It was simply that MGM changed its mind because another moviemaker used the theme of a Jew-Gentile marriage, without success.

But that lump of money didn't stay with the author. The Canadian Department of National Revenue took about half, which stirred the CAA national president's ire. Why should this writer be taxed in one year for a work that took at least three years to accomplish? Rod Kennedy knew he would fight more valiantly than the author, and headed this part of his cabinet himself, with Hugh MacLennan his staunch lieutenant. MacLennan and other authors had been complaining that the Wartime Income Tax was unfair to writers. The Income Tax Act designated royalties as "unearned" income. The term obviously applied to mining royalties, a misnomer when applied to money earned in writing a book. A current speech by James Ilsley, Minister of Finance, implied the possibility of allowing farmers and other "primary producers" to average their earnings over a period of some years. Great Britain and the United States in their Income Tax Acts recognized the special problems of book writers.

Say it takes three years to write a book, with no income coming in. Then in the first year of publication, the author receives sixty to eighty percent of the anticipated royalties. With the present high taxes, the writer will have little to live on for the next three years while writing a second book. If he could average-out his income for the past three years, that would bring it down to a bracket more in line with his needs.

How much money did the average author receive? No one knew, and Gwethalyn Graham's record was far from average. The authors were asked in confidentiality, and the CAA members readily sent in the information, by word and letter. Officials in the Income Tax office in Montreal proved courteous and helpful. "If you were to tabulate the information, maybe compare an author's income with a fisherman or salesman, you would give your presentation more punch," they advised. Back to the drawing-board.

Kennedy and his committee worked out tables to back their assertion that income from book writing is never regular, always sporadic. Thus a writer or other artist pays more tax in the few short years of good sales than a salaried store clerk of the same tax bracket. They made out tables comparing the two incomes over five year, two and three year periods, and proved that the writer paid more in every instance.

Table 3

Author takes 3 years to write books which earn $6,000 in total:
(20,000 copies sold @ $3 — royalty on each: 30¢)

	Income			Tax	
	Author		Salesman	Author	Salesman
	%	$	$	$	$
1st Yr	75	4,500	2,000	1,121.28	221.56
2nd Yr	20	1,200	2,000	— —	221.57
3rd Yr	5	300	2,000	— —	221.56
Total	100	6,000	6,000	1,121.28	664.68

Net income for 3-year period
for author. $4,878.72
for salesman. $5,335.32

Or average annual net income
for author. $1,626.24
for salesman. $1,778.44

Author pays $456.60 more taxes, has $152.20 less per year to live on.

Table 6

Author Takes 2 Years To Write Books Which Earn $9,000 in all. (30,000 copies sold @ $3 ---- royalty: 30¢ each)

Net income for 3 year period
for author.. $6,552.03
for salesman.. $6,757.44

Or average annual net income
for author.. $3,276.01
for salesman.. $3,378.72

Author pays $205.41 more taxes, has $102.71 less to live on.

In its submission to Mr. Ilsley, the committee quoted the Finance Act of Great Britain, urging him to adopt its principles in his forthcoming budget.

Furthermore, we ask the Minister to note that the term "royalty" in the War Tax Act is theoretically applicable to royalties on books, although nothing is more definitely "earned income."

The cases of spectacular hardship are rare, compared with the ordinary run of cases where the Income Tax acts as a heavy and continuous deadweight, without enough income being involved to impress.

In such cases of comparatively modest literary incomes the barrier against living by writing is commonly and impassibly raised by the Income Tax.

This version of the brief provides only a hint of the hours of work that went into its preparation, the many consultations with Finance and National Revenue authorities, who were sympathetic, but bound by Parliamentary decision.

On Monday morning of the 1946 convention in Toronto, National President Roderick Stuart Kennedy gave his presidential report, in which he contrasted the situation of 1921 with the present, twenty-five years later. He referred to the Copyright Act which called the Canadian Authors Association into existence.

It was a bad Act. Amendments have made it a worse Act. It allows the mighty Canadian National Exhibition, which pays huge sums for a famous band to play in its costly buildings — but it need not pay a cent to the composer of that music. When certain presumptuous writers and composers banded together to fight this law, another amendment forbade them to collect fees co-operatively, fees to which they were entitled individually, if they could collect. The CAA makes modest representations to the Secretary of State, and waits.

Back in 1921, the CAA knew that the Income Tax hit authors hard and unfairly, being designed for level annual earnings, whereas the author normally received seventy-five percent of his returns in the first year of publication, though it has taken him several years (without literary income) to write it. But the Income Tax was not staggering then.

But now it is 1946. Book earnings still come in chunks. But the Income Tax is changed. It has soared! There is now a CAA. It collects facts, it works out tabulations and calculations. It presents a Brief to a Finance Minister who finds it not unreasonable to suppose that it is as much a national asset for authors to live as for salesmen.

On Thursday, June 27, the budget was brought down in Parliament, and lo! the CAA Brief had been successful. Authors as well as farmers and fisherman could now average their income tax over a three-year period — provided they filed a notice of intent on a proper form and at a proper time.

In his excitement, President Kennedy threw grammar to the winds, and the conventioneers broke into wild applause.

This, as far as we know, is the first time an official Brief from the CAA has resulted in a specific remedy being provided for the hardship complained of.

But the good news came too late to benefit Gwethalyn Graham. She had docilely paid up in the usual way, and the relief was not retroactive. In 1972, the Income Tax law was revised, so that incomes were automatically averaged, with no need to file notice.

The news seemed a wonderful gift for a silver anniversary, and a good augury for the rest of the convention. Under branch president D.M. LeBourdais, with the assistance of his wife Isabel (Gwethalyn Graham's sister) the convention had a richness of texture, a brilliance of performance, a gaiety which had been lacking during the Depression and war years. Publishers lavished hospitality on their authors in an expansiveness of spirit that at times spilled over to the rank-and-file writers and poets.

Not so immediately successful was another probe. In the closing years of the war, Canadians had given a lot of thought to postwar reconstruction. Changes were imminent, and a new aggressive feeling of self-worth pervaded artists, musicians and writers. At government invitation, sixteen arts groups — painters, handicrafters, sculptors, architects, etchers, authors French and English, formed the Arts Reconstruction Committee, to brief a willing government on a program of development across Canada, to direct a national cultural program, including a National Library, enlarging the Public Archives and building a new National Gallery. At what was expected to be the final meeting of this Committee, Claude Lewis (Toronto) gave a report on its doings to the Canadian Arts Council, and two Toronto CAA members, Franklin McDowell and William Arthur Deacon recommended that the Committee become a permanent body, and this eventually became the Canadian Arts Council, of which the CAA is still a member. Dr. John Murray Gibbon (Montreal) headed the Copyright committee; Don LeBourdais that of Constitution. The whole weight of the conference was thrown behind a memorandum which the CAA sent to the Secretary of State, affirming the right of composers to be paid for the use of their musical works at fairs, and in churches and other public places. The composers won some minor concessions.

"But at present it seems as if the actual amendment will have to wait until the general revision of the Act," Dr. Gibbon concluded. (That time in 1981 is not yet.) The government received the briefs with an enthusiasm that eventually waned. It was only in 1951 that "the Massey Commission" produced its massive report espousing the same program, to be guided by a Canada Council.

And there were speeches, long and short, witty and profound, personal and instructive given by Hugh MacLennan, Mazo de la Roche, E.J. Pratt, Joseph Rutledge, Murray Gibbon, and Thomas Raddall. After such a rich diet, delegates could be forgiven if some thought a lecture on "Greek Literature and the Canadian Writer" might well be passed up. If so, they were the losers. The talk by Dr. W.G. Hardy, Classics Department, University of Alberta not only exalted the writing style of the ancient Greeks, but applied it to modern Canadian writing.

Dr. Hardy was a topnotch speaker, who knew how to make learning fascinating. (U of A students used to skip lunch to attend his noon-hour lectures.) His speech still evokes admiration and inspiration nearly forty years later, and the examples of Greek writing he incorporated in his talk, still move the emotions.

> The study of such writers can teach the Canadian author restraint, and dignity of expression, and to write with implication and understatement. . . . If the Canadian authors do not conform to the middle-class patterns in either ideals or actions, the public tends to be outraged. A derivative of the Greek emphasis on reason and freedom, is Greek frankness. No subject was taboo to the Greek, the sexual act or bodily functions. Nor was he afraid to express himself bluntly. But he did not wallow in either sex or the morbid.

> Along with rhetoric and romanticism, the Canadian who studies Greek literature will learn to throw overboard any striving for mere effect or for the bizarre. There will be no room for Art for Art's sake writing . . .

A new conference technique called Round Tables was reported for the first time. Five of these chaired by Kathleen Strange (Winnipeg), looked into the state of Feature Articles; Poetry, led by Leo Cox (Montreal); the Novel, chaired by Grace Campbell, author of *Thornapple Tree*; Drama by Percy Jacobson (Montreal); the Short Story led by Morley Callaghan. A seminar on Radio was conducted by Andrew Allan of the CBC, and discussion was so lively the stenographer couldn't keep pace. (Tape recorders had yet to be invented.)

The Annual Dinner held in the Royal York Hotel was a splendid affair. (Dinner jackets for men. Service personnel entitled to wear uniform.) His Excellency, Lord Alexander of Tunis was the chief guest. For the second time, a Governor General in person presented his literary awards. (The four silver-plated medals had cost the CAA $103.25, obviously not precious metal, as Earle Birney was later to remark, disparagingly.) Ross Munro, a war correspondent was on assignment in Europe, and his mother accepted his medal for *Gauntlet to Overlord*. (Joy Tranter's *Plowing the Arctic* had been a close second.) Evelyn Richardson had come from her Nova Scotia lighthouse to accept the Creative Nonfiction award for *We Keep A Light*. Earle Birney won his second medal in poetry for *Now is Time*. (A close runner-up was Charles Bruce's *Grey Ship Moving*.) There was no hesitation in the choice of the best Canadian novel of the previous year. The judges were unanimous in selecting *Two*

Solitudes by Hugh MacLennan, a title in constant reprint for four decades so far. The Governor General was presented with deluxe bound copies of the prize-winning books, and Lady Alexander with a bouquet.

Another highlight of the convention, and of the dinner was the specially arranged investiture of Capt. Jacob Markowitz, RAMC, the newly-elected CAA national secretary, with the insignia of a Member (Military Division) of the most excellent Order of the British Empire. "Marko" had been reported missing, presumed dead when the Japanese took Singapore. After a couple of years, word came that he was a prisoner of war. While in the prison compound, the doctor was joint originator and supervisor of a fully successful transfusion service, using the most primitive and improvised apparatus. At considerable personal danger, he taught other prisoners the technique and saved many hundreds of lives.

The dinner closed with an inaugural address by the newly-elected National President, William Arthur Deacon, literary editor of the *Globe and Mail*. He referred to the recent gratifying successes as the merest preliminary skirmish. He was pleased to see young vigorous writers conspicuous at this convention, ones willing to roll up their sleeves and work, and hold petty office, and he believed that the prima donna complex was fading rapidly.

> This, as yet small but professional class, whom so many have laboured so long to bring into being is the chief beneficiary of the practical work done in the last quarter-century. Non-professionals have been the mainstay of this Association. Until recently, they produced the whole of Canadian literature. My thanks to Rod Kennedy, who in uniquely difficult circumstances has concluded a most progressive administration. He is cautious. I am adventurous. I feel that this Association is miles behind the literary movement it is supposed to lead. I am impatient to get going. Mr. Kennedy thinks he is entrusting the controls to a rash youth. I am determined to pick up speed to overtake the procession.

When National President William Arthur Deacon gave notice that the prima donnas of the Association would be remodelled, it was in direct response to a petulant article in the *Canadian Author & Bookman*, written by a young Toronto member. He deplored the hoity-toity attitude which he encountered at branch meetings. When asked what he wrote, he replied frankly that he was writing short stories, hoping eventually to hit American slicks in time, as

Scott Young was doing. The condescending response, "But is that literature?"

"It will pay my income tax."

It was a period in Toronto branch history when F.R. Scott's derisive poem could fairly apply, when coteries gathered worshipfully around Sir Charles G.D. Roberts and Wilson MacDonald, to the neglect of ardent young writers impatient for information about contracts, income tax deductions, and, always, markets. This young Toronto member admitted that two or three branches seemed to be filling that mandate, but not the one he knew best. Nevertheless he made his sweeping statements, unaware of, or ignoring the solid achievements of the CAA standing committees, and he ended with a serious threat,

> Unless the CAA puts its feet on the ground, gets purpose into its actions, faces the hard practical facts of the writing life, unless it gets rid of the dead flesh and coaxes some fresh blood into the ranks — it will, and should, collapse like a pricked balloon.
>
> I do not want to start a new national organization of writers. Partly because I write for a living and cannot afford to devote my entire time to such a cause. Partly because I feel that the right machinery exists in the CAA and should be used. Sooner or later, some group is going to get sufficiently incensed about writers' problems to inaugurate a new national organization.

A sheaf of letters to editor Charles Clay from dissatisfied CAA members chorussed their agreement. Deacon waded into the fray, needling and upbraiding the dilettantes and sycophants, making them thoroughly uncomfortable. They were not turfed out of the Association, he just made them willing to go. The pruning job both thinned and swelled the ranks. As for the young malcontent, he proved a better prophet than writer, evidently.

Chapter 16
Bleak Decade

The 1950s witnessed a soaring prosperity in Canada, including a boom in book publishing as well as book buying. School library expansion took a spurt, not only in primary schools but in high schools, colleges and universities. Large companies built up impressive business libraries and government departments expanded their meagre shelves. The pace of public library building was stepped up, old ones expanded and modernized, and their torn grubby books replaced with the newest editions — in quantity.

Book societies flourished, as rental book collections diminished. Racks of cheap paperbacks sprang up in drugstores, tobacconists and even in corner stores. The wares quickly emerged from selling at twenty-five cents, and included more than light fiction. Casual readers picked up the book buying habit, no longer intimidated by library portals. Magazine racks were clogged with new titles — new markets for writers.

Members of the Canadian Authors Association felt the benefit of these new outlets, as well as of radio broadcasts. The membership increased to around 900 again, though the fee went from seven to ten dollars. All seemed to be going smoothly. The head office in Toronto occupied rent-free, the coachhouse-garage at the rear of Dr. Jacob Markowitz' residence. Joseph Lister Rutledge, retired editor of *Liberty* now edited the *Canadian Author & Bookman*. A pleasant capable woman, Ethel Whyte, ran the office, and stayed in the black in her bookkeeping. When Rutledge became ill, the competent Mrs. Whyte offered to put the magazine together until a new editor could be found. Naturally such a candidate was hard to find under the non-paying circumstances. Mrs. Whyte carried on as manager. The magazine was pretty much a paste-up job, containing few articles, a couple of pages of capsule book reviews and, what most people read with enjoyment, Joy Tranter's "Cross-Country Chat," a gossip column about the Canadian writing scene, emphasis on CAA members.

At the 1950 convention in Montreal, National President Will Bird (Halifax) was buoyant. We were at a crossroads, he said, and future looked bright. The Association was solvent, and the membership was almost back to its former peak, after the lean years of depression and war.

This euphoria was punctured by an article in the July 1950 issue of the *National Home Monthly* by Wallace Reyburn, formerly of western Canada, but now resident in England. In "The Canadian Authors' Dilemma" he disparaged the CAA and joyfully announced a new national organization, the Canadian Writers' Committee, founded by Len Petersen, Pierre Berton, Henry Kreisel, W.O. Mitchell and others, "which when it is in full steam, they expect will do much better than the Canadian Authors Association." After trotting out the old canards of pink teas, apocryphal yarns of amateurism, the age of members, and the Association's poverty, and a further mishmash of remembered gossip, he did give the Association some scant credit for accomplishment, but berated them for misdirection of effort.

> No amount of work done by the CAA is going to help young writers breaking into the book market. For the fact remains that Canada as a book market is very peanuts indeed. And sadly enough, Canada is the worst possible background from the writer's point of view. Canada isn't familiar enough — nor strange enough — to make Americans want to read novels about it. A Canadian background kills a novel for most publishers sight unseen.

(This belief still exists despite repeated proof by serious novelists, and even authors of thrillers set in Canada.)

Reyburn's article did contain one positive suggestion, though it was impracticable: "Why bother trying to bolster up Canadian writers' chances with Canadian publishers? Canadians are among the poorest book-readers in the world. Why not have a lobby down in New York with the express purpose of beating down US publishers' prejudices against Canadian background books? It's all a matter of educating the public." (Something of this nature was tried in the seventies when the government itself set up such selling agencies and bookstores as "Books Canada" in New York and London, and had to admit defeat. Foreign book buyers had not been sufficiently "educated.")

Since bad news sells more papers than good news, the editor cannot be faulted for using an expatriate's inept piece. The Writers' Committee, as such, never did get up steam. Some members of the CAA itself wistfully wondered why these young Turks did not take over the CAA and infuse it with new life.

Quite a different attack came a few years later, this time accusing the CAA of using its power and influence (!) to "muffle Canada's voice." Well, that was a switch, thought the members when their sardonic laughter faded. Lionel Shapiro, author of the Book-of-the-Month *Sixth of June* was newly home from a European career as a foreign correspondent. He admitted he knew nothing of the Canadian Authors Association, but waded into a lengthy diatribe in *Maclean's Magazine*. It was astounding.

> There is a group of people, based mostly in Toronto, with tentacles reaching deep into radio, television, publishing and the book pages of principal newspapers, that I like to call the Inner Coterie of Canadian Authors. Most of these self-appointed arbiters of Canadian culture are connected with the Canadian Authors Association. This group would seem to believe that a Canadian novel must restrict itself to Canadian characters, locales, situations and problems.

> Only in Canada is Canadian writing derided, decried and indeed dismissed as non-existent.... Canadian writers are being deterred by a home-grown legend that a Canadian has no writing tradition to build upon, that he is a mouse in the world of writing — not only a mouse but a mouse in diapers — that there is no distinctive Canadian literature in the English language.

National President Dr. Frank Stiling (London) disclaimed any knowledge of Shapiro's sinister "Inner Coterie."

> While members of the Canadian Authors Association are involved in radio, television etc., the Association certainly does not engage in the vain activity of telling them what they should and should not write.

> The Association's primary purpose is to safeguard the rights of

its members. Mr. Shapiro may be interested to learn that he benefits in more than one way from the work of this Association. I shall give only one example. Until 1947, a writer in Canada paid income tax on book royalties as "unearned income." The Association pointed out the injustice of the existing regulations, with the result that they were changed, the benefits of which accrue to Mr. Shapiro and all other Canadian writers.

But the 1950s had worse blows in store for the Association than verbal assaults. Perhaps it could be said that the Association was born old. Certainly those who had established themselves as authors (none full-time) were already mature when they brought the CAA into existence in 1921. And the years took their toll. Dr. D.C. Scott died in 1947, and his friend Dr. Pelham Edgar the following year, Arthur Stringer in 1950 (having produced sixty-five books), and that bright innovative music-lover, Dr. John Murray Gibbon in 1952, full of years and honours, author of twenty-five books; R.S. Kennedy in 1953, B.K. Sandwell in 1954, Katherine Hale Garvin in 1956, and Robert Stead in 1959. A crippling loss to an organization of any size.

Perhaps because the Montreal convention ended up with a deficit of $800 the spotlight was turned on head office in Toronto. Prosperity being an unfamiliar phenomenon to the Association, the national executive wondered what it had been doing right. Surely the increase in fees did not wholly account for the current freedom from stress. It didn't. The new national president, Dr. Wm. George Hardy (Edmonton) asked the headquarters committee to check the finances in view of the Montreal deficit.

What was the alarm of gentle Claude Lewis (Toronto) to discover not the vaunted efficiency of the office secretary, but a welter of confusion. Mrs. Whyte took off for England at the first breath of investigation. While embezzlement was suspected, it would be hard to prove, and no legal action was instituted. Still, by mid-March 1951 Lewis found unpaid bills to the tune of $6,000 and more to unearth. Arthur Child, treasurer of the Toronto branch, and a vice-president at Canada Packers, took on the headquarters committee and continued the search. He found income not entered, bills marked paid when they were clearly owing, bills tucked into queer corners and odd files, which took months to straighten out.

Child strong-armed one of his firm's accountants to set up a proper system of bookkeeping, and blocked out a budget. By June convention time, he could report that the Association had debts of

$10,332; had assets of $1,393; net deficit therefore $8,939. Antici-
pated revenue from delinquent dues and advertisers would reduce
the debt further. Some gifts from friends, such as senior members,
might be hoped for, and a drastic reduction of expense would be
necessary. That spelled the doom of an internal newsletter which
would provide only Association news. A bank loan of $900 would
be needed.

National President Hardy, always constructive, had to present
these unpleasant realities to the membership. The debt was more
than the entire income for one year. The delegates forgot the mag-
nificent scenery of Banff outside the windows and listened appalled
to the account:

> Our financial deficit was not caused by your present executive,
> but inherited. The background of this financial situation is that
> this Association has for years apparently been living beyond its
> income, and that the audited statements presented to the Asso-
> ciation's Annual Meetings have been misleading in that certain
> bills were not available to the auditors and not discoverable by
> them.
>
> Serious as the situation is, you have all the facts in the open.
> And since the Association exists from and for the members,
> capitations to the branches will have priority. The inefficiency
> of the central office has been rectified, the personnel changed, a
> proper set of books installed, and you have now elected Arthur
> Child as National Treasurer.
>
> For the time being, the *Canadian Author & Bookman* will be
> centred at Montreal under the editorship of Roderick Kennedy,
> and the *Canadian Poetry Magazine* at Ottawa, with Arthur
> Bourinot as editor.
>
> In addition, we hope for a substantial surplus from this conven-
> tion.

Part of that surplus came from the sale of the publishers' book
display, a sum of $300, part of which was remanded to the Associ-
ation for acting as booksellers and saving return freight costs.

All this Dr. Hardy had to make plain at the 1951 convention
held at the Banff School of Fine Arts. It was the first of many fine
conventions hosted by the Edmonton branch. The program and
other arrangements were convened by Marjorie Wilkins Campbell
(Toronto). She set up several panels of experts including editors.

Dr. Hardy's summary came as a great shock to most of the

delegates at the 1951 convention. After long and full discussion, it was agreed by all that the work of the Association was too valuable and important to be interrupted by a temporary financial embarrassment.

> It has become essential not only to authors, but to Canada, by its achievements through its Governor General's Awards Board, and in the fields of copyright protection, authors' income tax matters, publishers' contracts etc., by its publications, and above all by its contribution to Canadian culture as a corporate expression of the authors of Canada.

Despite the gloomy prospects, there was a feeling of optimism at that convention, a very heartening determination to cooperate in meeting the current difficulty. Dilatory members paid their fees promptly; each branch was inspired to be a little more efficient and effective, so that good came out of distress, though it was six years before the CAA books were again in the black.

While no person was blamed for the lack of supervision which permitted the financial bungling, no doubt the fiasco had a bearing on a book Arthur Child and Cadmus Bradford were asked to write for the Institute of Internal Auditors in 1954. They collaborated on the textbook, *Internal Control against Fraud and Waste*. Though it was much used in commercial schools, the taunt of one reviewer stung. "This book might be taken as a manual on how to defraud the boss rather than means for the boss to outwit pilfering in the front office."

Mary-Etta Macpherson, editor of the *Canadian Home Journal* spoke of the magazine situation in Canada, which she found very grave:

> So-called Canadian magazines (Canadian editions of American magazines, chiefly *Time* and *Readers' Digest*) are able to command a lion's share of Canadian advertising even though the rates are higher than those of Canadian magazines. Our publishing costs are higher because of our smaller runs. No other country in the world is so smothered by foreign imports. And though our rates to contributors are much higher than ten years ago, they still cannot compete with the dazzling sums which American magazines offer — though in proportion to circulation we pay higher. American editors are buying the product of Canadian authors to a much greater extent than in former years.

This problem of Canadian editions and Canadian advertising was not cleared up until 1975 when the Canadian government no longer allowed Canadian advertisers to deduct from their income tax the cost of advertising in a foreign magazine. *Time* bowed out (not meekly) as did several others. *Readers' Digest* (Canada) took out Canadian citizenship.

Margaret Arnett MacLeod (Winnipeg) was introduced as the only woman to have a book published by invitation of the distinguished Champlain Society, *The Letters of Letitia Hargrave*. Naturally she spoke on historical research, and Alice MacKay (Winnipeg), co-author of *The Honourable Company* followed with suggestions for historical articles and pamphlets and sources for such material.

> It used to be that articles were only a small part of magazines, then they became equal to fiction. Today, non-fiction outstrips fiction in both magazines and book club choices. This trend offers more encouragement to factual writers.

Dr. Douglas Leechman (Ottawa) author of *Eskimo Summer* agreed this was a fact, and gave practical hints on article-writing. Joan Huntley (Toronto) reported:

> On the whole this year's convention bore the stamp of professionalism. The congenital and lifelong amateurs were there, to be sure, but professionals set the tone and pace. It was a work conference first and foremost; practical sessions and panel discussions on the novel, creative non-fiction, writing for children, playwriting and radio writing — morning, afternoon and evening the delegates were hard at it. An innovation was coffee breaks halfway through the morning and afternoon sessions.

And yes, there was an afternoon off, for a picnic beside Lake Minnewanka. After ample lunch shared with a couple of mountain sheep, the men lolled back, hats over eyes, while the women watched with interest as elocutionist Phoebe Erskine McKellar (Montreal) prepared to recite. Her props in two boxes contained makeup and the scarves she used to dramatic purpose. As Mrs. McKellar got into the swing of her recitations, the women watched with horrified fascination, one sheep nibbling on Phoebe's cosmetics, while the other nosed into her scarves. Giggles roused the dozing men, who sprang up in alarm, frightening off the sheep. One got a couple of scarves caught in its corrugated horns, and whirling about took off up the mountain, with a scarf streaming behind. Phoebe, with admirable aplomb ignored the incident until the one breathless gallant returned from the pursuit, scarf in hand.

Juveniles came in for passing mention from Charles Strong, supervising editor of Standard Magazines of New York and slightly more from Dr. Donalda Dickie (Calgary). She found children not much interested in fairy tales: "Truck drivers are more interesting to them. So when you write for children, keep it lively, keep things moving. They'll yawn in your face if it's dull."

In Dr. Dickie's audience that day was one of her former Normal School students, Audrey McKim (Edmonton). She was awaiting publication of the first of her many books for children, *Here Comes Dirk*. Audrey Alexandra Brown (Victoria) and John Murray Gibbon read and spoke at the poetry session.

The annual banquet, now called the Awards Dinner, saw Governor General's medals presented to Germaine Guèvremont, Donalda Dickie and Marjorie Wilkins Campbell. Mazo de la Roche emerged from her habitual seclusion and overcame a bout of laryngitis to come to Banff to accept in person the first gold medal awarded by the University of Alberta for "distinguished contribution to Letters." She responded with a characteristically pungent and witty speech. But the liveliest memory of that occasion was Joy Tranter, caught in the act of switching place-cards.

"Well, I don't get information from dull types," she defended, "and I need it for my Cross-Country Chat."

Instead of snow-capped peaks looming around, London's first and to date only convention took place in a heat wave, at the University of Western Ontario, in 1952. For the first time, the program included an address on writing for television, the new medium just introduced to Canada. Mavor Moore spoke of how it differed from writing for radio, while Robert Weaver told about radio opportunities. Leslie Roberts spoke on article writing, and a lively panel on short stories including London's Elsie Mack, Frances Shelley Wees and Scott Young (Toronto), was chaired by Leslie Gordon Barnard. A panel discussed the novel, with so much interest and information that it was carried forward to the next day when five book publishers told what they were looking for in fiction. John F. Hayes gave a splendid talk on writing for boys. Governor General Vincent Massey was on hand to distribute medals to Josephine Phelan, Charles Bruce, E.J. Pratt, Morley Callaghan, Frank McKinnon, Jan Hilliard, and John F. Hayes.

The convention returned to Toronto in 1953, and according to those who were there, it was the best yet, and the credit rightly went to Isabel LeBourdais, who didn't hesitate to "reach for the top." It was held at Hart House, and chief drawing cards were Nicholas Montserrat and David Walker. The convention was a miracle of smooth timing, graciousness and top-flight speakers.

National President Dr. Paul Kuhring (Montreal) suffered a severe heart attack, and Dr. George Hardy filled out his term of office. Thus the 1954 convention was held again in Banff. Addresses were given by D.M. LeBourdais, by Dr. Lionel Stevenson and Josephine Phelan on writing biography. "Writing for Teenagers" was a lively panel composed of Olive Knox (Winnipeg), Mary Carr Wright (Victoria), Audrey McKim (Edmonton) and Harlan Thompson.

The 1955 convention was held for the first and only time at Queen's University, Kingston, Ontario. Panels were popular — on the short story; publishers; and television, conducted by Esse W. Ljungh, and one on French-Canadian letters chaired by Dr. Guy Sylvestre (Ottawa). A social event was a trip to Bon Echo to view the memorial to Walt Whitman. But perhaps the most striking memory was that Laura Berton (Vancouver) fell on the stone steps and broke her leg. Or it may have been Vinia Hoogstraten's incarceration in her bedroom due to a freshly-varnished door, when she should have been at the Awards Dinner. Also notable was Helen Creighton (Halifax) speaking on "Songs, Spectres and Specie."

The convention in 1956, was held in Halifax, and was notable for the prizes and awards handed out: the Governor General's medals, the Ryerson Fiction Award, the *Maclean's Magazine's* $5,000, University of Western Ontario President's medal, and the Beta Sigma Phi Sorority prize. Lionel Shapiro accepted the medal for fiction with his *Sixth of June*.

By 1957, the convention was back to Winnipeg for the first time in thirty-two years. Entertaining speakers were Paul Hiebert (Winnipeg), Ross Annett (Edmonton) and Winnipegger Adele Wiseman, whose first book *The Sacrifice* was picking up awards right and left. To this meeting came a wide-eyed neophyte from Yorkton, Saskatchewan: Stan Obodiac had had a book published at cost of $2,900 by a vanity press, and was flogging it wherever he could. Joe Holliday, editor of the *Canadian Author & Bookman*, saw a story in him, a warning of the hazards of vanity publishing. Undaunted, Obodiac self-published another book, *My Experiences at a Canadian Authors' Convention*, of which gossip was a prominent feature. Delegates were later startled to find a copy in their mail-boxes along with a bill for two dollars. National Treasurer Elsie Pomeroy (Toronto) enraged, flung her copy into the garbage, when she found he implied that her long friendship with Sir Charles G.D. Roberts was a one-sided love affair.

Dr. Watson Kirkconnell of Acadia University had been persuaded to take on the national presidency for another term in 1944, despite his busy life and all the services he had already rendered to the Association. He gave a very full, long report on the Association's affairs, beginning with the happy news that the Association was now clear of debt. (Applause.) Membership had slipped to 650. (Consternation.)

Why had the membership sagged so badly?

There is a tendency in any organization for an extremely efficient member to forget the parameters of his/her duties and exceed them. Arthur Child, in charge of headquarters and also National Treasurer felt, not unreasonably, that he was doing more for the Association than anyone else. Was he not also gathering advertising for the Association's two magazines, using his business connections? He had a dream of how the CAA should be run to make it truly dynamic. It needed an Executive Secretary, one who could and would be supervised closely,

But first the constitution must be changed. More easily planned than accomplished. The CAA had already had four short-lived constitutions, largely hewing to the lines Gibbon and de Montigny had worked out in 1921. The Incorporation Constitution of 1947 was only slightly changed. It had been circulated to every member, and decisions requested on every article and by-law and every subsection, so that eighty-seven specific points were balloted on by every member. No one cared to go through that experience again.

In 1945, Charles Clay, National Secretary, could write to National President Watson Kirkconnell in ironical amusement: "You will, I am sure, be delighted to hear that the constitution over which we laboured so lovingly last year is not only full of holes big enough for elephants to caper though, but that the elephants are actually capering through them with high glee."

Exaggeration, undoubtedly, for very slightly modified, it satisfied the corporation lawyers of the Secretary of State's department in Ottawa. Now in 1954 Child proposed changing it again, and worked out a constitution which would do away with the advisory

National Council entirely, and effectively place control in the hands of a National Executive Secretary. This constitution was circulated in mimeographed form, and won many adherents. But Isabel LeBourdais, president of the Toronto branch, viewed it as undemocratic and dangerous to the well-being of the Association, and campaigned vigorously against it. It was perhaps an idea ahead of its time, and certainly beyond the current finances of the Association. Still, the controversy rose to remarkable heights, and wounded egos. Long-time friendships were broken, not to be healed for many years, and that year of crisis saw resignations of many partisans. Then Child transferred to western Canada and lost interest in the Canadian Authors Association.

More major disappointment lay in store for the Association before the fifties ended. In his presidential report on the past year, Dr. Kirkconnell filled in the delegates in Winnipeg on his progress in approaching the newly-formed Canada Council, which he had investigated earlier in the month:

> Finally, let me come to a matter of profound interest to us all — the setting up of the Canada Council and the probable relevance of that step upon the future of the Canadian Authors Association. On April 18, 1957, at the National Executive meeting, a committee was appointed to prepare a Brief for submission to the Canada Council which was to go into operation in the fall. The committee consisted of Leslie Gordon Barnard, Dr. Constance Beresford-Howe (Montreal) and Don Thomson (Ottawa), and the branches were asked to send them their suggestions. They worked well, and on June 9, Mrs. Barnard handed me a bulky envelope with the committee's report.
>
> The next day in Ottawa on business for the Royal Society, I learned that the Canada Council was almost ready to function, that its secretarial staff was complete, that it was to move into its new quarters on Wednesday, and was to strike a tentative budget on Thursday. Ottawa was full of organizations that were interviewing the chairman, Mr. Brooke Claxton. I therefore sought out an interview with Mr. Claxton myself.
>
> I discussed our Brief with him off the record so as to get his judgment on things that might or might not be favourably considered. On this his views were clear-cut. He vetoed travel grants to assist conventions or to bring speakers to national or branch meetings, and lecture tours abroad, at least for the time being.

On the other hand, fellowships and grants in aid of publication would at least be given sympathetic consideration. He urged me to put in a Brief immediately, bearing in mind that the funds thus far available are a very small fraction of what will ultimately be needed. For example, merely to implement the scholarship provisions of the Massey Report would take seven times the total present income of the Canada Council.

I dropped all my Royal Society meetings for twenty-four hours, and re-wrote the committee's Brief, omitting all items that Mr. Claxton had denounced and reorganizing the remainder into a new pattern. Telephone calls to Don Thomson kept me in touch with his point of view, and on Wednesday morning, I had the Brief typed out by a public stenographer and handed it to Mr. Claxton's secretary at twelve noon.

Let me read you the document:

"(i) We strongly recommend that a Canada Council Prize of at least $1,000 be attached to at least three Governor General's Medals each year. We also recommend that the administrative costs of the Governor General's Awards Board be borne by the Canada Council.

(ii) We would strongly recommend a system of Canada Council Fellowships and Grants-in-Aid for creative writers. The novelist, the playwright, the essayist are rarely even the step-children of the Humanities and Social Science Research Councils. We therefore suggest fellowships of from $500 to $1,000 for young writers; and an occasional $2,500 to $4,000 to a mature writer of proven competence.

We recommend still more strongly a system of Canada Council grants in aid of publication for works that a panel of experts may recommend for printing. In the present state of the publishing business, grants of $500 to $1,000 may well rescue from oblivion works of profound literary merit for which the realistic publisher would anticipate no large popular sale.

(iii) On page 381 of the Massey Commission Report, special consideration is urged for 'the strengthening, by money grants and in other ways, of certain of the Canadian voluntary organizations on whose active well-being the work of the Council will in a large measure depend.' We submit that the Canadian Authors Association is one of those voluntary organizations, 'whose work is of national importance but whose resources are inadequate for their growth.'

243

For thirty-six years, we have borne the burden and heat of the day' and have struggled with the slenderest means and heroically voluntary labour on behalf of authorship in this country. The editors of our quarterlies work without reward, for we have no money to give them. Again and again our deficits have threatened to swallow us up and only sacrificial giving has bridged the muskeg.

We therefore submit that ours is one of those voluntary national organizations envisaged by the Massey Commissioners for which a substantial annual grant of perhaps $5,000 would assure a proper headquarters, proper secretarial and clerical help, and the survival of our publications: the *Canadian Author & Bookman* and the *Canadian Poetry Magazine*.

The foregoing appeals may be summarized as follows:

(a) Prizes for Governor General's Medal winners.... $ 3,000
(b) Administration of the Awards Board............ 500
(c) Canada Council Fellowships.................... 5,000
(d) Grants in aid of publication.................... 2,500
(e) Maintenance grant for Authors Association...... 5,000

Annual Total $16,000

We submit that such an annual grant would be only modest encouragement for the non-academic authorship of a nation of sixteen millions. While it is less than one per cent of the Canada Council's annual income, we realize that many other phases of Canada's arts and letters are by their very nature vastly more expensive, and we have purposely kept our petitions within humble bounds.

While the relief and pension activities of the Canadian Writers' Foundation fall outside of our organizational orbit, we should like to commend them also to your sympathetic generosity."

Surely a modest enough proposition, even before inflation set all currency askew. In the finale of his address, Dr. Kirkconnell hoped the delegates at the convention would not criticize his action too fiercely.

There seemed to be a real danger two weeks ago that we should actually be left out in the cold in the striking of the first budget of the Canada Council. I would hope, therefore, that this Convention would not only condone what I have done but would decide not to confuse the issue by sending along any supplementary recommendations that have not passed through the CAA's drafting committee or my interview with Mr. Claxton.

244

Much may be hoped for if we act with dignity and discretion.

Far from criticizing their president's activities or attempting to modify his appealing brief, the delegates at Winnipeg gave him a hearty round of applause.

But the hopes of all were shattered when the Canada Council brought down its budget, with not a dime earmarked for the Canadian Authors Association. Although requests for assistance have been made since, with dignity and discretion and from various aspects, the Canada Council has remained non-supportive, on the grounds that non-professional writers comprised too large a percentage of the membership of the CAA. Nonetheless in the late seventies the Council contributed some funding for outside speakers at Conventions.

One final act remained in the business session. Should we continue our Book Week activities? The National Executive had decided against it, but the branches were free to do as they wished. Lacking an advertising agent, the magazines drew no support from the publishers, and the two editors were too busy doing non-paying editorial work to drum up advertisements. The decision was made to drop Book Week officially.

However, the Vancouver branch under President Alban Winspear, rented a booth at the Pacific National Exhibition for eleven days to display books written by B.C. writers, and other books about British Columbia. Eastern publishers cooperated splendidly, and even local booksellers finally responded. It was the last hurrah.

The 1958 convention returned to Montreal, and was reported as excellent for the quality of its speeches, among them Joyce Hemlow's account of how she discovered the Fanny Burney Papers, and Pierre Berton (Toronto) telling of how he wrote *Klondike*. Frances Shelley Wees and Marjorie Wilkins Campbell (Toronto) rounded out the cast of fascinating speakers.

Star speakers at the final convention of the fifties who held forth at the only convention held in Windsor, Ont. were Arthur Hailey, Laura Goodman Salverson (Toronto) and the Hon. Paul Martin, once honorary counsel for the CAA. It is interesting to note that at this convention, Pierre Trudeau was named winner of the President's Medal for the best scholarly article submitted.

And so closed a stormy decade of lowering clouds and chill winds and the bleakest of prospects. All hoped the next decade would be more serene and optimistic.

245

Chapter 17
Poets and Poetasters

"Why doesn't your Association offer worthwhile prizes for poetry instead of piddling little twenty-five, fifteen and ten dollar awards? They should start at a hundred dollars," read a strident letter to an editor of the *Canadian Author & Bookman*. He, of course, had nothing to do with the prizes except to report them.

Many of the branches had poetry groups, some of which issued a slender volume of verse from time to time, either their own or the winners in competition. (This probably launched the humbug that the CAA was composed of self-published writers.)

"As might be expected," an article on Canadian literature in the June 1887 issue of the *Canadian-American Magazine* had run, "Canada has been most fruitful of poets. Canadian poets are almost as numerous as the birds in the wood: but on the whole, the birds have the best of it. In front stands Charles G.D. Roberts, a poet of whom any literature might be proud."

Canada *was* proud of Roberts, especially after he returned from abroad to live in Toronto. His poetry was among the first to be recognized by school boards in Canada. A dapper small man, he was not shy. In fact, Thomas Raddall considered him something of a *poseur*. Probably he had more showbiz than most, and who could be called "the Dean of Canadian literature" without taking on some airs, especially with his literary record? Had he been willing to settle in the States, he might well have been honoured there as superior to Robert Frost or Carl Sandberg, according to some. The poetry group in Toronto revered him for his work, and loved him for his kindness to young writers. "Perhaps it's a good thing that someone holds a laurel wreath, if not a halo over his head," mused a critic. "The halo wouldn't fit."

In 1925, Bliss Carman made a highly successful reading tour to western university campuses. The following year Roberts repeated the feat to considerable acclaim in high schools and church audiences.

Of all the groups — drama, short story, article, novel and radio — formed in the Association's early years, poetry was the most popular and most durable. Here many women found their voice, though few achieved the renown accorded the more sonorous male tones. The branches found that those interested in a particular aspect of writing coalesced to the relief of other members less interested. The poetry groups not only wrote, read, criticized their poems, but studied techniques be it concrete poetry or haiku. They promoted the reading of poetry outside the Association, not for a fee but in the desire to open ears. Paying markets were scarce, though most magazines and newspapers used verse as fillers, and Canadian poetry (the rhyming kind of course) had infiltrated school textbooks.

Fred Swayze (Ottawa) poet and high school inspector, and author of *In the Egyptian Gallery*, who would have become an important name in Canadian literature but for his untimely death, had words of commendation and warning for the group system:

> Craft groups are worth their weight in Canadian currency. A branch that devotes as much time to organizing study groups as it does to entertaining visiting celebrities is giving good value. In such groups we experience the stimulus of encountering lively minds and the bittersweet of subjecting our work to criticism.
>
> Membership requirement should be an agreement to write something for critical appraisal for each meeting. And an understanding that each member will send out his/her work, submitting it to editorial judgment. It is fatally easy to dissipate the energies of a good leader and a talented group by suffering parasites to belong.
>
> If the critical appraisal is as frank as friendship can stand, the problem of membership is solved. Anything less than honesty destroys the validity of criticism. Praise of the mediocre is dishonest. Better to point out one phrase or line or paragraph, and scrap the rest. Better to invite a sound critic as guest executioner and benefit from his comment. The group can provide criticism

at a time when it can be effective — before publication.

I have been most grateful for these craft groups. The unselfish men and women who have associated themselves with this work have earned the gratitude of all . . .

Dr. Don W. Thomson, a past National President remembered:

The Ottawa poetry group was later in starting but has persisted for forty years since 1940. The group seldom exceeded ten at any given time. In its initial years, the group was convened by Lilian Found, with Wilfrid Eggleston as mentor. Since those early days more than a score of chapbooks have been produced by individual members. The group, as such, was instrumental in the publication of three major collections of verse: *Profile*, 1946, the best poems from a nation-wide contest; *Poets of the Capital*, 1973; and *A Flock of Bards*, 1975, an anthology featuring the work of twenty-three Ottawa poets.

The group has been far from an inward-looking aggregation. For fifteen years it organized annual poetry contests in Ottawa area schools, an activity mainly directed by Winifred Horne. Group members visited schools in the city from time to time. Guest critics have included Dr. Arthur Bourinot, A.J.M. Smith, Dr. Fred Cogswell and Dr. Wreford Watson.

In the foreword of Montreal's 1946 Poetry Yearbook, Lily Barry claimed her group was the first formed in Canada. Montreal began small with five poets who met in one another's homes, until the enthusiasm spread to about fifty more. Then meetings of the group took place in the studio of photographer Charles Rice. In 1925, the group decided to hold a poetry competition. Small cash prizes were offered, for the best poem submitted by a group member; for the best unpublished poem in French or English by a Montreal student; and similar for the province of Quebec. In all there were eighty-four entries, and the Montreal student who won the ten dollar prize was A.J.M. Smith, later anthologist of the *Oxford Book of Canadian Verse*.

The poetry group in Victoria was long under the capable leadership of M. Eugenie Perry, and in Vancouver of Marion Angus. The Calgary branch began after studying the regular advice columns of Donald G. French in the *Canadian Bookman*. Elaine Catley led the group for years. Many of the poetry groups produced a chapbook or yearbook of the best poems. The Regina branch was perhaps the trailblazer with the undated publication of the chapbook *Saskatchewan: Her Infinite Variety.* In 1925 Montreal produced its first yearbook of a series that went on until 1950.

In 1934, Prof. V.B. Rhodenizer edited *At the Sign of the Hand and Pen* for the Nova Scotia branch. Edmonton's *Alberta Poetry Yearbook* was first published in 1930 and has continued annually for fifty years. Winnipeg branch published in 1933, Regina again in 1935, Victoria in 1938, Ottawa 1946, Okanagan 1971, and Sarnia produced *Polished Pebbles* in 1974, and sold every copy. Chapbooks were much esteemed for use at Christmas, as saying much more than a commercial card.

The Toronto poetry group began in 1932 when Donald French was branch president. Reminiscing two decades later, Amabel King recalled:

> The history of Toronto poetry group goes back a long way — to the time when dinner jackets were a uniform for the gentlemen who attended. There were sixteen members fairly consistently. Peak attendance was in 1941, with forty members.
>
> That year, the Toronto group sponsored an anthology, *Voices of Victory.* The group invited the major poets of Canada to contribute. None refused, and seventy were printed. A newspaper commended the idea, but said it would take a year to complete. It took four months. The Macmillan Co. delivered it on the very day of a Book Fair held in the branch clubrooms. The first edition sold out early in 1942; the second was bought by the IODE for their war work. The poetry group was able to hand over to the Red Cross for British Bomb Victims more than $1,000. Agnes Aston Hill (Calgary) took the silver medal offered by the Earl of Athlone and Princess Alice.

Many factors play a part in such an undertaking as this. Someone has the idea. The group or the branch decides to act on it. Hard work follows. Rules, fees, judging, publishing costs have to be considered. Then put into operation. The palm for longevity must go to the Edmonton branch for its Alberta Poetry Yearbook. It began in 1930 with a poetry contest limited to residents of Alberta, with the intent of encouraging the poets of the province to practice their craft, and possibly see their work published. Alberta Scouten mothered the Yearbook for the first fifteen years, the most difficult period, and due to her determintion, the Yearbook flourished for fifty years.

The first issue published the award winners, as well as other poems. Magistrate Emily Murphy ("Janey Canuck") wrote the foreword: "It is to be sincerely hoped that the Canadian Authors Association may definitely continue in the role of foster father to the versifiers. Our land must not be songless." A feature of the Alberta Poetry Yearbook was its unique Judges' Report in each volume. This has been valuable to the fledgling poet who studied the comments made and attempted to apply the advice to his/her own work. Over the years, the judges perused more than 50,000 pieces of creative work by writers living in Canada. One-tenth were found worthy of publication, a proportion representing 1,600 writers.

June Fritch (Edmonton) filled the editorial chair for the final twenty-seven years, growing in expertise. She recorded:

> That first Yearbook contained twenty-four poems and thirty-one pages, with nominal awards to three winners. The final edition contained eighty-eight poems on sixty-four pages, with awards going to sixteen writers.

> We have been fortunate in having had competent judges. Their task was difficult, for in recent years as many as 1700 entries have been submitted, and the task of sifting the good from the not-so-good has been arduous. The final selection could be heart-wrenching. The last judge to evaluate 1500 submissions was Dr. John Chalmers. (Edmonton).

> In 1979, cash awards of $225 were spread over four categories. Book awards memorialized Alberta Scouten, Georgia May Cook, Jessie Boyd. (In recognition of their long-continued interest in Canadian poets and poetry, the 1955 Yearbook was dedicated to Ethel and Jessie Boyd (Calgary).

> It is interesting to note that while most of the judges have been men, the editors were women. But where is the writer now who is able to devote 500 hours of time to this project? The most devoted woman wearies of this expenditure of her time and talent.

> In 1979, the contest and Yearbook were discontinued. The Edmonton branch took this decision with regret, largely because the rising cost of publication prohibited selling the product for a nominal $3 and this in spite of cultural grants in recent years.

> Dwindling distribution was another factor. The thousand copies of recent years were distributed through book stores,

standing orders, circulars to schools, and a copy to each contestant. Back issues are in libraries in Europe, the United States and Canada. It is on microfiche at the National Library in Ottawa.

But Cora Taylor (Edmonton) picked up the challenge in 1980, and the Alberta Poetry Yearbook continues.

The genesis of the *Canadian Poetry Magazine* in 1927 was nothing like so businesslike, as W.A. Deacon recalled forty years later. The successful tours of Carman and Roberts set the young Canadian Authors Association brimming with unfounded optimism. Obviously Canadians liked poetry. Then why not publish a magazine for and of Canadian verse? It would be a further service to the membership.

A dozen male members of the Toronto branch blithely launched a quarterly with E.J. Pratt as editor. One of the lot professed to know the business of setting up, getting advertising, and would handle that end of things. The others left it to him. Pratt edited the first number, which was printed in the thousands, but never distributed! The self-proclaimed expert couldn't raise even Pratt's salary of twenty-five dollars. Deacon doubted (correctly) that the printer was ever paid.

A few years later the subject cropped up again. The Montreal poetry group thought they could manage a poetry magazine. Cannier than their predecessors, the Montrealers set up a feasibility study. What would it cost to produce a national poetry magazine of five issues a year, the fifth replacing the poetry group's yearbook? Too much.

Then why shouldn't the Association publish a quarterly, two dollars a year to subscribers, small cash awards to contest winners? After some nagging from the poet-members, the National Executive raised the matter at the Kenora convention of 1934.

If feasible, the Executive would sponsor the project to the extent of naming an advisory council, thus giving the magazine a national character. But not be responsible. The Association could not afford the luxury.

Dr. E.A. Hardy (Toronto) stressed that this could be a practical service to the Association, increase its membership, and assure members it was being constructive.

John Murray Gibbon thought that a national magazine rather than a branch project might bring about a national list of subscribers or guarantors.

251

Gibbon therefore moved at the 1935 convention in Montreal,

> that this convention approves the re-consideration of a poetry
> magazine, and that the Executive be empowered to arrange for
> its editing and publication, if it be financially within our means.

Albert H. Robson (Toronto) seconded the motion. Leslie Bar-
nard thought it a good idea, better than a branch project. Charles P.
Rice (Montreal) queried about combining it with the *Canadian
Author*.

That would not satisfy Gibbon. "Type-face and format will
have a lot to do with success, and the *Author* wouldn't appeal to the
public." Rod Kennedy opposed the notion of multiple editors: "Too
much compromise." R.J.C. Stead, known as "the poet of the prairies" predicted a considerable sale for a bound volume of the
year's issues. Elizabeth Bailey Price (Vancouver) believed the magazine would find strong support from all the poetry groups.
"There's only one way to be sure of how it will work," Leslie Gordon Barnard contributed, "and that is by trying it out."

Dr. E.J. Pratt (Toronto) good-humouredly accepted the
editorial chore, with an advisory board of five, comprising Sir
Andrew Macphail (Montreal) essayist, critic; Katherine Hale
(Toronto) poet-essayist; Sir Charles G.D. Roberts (Toronto) newly
knighted; Dr. Duncan Campbell Scott (Ottawa) and Albert H. Robson (Toronto) knowledgeable artist. Funded (though barely) the
Canadian Poetry Magazine came out first in 1936, hardly surviving
its infancy. The next issue was larger, with an article by Dr. Lorne
Pierce. It was soon apparent that poets alone would not sustain
publication. CAA members, whether or not they wrote poems,
were implored to support the publication. A free subscription was
offered for every five new subscribers. Pratt urged members:

> The poetry is well above the average. I have great hopes for the
> magazine's future. We've proved the existence of high-grade
> ore. Our appreciation goes to the donors who manifested their
> faith in the beginning, and to the Press for the encouragement
> that has greeted each number. But a great deal of further effort
> is needed to lift us out of the mists. Much of the work in promo-
> tion, and even the actual production is voluntary. It is not run
> for profit: it has no other objective than the enlargement of the
> poetic vision of Canada.

(One whose contribution never made print was his wife. Viola
Pratt's work as editor of a Sunday school paper provided the exper-

tise in layout and editorial experience. Frequently she pasted up the copy for the printer.)

Yet issues constantly lagged behind publishing deadlines for lack of staff. "A depleted treasury accounts for our belated appearance," the editor admitted in the April 1937 number. "We are convinced that out of a population of nine or ten millions in Canada, a constituency could be discovered to support one magazine devoted exclusively to poetry. The *Canadian Author* of December 1935, quoted Dr. Wm. Lyon Phelps of Yale University, whose article praising *La Vérendrye*, by A.M. Stephen (Vancouver) was syndicated in forty American papers: "For a number of years I have felt sure that Canadian poetry has been too much neglected both by Great Britain and the United States. In fact the surest way to obscurity is to be a Canadian poet."

"Is it possible that Canadian poetry is more neglected abroad than in its native land?" queried the editor acidly. "Canada lacks neither quality nor quantity of poetic production, but lags far behind other countries in its encouragement. The United States, besides offering substantial prizes keeps alive, if not flourishing, more than forty magazines that publish nothing but verse and critical comment, and a few of these are responsible for the discovery of several major American poets of the twentieth century. The time is well advanced for Canada to initiate its own movements in the same direction."

Robson, the business manager, could announce soberly, "We have less than six hundred subscribers. We need a thousand."

Help was at hand. Nathaniel Benson (Toronto), an energetic young advertising man and poet, proposed holding a Canadian Poetry Night in Convocation Hall. "People will come to hear the Governor General even if they don't care about poetry. He can hand out his Tweedsmuir medal, and the Governor General's medals at the same time." The University of Toronto generously loaned the hall, but did not allow any admission fee. Instead fifty ushers organized by Amabel King, sold 500 subscriptions to the new magazine, to a full house.

The program was well-paced. Sixteen separate events in two hours. Dr. Edgar occupied three minutes in introductory remarks, National President Leslie Gordon Barnard took five minutes in conclusion to wrap up an appeal for subscriptions, donations or endowment. By choice, Lord Tweedsmuir spoke first, followed by Sir Charles G.D. Roberts, who kept within the allotted six minutes.

Wilson MacDonald, home from Boston for the occasion, read his popular "Song of the Ski." At half-time, a soloist sang Duncan Campbell Scott's "Imogen's Wish" and Millicent Payne's "Dressmakers," musical settings by Leo Smith. After the medals were presented, Prof. George Herbert Clarke of Queen's University read half the award-winning poem; two of Norah Holland's poems set to music by Dr. Healy Willan were sung, followed by short poems by Katherine Hale and Nat Benson. Afterwards, Amabel King entertained in her Forest Hill home for all participants. (Her literary parties were a feature of Toronto society for two decades.)

For the next three years, the Toronto branch staged an annual Poetry Night in the Heliconian Club raising money for the support of the *Canadian Poetry Magazine.* Yet for all the goodwill, *CPM* lurched from crisis to crisis.

E.J. Pratt formulated his policy for the magazine: "It is intended to be a national vehicle of poetic expression, and aims to preserve a sane balance between tradition and experiment. We particularly hope to hear from young writers." He was deluged with verse, good, bad and indifferent, and while accepting the good and best of the indifferent, he leaned away from the versifiers to the modern. Among his contributors were Raymond Souster, Earle Birney, Ralph Gustafson, Leo Cox and Dorothy Livesay.

Pratt stuck it out for eight years. Often the quarterly deficit had to be bailed out by the National Treasurer, who after the war was Dr. Jacob Markowitz. The beloved "Marko" sometimes dipped into his own pocket to make ends meet. When Pratt vacated the editorial chair, Sir Charles G.D. Roberts moved in for a single issue. However, his introduction was to become his obituary. Major A.H. O'Brien, a Toronto lawyer headed the management committee, pulling hard on the purse strings.

While the CAA looked for another altruistic editor, Dr. Watson Kirkconnell shouldered the burden. Later he recalled,

> The editing had to be done with the little finger of my left hand, for I was carrying a full load of teaching, research and publication, and was helping to organize the Humanities Research Council. The best that can be said is that I was keeping the magazine alive when no one else could be found to take it on. Obvious symptoms of my professional incorrigibility were my class-room style editorials on imagery, tempo, pattern, rhythms and tone colour.

Back in Toronto, W.A. Deacon conscripted Prof. Earle Birney just home from the wars and with two Governor General's medals for poetry. Birney allowed himself to be inveigled, having a dream of his own, to print the best poetry available in Canada, and make it known outside as well as inside the country. Birney moved to the University of British Columbia and gathered helpers there. He was proud to print verse by all the young leading poets of the forties — among them Finch, Bruce, Anderson, Waddington, Klein. Some poems in French were published, some Eskimo translations, and he went outside Canada, even to swapping with the London *Outposts*, for which he edited a Canadian issue, and devoted a corresponding issue to English poetry.

Circulation doubled, critics paid attention, but the rank and file subscribers whose magazine it actually was, felt bewildered. This new editor was rejecting their work consistently, and they felt unable to change. Indeed they were reluctant to support a magazine that didn't carry their work, or something equally comprehensible. The end came in two years. Birney wanted to raise the price from two dollars since every new subscription was actually a liability. But the manager back in Toronto refused to budge; was too old to seek advertising or donors, and considered the contents "rubbish."

Said Birney:

> His way was not our way. The Toronto versifiers organized a systematic cancellation of subscriptions within the CAA and sent a steady stream of complaints to the National Executive, and even threatened to drop their membership unless we opened our doors to them and excluded the moderns. When the hostility in the managerial office began to involve book-keeping and payment of certain contributors, I found the situation too exhausting, and too compromising. My staff resigned with me.

Dr. Arthur S. Bourinot (Ottawa) poet, painter, lawyer, took on the task from 1948. He wrote:

> My memories of editing *CPM* are pleasant. I tried to encourage young and unknown writers, some of whom became well known, such as Al Purdy, Arthur Stringer, Goodridge Mac-Donald, Fred Swayze, Sarah Binks (P.G. Hiebert) and a host of others.

Leo Cox (Montreal) succeeded to the post in 1955. He had been associate editor under Pratt and Kirkconnell. Cox felt that poetry needed no garnish of comment or book reviews, but substituted cogent quotations about poetry. His contributors included Miriam Waddington and Fred Cogswell. Associate editor Prof. V.B. Rhodenizer (N.S.) took over in 1957, and held the office for three years, when eye trouble forced him to resign. He was a traditionalist.

Though most of the contributors were women, nearly all the editors of CPM were men. In 1960, a triumvirate of Montreal women volunteered their efforts. Editor Bluebell Phillips and her associates Malca Friedman and Catherine Bagg fought tirelessly for three years to keep the magazine alive on a diminishing budget. It was a hopeless task. Still, there was a bit of life stirring. Dublin-born Pādraig Ō Broin, (Toronto) poet and editor had some experience in editing a poetry magazine of his own, and gave the CAA's problem child his attention. He shortened the title to *Canadian Poetry*, and his aim was to make it of, and about, poetry, not merely competent verse. "Emphasis should be on Canadian writers, for it is they who make the literature by which their country's true achievement will be judged."

Ō Broin "greatly began," but his early death five years later brought an end to the struggle. *CPM* was merged with *CA&B* in 1968 and the poetry limited to about four pages. Peggy Fletcher (Sarnia) and Bernice Lever (Toronto) became Poetry Editor in succession.

Poetry reading and discussion of contemporary poetry were a feature at every convention, and frequently at branch meetings. It was the subject of several controversial addresses at the Vancouver convention of 1936. President Dr. Edgar handled it obliquely in his luncheon address, hosted by the Women's Canadian Club. With his gentle good humour, he said:

> Creative writers are the most egotistic people in the world. Their productions flow from an inexhaustible fountain of self-esteem, and when a critic informs them that they are not impeccable, they fly into a rage, as Tennyson did for ten silent years. Poets, especially are thin-skinned. The dominant need in Canada is for discernment in the evaluation of our output. Some of our critics, chiefly in the academic camp, think that Canadians cannot write, and at the other extreme another group exalts mediocrity far beyond its merits. It makes one wonder whether we wish to be saved from our enemies or from our friends! It is high time, at any rate, that we should pass out of

the parochial stage; our critics must learn to deliver their blows fairly but firmly, and the writers must learn to take their knocks. . . .

The poet and anthologist, A.M. Stephen (Vancouver) was less cheerful.

Poets should practise a healthy self-criticism, of which there is a serious lack.

Why is that true? Why is it possible that the new order of poetry coming to birth in Canada may remain in obscurity? The answer lies with the critics, or rather the dearth of creative criticism in Canada. If the Canadian poet has not an appreciative audience at home or abroad, he must have the field prepared for him by criticism that is creative and constructive. We may search in vain for help and support.

While English authors enjoyed the benefits of criticism emanating from men of culture, Canadians had to endure the extravagant indiscriminating praise, or the unintelligent censure of hack writers imbued with an aggressive Canadianism of the parochial variety.

Or they had to meet the supercilious ignorance of British-born reviewers incapable of seeing outstanding value in anything Canadian — who feel that great art cannot flourish beyond the rumble of a London omnibus.

Stephen censured Toronto reviewers for regionalism, which resulted in the creation of cults centred about the names of eastern writers whom these misguided enthusiasts were determined to force upon the public as paragons of literary excellence. (A voice in the audience murmured "*Toronto delenda est.*")

He slated *Highways of Canadian Literature* by Logan and French and also MacMechan's *Headwaters of Canadian Literature* for opposite reasons. He found flaws of subject matter in Lampman, Carman and Roberts. E.J. Pratt had infused into our poetry a fresh character of red-blooded realism and masculinity. Dorothy Livesay's work showed possibilities.

"Proletarian Poetry" was the title of a talk by Mary Elizabeth Colman (Vancouver) who had found wide acceptance for her traditional verse in Canadian, American and British journals. In a candidly critical but not unsympathetic spirit, she talked of the poetry written by an increasing number of younger poets, stating that much of the day's poetry had as its main preoccupation the present economic and political struggle and offering as solution a romantic Communism.

Poets who had survived the Great War were old, bitter, dissatisfied with the poetic conventions of the past, but incapable of initiating new ones. From the despair and disillusion of the postwar period emerged a new poetic formula — speech rhythms, a new freedom in the handling of metric pattern, a diction closely related to the speech of everyday, the engineering motif in simile and metaphor, a revival of counterpoint and dissonance.

Here then were all the materials for a new poetic convention, when a new cataclysm interrupted the course of events. The young poets arrive at the age of expression at a time of universal unparalleled social and economic distress, when apparently our most trusted institutions have failed — democracy, religion included.

Subjectively speaking, all poetry is escapist. There is only one justification for writing poetry — an irresistible compulsion. It is not surprising then that the youngest generation of poets should turn to Communism as a solution to the world's ills and their own spiritual problem, for it is the revolutionary temperament that is responsible for much of our romantic poetry.

The new poetic convention is not to be sought in the humanistic ideals of Communism or Facism, which have no place in their philosophies for unsubmerged individualistic expression. Poetry must seek some other lodestar — no system of politics will serve."

Colman felt that Dorothy Livesay (Vancouver) had written the most successful poem of the proletarian mode, *Night and Day,* "though it impresses one as a clever piece of rhetorical propaganda, lacking emotional depth." The work of the Montreal Four — Smith, Scott, Klein and Leo Kennedy — was little more than maudlin.

In rebuttal, Dorothy Livesay defended poetic expression of political opinion, remarking that art must embody ideas, otherwise it is spineless. And if it embodies sound ideas, it cannot help being propaganda. We do not write because we want to be smart, but because we are forced to write. We feel that war may come, or fascism. That is why writers have turned away from all the superficial claptrap of other poetry and allied themselves with the progressive movement.

The delegates felt that war of a kind had already come,

mopped their brows and cooled off on a motor launch excursion up Howe Sound.

Chapter 18
Medals and Money

The Governor General's literary awards are still the most prestigious in the country. But they were neither the first nor the greatest to come to Canadian authors. Was an 1886 short story contest sponsored by the *Family Herald* among the earliest? It was won by a twelve-year-old named Lucy Maud Montgomery, living on a Prince Edward Island farm.

It is, of course, impossible to list all the contests noted in the *Canadian Author & Bookman*, their sponsors and winners. What follows is a backward glance at the scattered achievements, principally of the Canadian Authors Association members.

In 1899, Marjorie Pickthall, at sixteen years of age (later of the Victoria branch) took first prize in a *Mail & Empire* poetry competition. Marshall Saunders (Toronto) was a mature scribbler of thirty-two when she entered an 1893 contest sponsored by the American Humane Society for a book "inculcating intelligent sympathy for animals," a second *Black Beauty*, in fact. Saunders won with her *Beautiful Joe*, the first Canadian book to sell over a million copies.

American publishers' competitions brought Canadian authors their first big encouragement. Martha Ostenso rocked the country by winning a fabulous $13,500, in a Dodd Mead-Pictorial Review competition in 1926, with her manuscript *Wild Geese*. Mazo de la Roche did it again the following year by winning $10,000 in the *Atlantic Monthly Press* contest with the durable *Jalna*. Dodd Mead Intercollegiate Literary Fellowship of 1936 was won by Constance Beresford-Howe. She was only twenty-one when she wrote *The Unreasoning Heart*.

That same year Oxford-Crowell awarded $500 to each of two winners — Christine Van der Mark (Edmonton) for *In Due Season*, and Angélique Hango (Montreal) for *Truthfully Yours*. Miss Hango also picked up a Leacock Medal and apparently vanished from the Canadian literary scene. Not so Kathleen Strange (Winnipeg), whose *With the West in Her Eyes* won the McLeod-Dodge award in 1936 and is still being reprinted.

In 1941, the Ryerson Press launched an award of $1,000 for the best fiction submitted during the year. Will Bird (Halifax) won twice, as did Gladys Taylor (Montreal). More substantial bait was dangled by Doubleday in its $10,000 award for outstanding fiction. Arthur Hailey (Toronto) and Thomas Raddall (N.S.) were among the recipients.

The Lorne Pierce Medal, established in perpetuity for "Fellows of the Royal Society . . . or others of conspicuous literary merit" was first presented in 1926, to Dr. Charles G.D. Roberts. Other gold medalists included CAA members D.C. Scott, Bliss Carman, Pelham Edgar, Watson Kirkconnell, Mazo de la Roche, John Murray Gibbon, Bruce Hutchison and Marius Barbeau.

The J.B. Tyrrell Medal for historical writing was won by men like Lawrence Burpee (Ottawa), Judge Howay (Vancouver), J. Clarence Webster (N.S.) and Col. Stacey (Ottawa). Edgar McInnes won the Newdigate Prize in 1924 with *The Road to Arras*, and in 1930 was the first Canadian to accept the Royal Empire Society's gold medal for his book on Lord Durham.

The Canadian Authors Association launched the Governor General's Literary Awards in 1937 for the best books of fiction, non-fiction, poetry/drama published the previous year.

This was not the Association's first link with vice-royalty. Before the CAA was a year old, someone (probably J.M. Gibbon, the first president) approached Government House with the request that Baroness Byng of Vimy, herself an author, would honour the young Association by becoming its Honorary President. Lady Byng graciously accepted, for a Canadian edition of her two light romances *Anne of the Marshland* and *Barriers* had been published. The CAA realized that official duties would not leave their honorary president much time for the colonial literary group. They guessed rightly, for beyond a reception at Rideau Hall to launch the 1922 Book Week, there is no mention of Lady Byng's further interest.

Governor General Lord Willingdon established the Willingdon

Arts Competition. Included in the 1930 regulations were two prizes of $100 each for essays of 5,000 to 7,500 words in English or French on selected historical/literary subjects.

In 1933, former National President Robert J.C. Stead introduced Book Week with a message from the King's representative, Lord Bessborough:

> The Governor General sends his best wishes for the success of Canadian Book Week. He hopes that this movement may stimulate Canadians young and old to read the literature of their own country and thereby develop pride in their national culture which is so essential to the progress of a great people.

Evidently the Bessboroughs were more interested in drama than in books per se, for the Bessborough Trophy was awarded for the best production in the Dominion Drama Festival founded in 1933. Various individuals awarded prizes for the best presentation of a play in English and in French, as well as a hundred dollars to the author of the best presented Canadian play. "There is no doubt that the wisely ambitious work of Lord Bessborough in initiating the Dominion Drama Festival is already having an effect not only on the acting and production of plays, but on the art of writing them," was the opinion of the *Canadian Author*.

The English adjudicator Grenville Barker, on the closing night of one festival in Ottawa, commented to the audience which included Their Excellencies and Prime Minister Mackenzie King:

> It gives me great pleasure that more Canadian plays were entered in the Regional Festivals this year than ever before, and that four of them won through to this final week in Ottawa.
>
> I have pleasure in announcing that the Bessborough Trophy goes to the London Drama League for performance of *Twenty-five Cents*, and also the Sir Barry Jackson Award for the best presentation of a play written by a Canadian. Furthermore, the author W. Eric Harris of Sarnia receives the $100 award for the best play written by a Canadian.

A few years later in 1937, the final adjudicator was a French playwright-actor, who found Canadian dramatists too gloomy. Governor General Lord Tweedsmuir agreed. So did the regional adjudicator, who lamented that he had been witnessing death and disaster on the amateur stage from one end of Canada to the other. Naturally then, their choice of a play written by a Canadian went to

John Coulter of Toronto, for his Irish-Canadian comedy *The House in the Quiet Glen*, which meant that the playwright also took the Jackson Trophy and the hundred dollars. The Bessborough Trophy for best presentation went to the Toronto Masquers, for their production of the same play.

The reporter for the *Ottawa Citizen* had an explanation for the comedy's sweep of prizes: "There is really a shortage of bright and witty one-act plays ... There is the youthful preoccupation with serious themes. The tendency to sombre drama will remain as long as most of the play producers and actors are youthful and the time is out of joint."

Ottawa branch member, Mrs. Roy MacGregor Watt, became chairman of the Canadian Playwriting Competition Committee for Ottawa Little Theatre Workshop, for original one-act plays.

Captain John Buchan had endeared himself to Canadians on an earlier visit to Canada, and proved himself keenly interested in the Canadian Authors Association on the literary tour of 1933. When it was learned that he, now Lord Tweedsmuir, would succeed Lord Bessborough as Canada's next Governor General, the national executive wired congratulations and asked him to become honorary president. Without hestitation, he wired his acceptance, "deeply honoured by the invitation."

Here is how the Governor General Medals came about. Albert H. Robson, author of *Canadian Landscape Painters* and friend to artists of every stripe, as president of the Toronto branch of the CAA queried William Arthur Deacon on practical steps to benefit Canadian authors. Deacon suggested awards. Medals were then in good repute, even without the dollar sign. They meant recognition.

Robson consulted the founding president J.M. Gibbon, and National President Pelham Edgar. In view of Quebec's generous awards to French writers, they suggested the next batch be for writing in English. Edgar recalled John Buchan's strong encouragement of Canadian literature, and believed Lord Tweedsmuir would be happy to endow some medals as further stimulation. The National Executive dusted off the prospectus it had unsuccessfully presented ten years earlier to the Confederation Jubilee Committee, updated it, and Dr. Edgar went off optimistically to Rideau Hall.

Whether there was really "a colossal row" as Kirkconnell guessed, no one will ever know, but certainly John Buchan saw no need to back up his rhetoric with a hundred thousand dollars. All Edgar took home was permission to use the name of the Governor

General's office in perpetuity, provided the Association took full responsibility for financing, judging and all other administration.

Later, Tweedsmuir relented, and offered a gold medal for the best poem appearing in the new CAA quarterly, *Canadian Poetry Magazine*, first published in Dr. Edgar's presidency, and at the same time he would present the Governor General's medals.

To avoid any charge of nepotism, the CAA approached the Royal Society for judges. Several members agreed to take on the task, but they were so dilatory about reaching their decisions that the books selected for judging in 1936, were not awarded until April 1937, by which time one of the authors had died.

Poetry Magazine Night was held in Convocation Hall, Toronto, when Lord Tweedsmuir addressed a full house on the subject of Poetry, followed by sixteen poets reading their own verse. The best single poem appearing in the magazine in its first year was judged "Hymn to the Spirit Eternal," by Prof. George Herbert Clarke of Queen's University, and the winner accepted his gold medal from Lord Tweedsmuir, for the first and only time.

The Governor General's medals were of baser material — bronze. That for non-fiction was awarded posthumously to T.B. Roberton (Winnipeg) for a collection of newspaper essays. Bertram Brooker (Toronto) received the fiction award for *Think of the Earth*. He said later that he had originally entitled it *Candle in the Sun*, but the publisher had changed it because that title had recently been used. Perhaps the indifferent title was to blame, or Brooker was a better art critic than novelist, for the book sold only eight copies.

Lord Tweedsmuir died unexpectedly in 1940. In answer to the Association's telegram of sympathy, Susan Buchan, Lady Tweedsmuir, replied:

> My husband was deeply interested in the work of the Canadian Authors Association, and was so keen to help them in every way that he could. I hope very much that the Canadian Authors will remember how much he was one of them, and will go on with their work encouraged by what he was able to do for them.

Thereafter, most of the Governors General have stood as patrons to the CAA, from the Earl of Athlone in 1940 to His Excellency, the Right Hon. Edward Schreyer at present.

Dissatisfied with the learned judges, the National Executive undertook the judging themselves, farming out the selected books among friends, employees and relatives, anyone who had time to read and comment wisely. Correspondence was heavy, and distributing the books onerous especially in wartime. Costly, too, even at the low postal rates of those days. Since the budget-conscious Association had to foot the bill for designing, casting and material, the medals at first were bronze. In 1942, bronze was reserved for the war effort and the medals went to silver.

(At the National Book Festival presentations in Vancouver in 1979, Dr. Earle Birney, introducing a waggish note to enliven the proceedings, mentioned that he had won two of the early medals presented by a minor organization that did not represent the major authors of Canada. He had wanted to hock them, and taken them to a jeweller for appraisal. "Not worth more than five dollars each," said the expert. But as a member of the Association Birney must have known their worth at the time, for the unimpressive cost had always been itemized in the Treasurer's report.)

In 1943, the drama category was dropped, since it seemed adequately covered by the Dominion Drama Festival, and the non-fiction was split into Creative and Academic. The former medal was awarded to Bruce Hutchison (Victoria) for his *Unknown Country*, the latter going to Edgar McInnes for his *Unguarded Frontier*.

At the 1944 convention in Hamilton, it was decided to set up a standing committee, a board representing the five regions of Canada. This device was hailed with a collective sigh of relief. The chairman of the board would serve five years, the others, three for the sake of continuity, but the personnel would thus change yearly. The board was self-perpetuating, and autonomous, except that any change of policy must be vetted by the National Executive.

The CAA urged its affiliate *La Société des Ecrivains Canadiens* to strike medals for French-Canadian literature. In the meantime translations of French-Canadian writing were honoured. The first was *Thirty Acres* by Ringuet (pseud.) in 1940. Gabrielle Roy won twice, and Germaine Guèvremont with *The Outlander*. At the 1946 convention in Toronto, well-attended by members of *La Société*, the Board offered to share the glory of the medals, *La Société* exercising its own control, but announcing jointly. The offer was declined.

"Why not an award for juvenile books?" some demanded.

The board deliberated, and in 1948 got as far as a citation to Roderick Haig-Brown (Victoria) for *Saltwater Summer*. No medal. No money.

The Awards Board chairman W.A. Deacon reported:

This brings to a head discussion that has been going on for years privately and in the National Executive. The attempt to establish a medal for the year's best juvenile has always been defeated by conservative officers who argued that the value of the present awards would be weakened if any further categories were added, and that there are not enough Canadian juvenile books to ensure a suitable winner, especially with the caution of Miss Lilian H. Smith, Head of Boys and Girls House (she disliked the term "juvenile") who said:

> "The greatest danger is that a committee should feel that an award must be made in a year when no book worthy of one has appeared. The newly-formed Canadian Association of Children's Librarians will give an annual award for an outstanding children's book by an author resident in Canada, but will withhold it if nothing suitable appears."

The problem went into hiding, but resurfaced almost immediately, and a new category Governor General's medal went to R.S. Lambert in 1949 for *Franklin of the Arctic*. This set the historical tone which carried through the next decade to end with *Nkwala* by Edith Lambert Sharp. *Nkwala*, an exceptionally good Indian story, was also first to win the Little, Brown Canadian Children's book award in 1957.

The Canadian Library Association felt compelled to recognize good Canadian writing, and in 1947 the CLA established its bronze Book of the Year medal, (now for both English and French). The first medal went to Roderick-Haig Brown for *Starbuck Valley Winter*, still a prime favourite. He took another for *The Whale People* in 1964. Books of Indian legends have been popular choices, and modern subjects are still shunned. The CLA regrets that its medals are still not accompanied by a cheque. Yet authors admit that the repeated listing of a title guarantees not immortality perhaps, but at least long shelf-life.

A good year for authors of juveniles was 1962. Macmillan launched the *Buckskin Books*, a series of short historical fiction. The preliminary competition was won by Adelaide Leitch's *Great Canoe*, Lorrie McLaughlin's *West to the Cariboo*, and Beulah G. Swayze's *Father Gabriel's Cloak*, all of Toronto branch. All continued writing, and Macmillan continued the series for some years. That same year, Gage held its "Writing for Young Canada" contest. Two anthologies, entitled *Nunnybag* and *Rubaboo* edited by Helen Morrison left the librarians cold, the publisher poorer and many writers richer by $300 per item.

Also, Vicky Metcalf (Toronto), author of *Journey Fantastic*, generously launched her annual award of $1,000, administered by the CAA, not for a single title, but for a body of work inspirational to Canadian youth.

> The prize is given solely to stimulate writing for children. We do not have enough children's books that are written by Canadians, and I do not think we should lag so far behind the United States in this respect. The prize is intended for a number of strictly children's books by any Canadian author. The books may be fiction, non-fiction or even picture books. There is no set formula.

A reporter's snigger watered down "inspirational" to "of interest to." But the intent remained the same. Mrs. Metcalf meant to encourage wholesome social and moral values. The prize went first in 1963 to Kerry Wood of Red Deer, Alberta, author of *Wild Winter* and many other books for young people. It has been awarded every year since, a truly impressive total. One winner bought an electric typewriter, another a new furnace, another financed a field trip to India. All continued to write books that won favour with young Canadians, thus fulfilling Vicky Metcalf's purpose.

Then in 1979, to encourage writers of shorter fiction, Mrs. Metcalf presented an additional award of $500 for "the best short story published in a Canadian children's periodical or anthology during the previous year." It was first won by Marina McDougall (Toronto) for "The Kingdom of Riddles," and by Estelle Salata (Hamilton) in 1980 for "Blind Date," both in Holt Rinehart anthologies for young readers.

The Awards Board alone knew the identity of judges scattered across the country. When authors wondered where to submit their books for judging, they were told simply, "You don't submit — they pick the likely titles and get sample copies from the publishers." Even the judges in the same category didn't know who the other judges were. This was found advisable to prevent any individual from being pressured. In the event of a tie, the Executive was called in. In fact, it was rumored that on one occasion the girl-in-the-office cast the die for one competitor "because he's such a nice man." Maybe.

267

At the outstanding Toronto convention of 1946, Governor General and Lady Alexander were honoured guests. An official reception was held, at which the award winners and the National Executive were presented to Their Excellencies. In presenting the medals, Lord Alexander began:

> I am thankful that Mr. Gibbon who is with us tonight and Mr. Leacock did not follow the advice of another illustrious writer, Thomas Macaulay, when they founded the Canadian Authors Association. Macaulay said that he detested all such associations, and that the less authors had to do with each other, the better it would be. That is not necessarily true, of course. Your work has been judged by your peers and not found wanting. You have created something which is a tribute to your art and a contribution to Canadian literature.

Hugh MacLennan (Fiction) replied briefly and graciously. Evelyn Richardson (Creative Non-fiction) said: "These three days have been most exciting to a lightkeeper. I'm sure I will think it all a dream." Earle Birney (Poetry) said: "I would like to express something of the honour I feel on this occasion. I am deeply grateful to the judges who have twice honoured me ... Finally, I am more honoured than I can express to receive the medal in person from Your Excellency." Mrs. Munro accepted the medal for her foreign correspondent son, Ross Munro.

Some awards were very localized, such as the Lady Eaton prizes for short lengths, administered by the CAA Winnipeg branch, and the Hudson's Bay Co. "Beaver" Trophy and $500 for an unpublished manuscript, adult or juvenile, administered by the Edmonton branch, not to mention the various awards of the IODE, provincial and municipal. In Alberta, Barbara Villy Cormack's *Local Rag* and Audrey McKim's *Lexy O'Connor* (both Edmonton) tied in 1952, and the IODE awarded two prizes of $200.

Since the Governor General's Awards Board seemed to have a workable set-up and had developed so much expertise, other bodies came seeking assistance. The first such independent award entrusted to the G.G. Board was that of the Stephen Leacock medal for humor, donated by the town of Orillia at the suggestion of William Arthur Deacon, literary editor of the *Globe and Mail*.

The silver medal designed by sculptor Emmanuel Hahn was first presented at a dinner in Orillia in 1946. W.A. Deacon spoke:

> In establishing this special prize, the surviving friends of

Stephen Leacock have done Canada a great service. Canadian writers as a whole are deadly serious; and this is strange in a country that has produced famous humorists for a century.... We need a group of writers who will be amusing, whether as idle recreation, or with the desire to teach, as in satire. Canada needs to laugh oftener, and this monument to a great humorist should encourage more writers to see and express the funny side of life.

The medal has done just that. The first winner was Harry L. Symons with *Ojibway Melody*, a volume of word-sketches of life on Georgian Bay seen through the eyes of a summer visitor. The humor is gentle, friendly rather than satirical. The judges agreed without a dissenting vote, and the awarding of 1946 was unique in its unanimity.

Certainly there were disagreements among the judges, in spite of the point system and the anonymity. And there were complaints after the decisions, of course. Deacon, first chairman of the Board could report of 1946 winners:

For the first time there were no protests that medals went to inferior books while superior books failed to win. We got two protests once that Gwethalyn Graham's *Earth and High Heaven* was an immoral book. We ignored letters from non-writers.

(A detail about those medals which Lord Alexander presented in 1946 is that, due to the dawdling of the first set of judges, medals were engraved with the date of presentation. The medalists of 1946 preferred to have the engraving record the year of publication, so that two sets of medals bore the date 1945.)

When in 1949, W.A. Deacon had served his five years as chairman of the Board, Franklin Davy McDowell was chosen to succeed him. He wired a reluctant "Not me!" But he was cajoled into office with all its petty deliberations, and it expanded under him.

Scott Young, president of the Toronto branch in 1950 made the suggestion that the short story should be recognized by the Board as an art form. Young was selling consistently to high-paying American slicks, and was in no way self-seeking. "But hardly as Governor General's Awards," came the protest. "We're splintered enough now. Why, that would inevitably lead to awards for an article, even a single poem!"

Shortly afterwards, Young had occasion to speak with Dr. G.E. Hall, president of the University of Western Ontario, and expounded his theme. Dr. Hall was known to be keenly interested in Canadian writing, and after some correspondence, in 1951 he inaugurated The President's Medals for the Short Story, Article, and Single Poem. The response was overwhelming, and Dr. Hall found that he had to divide the Article category into Popular and Scholarly.

For some years, the medals were presented at what came to be known as the Awards Dinner, the finale of each CAA convention. One UWO professor too often delegated to make the presentations, was heard to mutter to his dinner companion at head table, that he was embarrassed at having to present only medals. In fact, he would refuse to perform next year. "Why, we don't even offer winners their fare to pick up the prize." The following year, the Association of Canadian Magazine Publishers donated $250 to accompany each medal.

The year 1951 also marked the inauguration of the University of British Columbia medal for popular biography written by a Canadian citizen. President Norman A.M. MacKenzie had long felt the lack of an award which would draw attention of Canadians to their own outstanding citizens past and present, and said so in print. He was ripe for Dr. W.G. Hardy's suggestion that the university might rectify the omission by awarding an annual medal.

That same year, Dr. Hardy, who had brought great credit upon the University of Alberta not only by his lectures on the Greeks and Romans as well as popular radio talks on Classical subjects, but also by his novels, short stories and radio dramas, spurred President Dr. Andrew Stewart into originating the University of Alberta award for Distinguished Contribution to Canadian Letters. The gold medal was presented for the first time at the 1951 CAA convention in Banff to Mazo de la Roche, Toronto's prolific novelist. Though this award came entirely under the jurisdiction of the University of Alberta, both the CAA National President and the chairman of the Board were consulted. As with the Lorne Pierce gold medal and the Vicky Metcalf Award, the prize was not for a single volume but for a sustained output.

By 1952, the Awards Board was being entrusted with a dozen literary awards, a tremendous load of voluntary effort, even though it insisted on one of the judges being a member of the donor organization.

Small wonder that Franklin McDowell was happy when his term ended in 1954, and he could shuffle the burden on to Dr.

Frank Stiling (London) of the University of Western Ontario. Dr. Stiling found it increasingly difficult to find judges prepared to devote their leisure time to assessing books, gratis. Or indeed to spend that effort on behalf of winners who didn't even show up to receive their medals. Not one was present at the 1958 convention. And who was available to serve as next chairman?

Since the Board had been self-perpetuating for fifteen years, Stiling forgot or ignored its obligations to the Canadian Authors Association. He did not contact the National President H. Gordon Green (Montreal) but when his term ended in 1959, went in despair directly to the Canada Council with a request for $2,000 to accompany each medal, and some stipend for administration. The Canada Council gave polite attention, then brought forth a counter-proposal. The Council was prepared to fund the medals to the tune of $1,000 each and take on the administration if the Board would surrender the Governor General's Literary Awards completely.

Dr. Stiling, already ill (he died not much later) agreed, and apparently turned over his files to a new Governor General's Literary Awards Committee funded by the Canada Council. Chairman Douglas Grant, reporting on the first year of the re-organization in 1960, said:

> Credit for the inception of these medals belongs entirely to the Canadian Authors Association, whose initiative conferred a great boon on Canadian letters, both in helping to stimulate the writers themselves and in encouraging a deeper interest among the general public.
>
> I am doubtful whether money can add to the intrinsic honour of such awards, but as our society has chosen to measure success by its standard, it has been a disadvantage in the eyes of many that they were confined to a medal which could not be decently disposed of.

The awards were cut back from five to three — fiction, non-fiction and poetry — and doubled to include French in each category. In 1975, the children's award was resumed, in both languages, and extended to illustrators of children's books. Bill Freeman of Toronto was the first recipient, with *Shantymen of Cache Lake*. The accompanying cheques swelled to $5,000.

Some members of the Canadian Authors Association, unaware of the background events, were resentful that the Canada Council had "snatched" the Governor General's Awards. That was not precisely the case.

H. Gordon Green wrote:

> I was National President of the CAA when the transfer was made, with neither the consent nor prior knowledge of the Association. However, I think I can say that the feeling of the membership was generally in favour of the change. It seemed to me that the Association had not lost any prestige by the move, and felt a measure of pride that the awards we had created were still the highest that Canada had to offer, and that a cheque would now go out with each.

Any contest can expect gripes when the results are announced — the selection of winners, the lack of publicity or follow-up. They plagued the new administrators as they had the Canadian Authors Association. One year Margaret Laurence's splendid *Stone Angel* was by-passed, and critics raised such a furor that the following year she was accorded the honour for a lesser work. Some Quebecois authors refused to accept the honour, declaring that to do so would be to acknowledge "foreign rule" since the Governor General was the representative of Her Britannic Majesty.

Should the name of the awards be changed? Medalists with a feeling for tradition protested vigorously. Yet when awards for children's books resumed, they were designated "Canada Council" awards. Medals were scuttled early and replaced by a specially-bound copy of the author's book.

The award-giving ceremony took place in Rideau Hall, where television cameras were not permitted. So in 1980, the ceremony formed part of the National Book Festival held in Vancouver. Another departure from custom was the advance announcement of the "short list" of contending books, in the hope of generating more attention and public speculation.

The selections made during the thirty-three years in which the Canadian Authors Association administered the G.G. awards have stood up fairly well. Many of the titles are still in print, and the authors did continue to produce publishable material.

Hugh MacLennan took the record, winning five medals. Triple winners have been Bruce Hutchison, E.J. Pratt, Thomas Raddall and James Reaney. Double winners make a longer list: Marjorie Wilkins Campbell, N.J. Berrill, Pierre Berton, Earle Birney, J.M.S. Careless, D.G. Creighton, R.M. Dawson, Robert Finch, Gwethalyn Graham, John F. Hayes, Douglas LePan, Dorothy Livesay, A.R.M.

Lower, Edgar McInnes, Gabrielle Roy, Laura Salverson, David Walker and Kerry Wood. Of 134 awards presented over the years, only 27 have gone to women.

Medals with honour but no cash have been part of Canadian literary history. The Leacock Memorial medal has been presented annually since 1947, though humor is not believed to be a Canadian strong point. Paul Hiebert's *Sarah Binks* of 1948 has proved durable. Eric Nicol won the silver medal at least thrice. After winning with *Shall We Join the Ladies?*, he said, "I will," and went off on a honeymoon. A medal is not to be despised. Time and again, the medalist has gone on to win a cash award or another contract from a book thus highlighted.

Evelyn Richardson's *We Keep a Light* won a Governor General's medal, and her next volume, *Desired Haven* took a Ryerson Press award as did Joan Walker, winner of a Leacock medal. Colin McDougall expanded a prize-winning short story into *The Execution*, received the G.G. medal for fiction, and topped off with a Beta Sigma Phi award of $1,000. Adele Wiseman's *The Sacrifice* took a Governor General's medal in 1956, plus the Beta Sigma Phi, and won a fellowship of $2,700 from the Canada Foundation.

In 1973, the Canadian Authors Association, feeling that the books winning the Governor General's Literary Awards "were apt to appeal to a relatively small and supposedly select readership, being frequently academic and arty rather than popular," passed a resolution:

> Since this Association is comprised largely of writers who hope to communicate with a wide and varied audience, and since the original awards were instituted in the belief that literary excellence and popular appeal are entirely compatible,
>
> Therefore be it resolved that this Association originate a set of prizes to be known as the Canadian Authors Association Awards: these to be medals or any other trophy the Executive may select. Carried.

In 1975, the CAA Awards were a reality — a handsome silver medal bearing a modernistic owl design plus $1,000, funded by Harlequin Enterprises Limited of Toronto. They applied in four categories:

1. Prose fiction
2. Prose non-fiction
3. Poetry
4. Drama (for any medium)

and stipulated:

> Entries should be submitted by December 31 of the year of publication, with five copies of the work. The awards may be won only once by an individual writer in any category. The trustees may choose not to make an award in any one year, if submissions are unsatisfactory.

Among the winners have been Jane Rule's *The Young in One Another's Arms* (fiction); Bruce Hutchison's *The Far Side of the Street* (Non-fiction); Alden Nowlan's *Smoked Glass* (Poetry); and Rex Deverell's *Boiler Room Suite* (Drama). See Appendix IV for the complete list.

The Drama selection was the most difficult, and no award has been given where too few plays of suitable calibre have been submitted for judging. But on the whole, the CAA Awards form a worthy alternative to the Governor General's.

Chapter 19
The Offbeat Generation

The sixties was a peculiar time in most lives, it seems. What with sit-ins, teach-ins, love-ins, hippies and flower children, a "quiet revolution" in Quebec, computers muscling in, women's lib, and a host of novelties enough to spin the heads of a senior generation, it was a lively decade. By comparison, the soaring cost of paper and printing seemed thoroughly comprehensible, though it almost capsized the *Canadian Author & Bookman*. Editor Joe Holliday (Toronto) had turned it into a highly readable little magazine, chock full of interesting articles and snippets of information. Not so long-hair as some of his predecessors, he grew into the job, having taken on the task of business manager soon after he joined the Association — soliciting advertisements, handling subscriptions and keeping track of printers.

When Dr. Bourinot's year ended, Holliday reluctantly became editor at a stipend of one hundred dollars per quarter. This editorial sideline meshed with his daily work as editor of a company publication. He was able to obtain cuts at little cost, and the *CA&B* was illustrated as never before with snapshots taken at conventions. But it seriously interfered with his fiction writing. He wrote a dozen *Dale of the Royal Mounted* series, and some others.

Holliday's editorial policy was: "Craft aid, healthy critique and exciting controversy." Sometimes the latter annoyed the membership — one member wrote a nineteen-page letter denouncing the editor's disparagement of Communist propaganda techniques. Holliday gave pages to attacking vanity publishing. He offended advertisers (book publishers) when he ran a gripe by Joan Walker, author of *Pardon my Parka*. She had been complaining about her book contract, and Holliday said, "Write that down!" and ran it as it came. She sarcastically advised:

> Don't Sign that Printed Contract. A publisher is in business to make a profit. Naturally he sends the author the worst possible contract he can dream up in the fond hope that the author will be fool enough to sign it without argument. An author is only competent to deal directly with a publisher provided he is a shrewd businessman who knows all the legal ins and outs of contracts. In short, you need an agent. He or she fully earns the ten percent charged.

(However, she later admitted that one agent had not lifted a finger for her.)

The editor gratuitously added boxed advice

Never Sign a Contract That . . .

1) does not give advance royalties, non-returnable
2) gives the publisher an option on the same terms
3) does not provide bi-yearly accounting
4) asks for more than Canadian book rights
5) allows a publisher more than 10% for selling subsidiary rights.

He should have added a No. 6 — does not include a publication date.

Courteous John Gray of Macmillan did not appreciate Walker's wit nor Holliday's strictures (nor did Dr. Lorne Pierce of Ryerson Press) considering them a slur on *all* publishers. He cancelled his membership in the CAA, Macmillan advertising in the *CA&B*, and apparently influenced other publishers to do the same. Marjorie Wilkins Campbell wrote to say that any writer intelligent enough to write a publishable book would surely have the sense to consult a lawyer before signing. (Few lawyers even today are skilled at understanding book contracts.) Two literary agents wrote in enthusiastic praise of the article. But the piece lost publisher friends — and their advertising.

Slightly repentant, Holliday offered to set up a contracts committee to meet with a publishers' committee for full discussion. He gathered a dozen contracts and made a chart, comparing them clause by clause with the Standard Contract devised by Gwethalyn Graham's committee of a decade before. Though several of his own suggestions were proved unworkable, the chart saved many a tyro from eagerly signing an unsatisfactory contract.

Thus in 1960, the magazine had to retrench, and went to mimeograph format for several issues, to the editor's disgust. He was anxious to get back to writing fiction, which had had to be laid aside for several years, and finally made his resignation stick. Lieut. H.R. Percy (Ottawa) having retired from the Navy, believed he could combine editorial work with short story writing. Percy had a different conception of what the magazine should be: more literary, more formal, less editorial opinion, less membership news. One memorable article in 1964 was a survey of the Public Lending Right and how it operated in Scandinavian countries.

This information had an immediate effect on the CAA membership, especially some in the Toronto branch. The subject had come up before in the Association, but only fleetingly, when A.P. Herbert attempted to get such legislation passed in England in the 1940s. Now Carol Wilson and Lyn Harrington, talked and wrote articles on the subject. They wrote letters to the Canada Council and to the Secretary of State. They compiled a brief and read it, with Wm. Repka (Toronto) and Don Thomson (Ottawa) to the Interdepartmental Committee on Copyright in Ottawa, and also presented it to Ontario's Royal Commission on Book Publishing.

They roused interest within the Copyright Institute, though all agreed that copyright was not the correct spot for the proposal. (In copyright, by the terms of the Berne Convention, such payment for the use of books in public libraries would necessarily apply to all authors, not merely nationals.) Their recommendations included:

> That a Board or Secretariat be set up to administer a Federal Fund established to annually recompense Canadian authors for the use of their books in Canadian libraries.

> Payments from the fund could be based on the holdings in libraries, or more expensively, on the actual circulation or reference use of individual titles. Figures would be based on a sampling system, at no cost to the libraries.

> We believe firmly in libraries. Equally we believe the author earns an income he is not getting. When a book is used by many readers, it is gross injustice that the author's only remuneration is the original ten percent royalty from his publisher. The author is forced into the role of public benefactor.

> Payments from the Federal Fund should be used exclusively for

277

the use of books written by nationals. Imports could scarcely come within this plan, for the Fund would then support far more outside authors than Canadian, and any reverse flow would be a mere trickle.

In April 1965, as part of Book Week, the CAA Toronto branch and the Toronto Public Library jointly sponsored a panel discussion on Authors' Lending Rights (now re-named Compensation for Authors).

In preparation for the 1965 convention in Vancouver, delegates were asked to make a preliminary survey in their local libraries on five books of fiction written by authors in disparate parts of Canada. Assuming a fee of (a) two cents per circulation (you could in those days count circulation by the date due stampings) or (b) count the copies listed in the card catalogue at, say fifty cents per holding. For example:

(a) Raddall, Thomas *Wings of the Night*. Retail price $4.25, therefore royalty from publisher 42¼¢. One copy had circulated 49 times. @ 2¢ per issue, the author would have earned .98, that is more than twice the royalty.

(b) MacLennan, Hugh *Watch that Ends the Night*. 7 copies. Retail price $3.95. Royalty on each therefore 39½¢. On those copies the author would have received $2.93 in royalties. $3.50 does not seem too great an extra.

The delegates gave good attention and applauded the notion and the idealism of the progenitors. But the authorities continued unimpressed; and the librarians, with mistaken visions of endless niggling bookkeeping, actively opposed it. The campaign faltered, until taken up in 1973 by the Writers' Union (est. in 1972) and the hope of realization was quickened. However, it was not until 1978 that the Canada Council recognized the strength of the demand.

A full-page advertisement in Percy's Summer 1965 issue also brought results. Headed "Freedom Under Fire," Gwethalyn Graham (Montreal), co-author of *Dear Enemies*, launched an appeal on behalf of Jacques Hébert, writer and publisher of Montreal. He had published his indiscreet book, *I Accuse the Assassins of Coffin*, convinced that Wilbert Coffin had not got a fair trial twelve years previously. Hébert was fined $3,000 and thirty days in jail for contempt of court. Graham, a member of the Committee of Appeal composed of twenty-one associations, wrote:

> Whether Hébert is guilty or innocent is not for us to decide. But we protest against the fact that he was prosecuted with exceptional procedure, arbitrary in form and inquisitorial in nature.
>
> From the moment an Attorney General chooses to prosecute a citizen for something he has written, by means of a process odious in itself and an outrage to the basic rights of man, the principle of freedom of expression is at stake. It is for this reason that we are asking the help of everyone concerned.

The Canadian Authors Association became the twenty-second organization to support the Appeal. Similarly in 1980, when Toronto writer Ian Adams was sued for supposedly basing his book *"S": Portrait of a Spy* on a living individual, the CAA and several branches contributed to the defence fund raised by the Writers' Union, believing that freedom of expression was in jeopardy. Hébert's two books on the Coffin trial had a wider impact than their sales indicated. Many Canadians felt there had not been sufficient evidence to justify a hanging, and undoubtedly this had an effect in rescinding the death penalty in Canada.

H.R. Percy stayed with the *CA&B* for four years, until he too found editorial deadlines cutting too deeply into his free time, which he wanted to spend in writing novels, and in fact did so successfully after laying down the blue pencil. Under Percy, the magazine was enlarged to *Time* dimensions, thus reversing the usual trend.

He was succeeded by the dynamic Gladys Taylor (Montreal), author of *Pine Roots*, and a past national secretary, the first woman editor in the quarterly's forty-six years. She discovered:

> Critics try to pigeonhole the *Canadian Author & Bookman* — as a literary magazine, as a craft organ, as a dilettante's gossip column. They are irritated when it defies typing. But it can never be strictly literary because in addition to its academic and Byronic members, the CAA numbers self-taught humorists, folk poets, limerick writers.
>
> It can never be strictly craft-oriented because its professional playwrights, novelists and journalists rub shoulders with amateurs and romantics. It can never be strictly dilettantish because one-poem hangers-on are far outnumbered by its prolific and/or best-selling authors.

> To be the house organ of a professorial-professional-dilettante group such as the Canadian Authors Association, it must have a slightly maverick personality. This has been both its strength and its weakness. Its longevity against staggering financial odds has made it a challenge.

Taylor drummed up advertising, as well as planning the contents and carrying a tremendous load of correspondence (without a secretary). Under her brief regime, the magazine grew in bulk as well as in circulation and interest particularly the four numbers celebrating the centennial year in 1967. Rather than reinstate branch news, Taylor badgered members across the country into becoming by-liners. When she moved to Alberta to found a publication of her own, so did the *CA&B*, but not together.

Dr. John W. Chalmers (Edmonton) author of *Horseman in Scarlet*, pinch-hit during the year when *Canadian Poetry* was absorbed into the *Canadian Author & Bookman* as an economy measure. Chalmers filled the post until the editorship could be taken over by Mary Dawe and Marjorie Morgan (Edmonton). Dawe continued in office until 1975, producing a consistently interesting magazine full of practical advice. When she left for the more lucrative editorship of *Alberta Heritage*, Duncan Pollock (Toronto) volunteered. Pollock, a teacher of creative writing courses, naturally envisioned the magazine as a teaching tool, a beginners' manual, a Canadian equivalent to the *Writers' Digest*, though lacking the latter's financial resources. Pollock, too, lasted four years, and when he resigned in 1980, again two women took over the editorial helm, both experienced in magazine production. Sybil Marshall and Bernice Lever (Toronto) had complementary talents.

Another CAA publication which had its origin in the 1961 convention in Toronto, experienced fewer vicissitudes. A stirring appeal was made for members to "put shoulder to the wheel" or at least come up with new ideas. Lyn Harrington, president of the branch though a fairly new member, proposed a Canadian market list for writers, and was promptly saddled with the job. Harrington's notion was that each branch would send in information of the local magazine field, an Association service that might even prove profitable.

And so it happened. The first edition appeared in 1962, forty-three mimeographed pages of detailed information that sold for a dollar. Its western information was channelled through Margaret

Johnston (Edmonton) and Betty Millway (Vancouver); eastern came through Helen Claire Howes (Montreal) and Marjorie Major (Halifax). This edition in its first year netted the Association $532. Nobody got paid, of course.

Lorrie McLaughlin (Hamilton), prolific author of children's books, edited and enlarged the second edition three years later. There was no intention of making the publication annual, partly from the labour point of view, mostly because the Canadian literary marketplace did not change greatly in the course of a year. The third, fourth, fifth and sixth editions of the *Canadian Writer's Guide* were researched and edited by M. Carol Wilson (Toronto) and Harrington. When they flagged, Betty Ross (Toronto) was asked to take on the chore, which she did admirably for the seventh and eighth editions.

Each edition more than paid its way, thanks to the volunteer effort. Since the returns were slender, no one was paid (originally all contributors were members). Bill Repka led a small delegation to the Ontario Arts Council and presented the case. To the happy astonishment of the editors, the OAC generously underwrote payment for contributors from the fifth to the eighth editions. A trade publisher, Fitzhenry & Whiteside, was found eager to accept the project, with results satisfactory to both parties, and greatly to the benefit of beginning writers across the country. Occasionally an item such as income tax, has been so valuable as to bear reprinting.

The 1961 convention in Toronto was memorable for many details, in spite of last-minute uncertainties. Perhaps the highlight was the luncheon address by Margaret Cousins, fiction editor of *McCall's Magazine,* and a hard-hitting, down-to-earth, witty as well as kind speaker. It took place at the Granite Club, thanks to the good graces of Lady Eaton (Toronto). During the course of her talk, Cousins singled out Sheila Burnford in the audience, whom no one knew until then, and informed the dazzled audience that never had the magazine experienced such reader response as it had to Burnford's novelette, *The Incredible Journey.* Or the highlight may have been the talk at the Awards banquet by Dr. Wilder Penfield (Montreal) author of *The Torch*, the banquet at which Burnford and Jean Little of Guelph received awards.

In 1962, the CAA Convention returned to Edmonton, where the outstanding speaker was Arthur Hailey (Toronto), author of *Flight into Danger* and many best-sellers since. An unusual and interesting panel was labelled "Toss us an Idea." John Patrick

Gillese, author of *Kirby's Gander* and literally thousands of articles and short stories, chaired the panel along with Dr. W.G. Hardy and H.R. Percy (Ottawa). The audience offered ideas for articles, which the panel developed in various ways for which they then suggested markets. Very stimulating.

Earlier that year, the Association was startled and somewhat bewildered when Walter Herbert of the Canada Foundation asked the CAA branches to play host to a UNESCO guest from the Ukraine, poet Alexander Pidsukha. Members across the country opened their homes and hospitality to the stranger, though they heard later that the Mounties had lost track of him for a week in Winnipeg. There had been considerable alarm at the Association being infiltrated by Communists, both crypto and avowed, during the dismal thirties, and particularly after the USSR had turned against the Nazis, and become an ally. But they made few converts. Indeed, the Governor General's Awards Board honoured defector Igor Gouzenko with the medal for non-fiction in 1954 for his *The Fall of a Titan.*

The 1963 convention in Ottawa was startled by a resolution that the CAA deplored the firing of Pierre Berton by *Maclean's Magazine* because of a controversial column on sex. Well, hadn't the CAA annually opposed censorship? From that resolution on, the capital city convention was "well in orbit" as the press put it.

The press showed less interest in the more important resolution that Canada should ratify accession to the Universal Copyright Convention, which had been hanging fire for some years. This resolution was moved by Gordon V. Thompson (Toronto) who as a music publisher had a vested interest in better copyright protection.

While Dr. George Hardy (Edmonton), chairman of the CAA's Centennial Committee gave his report, Thompson's mind turned toward the music of a century earlier. In 1860, the maple leaf had been adopted as Canada's floral emblem in Toronto. Alexander Muir, a young Toronto schoolmaster wrote "The Maple Leaf Forever!" and its catchy music, and sent them to a contest for patriotic songs in Montreal. Muir's entry came in second to a forgotten song about Ontario, and fetched him fifty dollars which he spent on having a thousand copies printed. He made about four dollars profit though the song caught on and was sung everywhere in the days before musical copyright. The song was taught in public schools. Thompson had learned it as a child, liked the tune, but thought the words too jingoistic for a later day. A renewal of the melody might be a meaningful contribution to Canada's hundredth birthday.

"But it would need new words," he said in conversation with Dr. Hardy. "Why not hold another contest, open to all Canadians? And make it a CAA project?"

Thompson agreed. He had done well with such patriotic songs as "O Canada," "There'll Always be an England," "Carry On" and other wartime favourites. He decided to offer as a prize, a $1,000 advance on royalties.

At a press conference, Thompson told reporters:

> You may have wondered why "The Maple Leaf Forever!," which was formerly regarded almost as Canada's national anthem, is not heard very much these days. The old song has a stirring martial air and should be one of Canada's best patriotic songs if a suitable lyric were written to Alexander Muir's music.

> On account of the references to wartime achievements such as the capture of Quebec, the song is not in harmony with Canada's thinking today.

> The Canadian Authors Association believes that a new lyric could be written that will help unite our country from coast to coast. Consequently our Association is sponsoring a contest for the best lyric submitted of stirring inspirational quality that can be sung by Canadians everywhere.

> It should appeal to New Canadians from all lands, as well as those of English and French descent. The lyric should be suitable for schools, churches and public occasions. The words should be simple, forceful and easily adaptable to the melody of "The Maple Leaf Forever!"

It was easy to sort through the 1,280 entries and cast out submissions obviously unsuitable, but more difficult to make the final choice. Representative adjudicators included Sir Ernest Macmillan, then probably Canada's most distinguished name in music; Dr. Helmut Blume, Dean of the Faculty of Music, McGill University; Dr. Helen Creighton, CAA National President and a well-known authority on folk songs.

The contest closed on May 24, 1964, and the judges' choice fell on "Our Home, our Land, our Canada," by Victor Cowley, a young poet of Ottawa. It was first sung at the Awards Luncheon in Wolfville, N.S. by Leonard Mayoh, head of the vocal department of

Acadia University:

> Our fathers came across the sea
>> Seeking peace and liberty
> To settle on this virgin land
>> Where all men can be free.
> Raise high our flag, our banners wave,
>> Let free men stand together
> United in our praise of thee
>> "The Maple Leaf Forever!"

Refrain:

> Our home, our land, our Canada
>> May we forsake thee never,
> But hold on high and proudly fly
>> "The Maple Leaf Forever!"

> Our rivers, lakes and mountain scene
>> Prairie acres, forests green —
> A wondrous land where Nature's hand
>> In its beauty can be seen;
> From east to west our land is blest
>> With men of high endeavour —
> Our voices ring and proudly sing
>> "The Maple Leaf Forever!"

> With flags unfurled from all the world
>> Can with native pride be flown,
> Where freedom's call is heard by all
>> And where brotherhood is shown.
> From end to end all races blend
>> To share this land together,
> From shore to shore forever more —
>> "The Maple Leaf Forever!"

At this 1964 convention, Dr. Creighton was succeeded as National President by Dr. R.S. Longley of Acadia University, author of a biography. Often he seemed bemused by what he had got into, but that was due to encroaching deafness.

Longley may have been grateful for that disability when he presided over the final banquet of the 1965 conference (the more dignified term was adopted in Vancouver) held in Victoria. After an interminable professorial speech during which several heads nodded, diners were electrified by a second speech from Roderick Haig-Brown (Victoria). The dinner was hosted by the provincial government, but Haig-Brown, arch-conservationist and nature-lover, used the occasion to blast the government for its forestry and land-use policies. Ever so embarrassing!

Quite different was the embarrassment suffered by the Winnipeg conveners of the 1966 conference, one of the best ever. It began with an eye-catching announcement so glamorous that it raised panic in the cost-conscious national executive, until it learned that the beautiful folder was a donation. Intriguing titles for the lectures piqued the most sluggish interest. "Naked with Beads on" proved a vibrant talk on modern poetry by Dr. Maara Haas. To this convention again came an uninvited individual, a middle-aged woman handing out race-hate literature. She was promptly invited to leave.

Dr. Hardy (Edmonton) gave a progress report on various CAA Centennial projects, on which planning had begun years previously. The Canadian Authors Association put a great deal into celebrating Canada's centenary. Every branch created a Centennial project of its own, such as the annotated list of Nova Scotia authors compiled in Halifax. Toronto was compiling a roster of writers, Dominion-wide, while Dr. Hardy planned a cross-country literary competition among students.

For funding, all projects had to go before the Centennial Commission, headed by John Fisher (Toronto). Neither the roster nor the competition was approved. But the Commission did approve individual projects by various members. It enthusiastically approved the idea of an anthology of Canadian writings in French and English intermingled. Dr. Guy Sylvestre, parliamentary Librarian and president of the affiliated *La Société des Ecrivains Canadiens*, was in charge of the selection of French writings; H. Gordon Green, fiction editor of *The Family Herald*, agreed to receive submissions in English from a selection committee, who chose fiction, non-fiction and poetry. Cdr. C.H. Little (Ottawa), fluently bilingual, acted as liaison. *A Century of Canadian Literature/Un Siècle de Littérature Canadienne* was published by the Ryerson Press early in 1967.

Green noted in the English foreword:

> We could not hope to offer more than a random sampling of our literary achievement. Our search was not only for authors of outstanding accomplishment, but for those who had some special ability to tell us what manner of man we Canadians were and how we got that way....

We have included writers whose appeal has been to the millions rather than to the professors. About half our space has been given over to writers of the last quarter-century. Not only have the earlier Canadian writers been honoured adequately by other anthologies, but there seems little doubt that what has been written in this country since 1940 will one day be regarded as more important by far than anything which preceded it.

The anthology was as well received by critics as any anthology could hope. It soon went into second printing, and was adopted for use by sundry CanLit college courses.

The forty-sixth annual meeting of the Canadian Authors Association took place in Montreal on the site of Expo 67. Everyone wanted to see this remarkable project — what better venue for the 1967 conference? The Rev. Fred Wilkes, Montreal branch president, acted as convention convener. He had soaring visions of a spectacular Universal Writers Congress. But where would he find the funds? He knew his project would require a mountain of correspondence, waiting around for answers, probably some travel, and much courage.

As a result, Wilkes' progress reports to the National Executive were exceptionally vague while he waited for responses and confirmations. Authors abroad were slow to commit themselves until travel funds were assured. At one point, National President Vinia Hoogstraten and her executive were so distraught by the mounting commitments that they wired a cease-and-desist order. They were considerably mollified to learn that the convener's European travels to contact available writers had been made at his own expense as part of a holiday abroad. It all left the Executive apprehensive.

Some writers proved no-show, but about ten arrived from as far distant as Australia, from Japan, Yugoslavia, France, Russia (their countries paid their way). Some spoke neither English nor French, which called for extra translation facilities. Morris West asked in ringing Australian tones, *"Ou sont les jeunesses?"* Of course, many young people had summer jobs, from which they could scarcely take off four or five days for a convention. Mordecai Richler thanked the Association for the free plane-trip from England to his home town, then read a published article in an inaudible monotone. Only later did the insulted delegates learn that Richler habitually displayed contempt for an audience. The applause was perfunctory. But he at least derived an essay out of the occasion.

The Association drew modest press coverage for a lacklustre program. The *Toronto Star* reporter honed his dull wit on the ladies' names. "Vinia was there, and Fanny was there and Bluebell and Una . . . and all the rest of the triple-named prairie poetesses."

La Société des Ecrivains were there in force, aloof from their Anglophone affiliates until someone realized they were shy, fearful of having their broken English ridiculed. From that understanding on, all was *bonhomie*. Except at the final banquet, which National President Hoogstraten remembered with a shudder. The head-table list went missing, and she had to cope with unfamiliar names and backgrounds. Fortunately, her French-speaking table companion knew most of them. Hoogstraten borrowed a pencil, jotted names on her menu in the right order. Suddenly protocol demanded that two more bodies be fitted in at head-table.

Someone fell off the too narrow dais. A presentation was made to Pierre Berton as "the writer of the Century," and the editor of the *Canadian Author & Bookman* was so preoccupied with justifying her nomination, that she forgot to hand him the framed screed. When Hoogstraten rose to deliver her presidential address the full skirt of her new evening gown was caught beneath her neighbour's chair, and she was forced to speak from a half-crouch. Never did president lay down the gavel more gladly.

But at least everyone enjoyed Expo.

The same could not be said of the Toronto convention the following year. The tumults of the sixties penetrated the halls of Glendon College. Young people were there, interpreting the generation gap to the veterans and not sparing the punches. One evening was turned over to a devoted young member for "A Happening." Poetry spewed from loudspeakers over deafening music — "something that had to be experienced to be believed," one delegate reported to his branch. Movie projectors cast their psychedelic colours on the ceiling and behind glass panels which the sensitive dared not examine too closely. There was a candlelight procession, with incense drowning out the aroma of marijuana (though most didn't recognize it, certainly not the conveners). Older members were outraged, and at the coffee party later, one asked a bearded, sandalled, long-haired hippie, "What does it all mean?" "What you want it to mean, man," the languid rhymster replied.

At least three good poems were written overnight by sleepless elders.

One aftermath. When the ladies of the Beta Sigma Phi discovered that their award of $1,000 for a first novel went to Scott Symons for *Combat Journal for Place d'Armes*, chosen by a panel of university professors, some of the sorority read the novel — and cancelled their award forthwith.

Whereas the Toronto conference had opened with skits at a wine-and-cheese reception, Edmonton in 1969 chose a Klondike theme and broke the ice with ballads of the gold rush days of '98. (Edmonton was the jumping-off-place for one horrendously difficult approach to the gold creeks of the Yukon) and Floradora costumes were rented for a gala dinner. President-elect M. Carol Wilson (Toronto) revealed shapely limbs in black fishnet hose. Quipped Max Goldin (Winnipeg) "Are these the legs that launched a thousand scripts?"

The conventions were much more than moments of unbuttoned gaiety in busy lives. There was final tribute to the Departed — among others, Gordon V. Thompson, E.J. Pratt, Lorne Pierce, Arthur Bourinot, Vincent Massey, Madge Macbeth and the beloved Allan Sangster, long Ontario vice-president — left the scene during the sixties. The conventions were occasions to hear serious and inspiring talks, to trade market information, to develop lifelong friendships and to hatch plans for the future.

Chapter 20
Outreach

Despite the persistent rain that attended the Golden Jubilee convention in Vancouver, the decade of the seventies began auspiciously. Forty-four CAA members had books published that first year, and immediately following the convention, the Okanagan branch was formed in Kelowna, through the energetic Rose Olivia Fry, in the presence of National President Carol Wilson (Toronto). The Kamloops branch took form four years later through the leadership of prolific freelancer Murphy Shewchuk, under National President Cdr. C.H. Little.

The Saskatchewan and Newfoundland branches folded, the Sarnia branch was formed, London and St. John branches revived. Cornwall branch sprang up, flourished briefly and dwindled away. CAA membership reached 969, but sagged when dues went up to forty dollars in 1978.

Death carried off distinguished members and branch stalwarts, among them: Watson Kirkconnell, Bruce Fergusson, Barbara Grantmyre and Evelyn Richardson (all N.S.), Del Young and June Fritch (both Edmonton), R.D. Symons (Sask.), Margaret Furniss McLeod and Margaret Barnard (both Montreal); and of Toronto branch: William Arthur Deacon, Lorrie McLaughlin, Charles Bruce, Joy Tranter, Joe Holliday and Mary Edgar. Ottawa lost Theresa Thomson. All left noticeable gaps.

The conference in Toronto in 1974 was graced by the presence of Victor Bonham-Carter, secretary of the Society of Authors (UK). The excellent program of the 1975 conference in Edmonton was shadowed by the passing away of Lena Newman in her sleep, en route to accepting the UBC medal for Popular Biography.

The 1976 conference in Montreal was a joint exercise with *La Société des Ecrivains*. A titled guest speaker at a Halifax conference displayed his eccentricity by visiting all the pay phones in search of leftover dimes. Perhaps he felt the fee was not enough? At the Winnipeg conference of 1980, the Bermuda Writers Club became an affiliate body.

The annual conferences alternated between Atlantic and Pacific and centrally, to customary satisfaction, culminating in the sparkling convention of 1981, when the Association returned to its birthplace, Montreal, for the sixtieth birthday.

At least the usual amount of writing briefs went on: to the Olympic Committee, the Ontario Royal Commission on Book Publishing, and the Federal Cultural Policy Review Committee in 1981. A resolution went from the 1979 conference in Ottawa, offering support for six writers in the Soviet Union who had challenged censorship in that country. Several branches contributed to the Ian Adams Defence Fund initiated by the Writers' Union. Adams did not reveal the sources of information used in his novel *"S": Portrait of a Spy* and was enabled to buy back the book rights. A small residue remained, a base for investigating "shield" laws.

All the branches took note of International Book Year, 1975, promoted by UNESCO. They took greater interest in the National Book Festivals inaugurated by Federal Government agencies in 1978, and now an annual event.

A phenomenon peculiar to the seventies was the explosion of creative writing instruction and writers' organizations. Marjorie Major (N.S.) launched a correspondence course in the craft. Throughout earlier decades, CAA members had visited schools to talk about Canadian literature or read their own writings, and proved that not all authors were dead and buried. Free, of course. That was in the days before school boards provided a little extra for pupils' "learning experiences," or the government subsidized reading tours.

Naturally the teachers' choice fell upon popular authors, who finally found such activities not only costly but time-consuming. Worse, they caused the writer to "break stride" in the full flush of composition. Requests became so numerous that authors eventually felt compelled to put a price tag on such cooperation. Even a small sum was more edible than a gift houseplant or odd cup-and-saucer. At last, Canada Council grants became available for these readings with hundreds taking place each year.

In many branches, members with a flair for teaching were invited to conduct creative writing classes in university extension or YMCA courses, and some went on to full-time positions in community colleges, where they were valued as having practical skills, not just book-learned knowledge. Hamilton, London, Toronto and Sarnia instituted day-long seminars for neophytes. Winnipeg and Edmonton branches were particularly active in evening classes.

In Winnipeg, Isabel Reimer and Dorothy Powell instructed high school evening classes in writing non-fiction and fiction. Both sold regularly to magazine editors, and knew whereof they lectured. Powell later turned to writing popular juvenile novels. Both were instrumental in mounting a successful campaign to prevent a provincial education tax on books and magazines, on the grounds that such a tax was self-defeating.

Winnipeg members also conducted classes with senior citizens, and some former pupils continued to meet and to write when the sessions ended. This natural course of events tends to have one disadvantage. The group may become ingrown, lacking input from other less chummy writers, and in fact usually fades out. Some former students joined the Winnipeg branch as Interim members, at a lower fee and for a limited time. After two years, the probationer must drop out or qualify as a member of the Association, either as Active (one who has had at least 25,000 words published or produced commercially) or as Associate (with no voting privileges).

Then in 1970, the Manitoba government became more culture-conscious, and the Allied Arts Association was founded with the blessing of the province. A few dedicated leaders and instructors were inspired to hold an Arts Festival at Gimli, a village on the sandy west shore of Lake Winnipeg. Vinia Hoogstraten agreed to instruct in writing and found the experience so rewarding that for several winters she continued weekly classes in several prairie communities.

In Edmonton, Margaret Coleman Johnston taught and supervised extension courses in high schools for nine years, drawing on the skills of the Edmonton branch members. Calgary branch president Ed Arrol taught classes in the city and in Cochrane, Alberta.

"The Alberta Story" began in 1972, when the re-organized Department of Culture, Youth and Recreation formed a Creative Writing Division, largely at the prodding of Dr. W.G. Hardy. John

Patrick Gillese, a prolific writer of thousands of articles, short stories and film scripts, was appointed director. To begin with, the Edmonton and Calgary branches formed themselves into the Alberta Division of the Canadian Authors Association, which gave the new director a pool of teaching talent to draw from.

Gillese brought to the job not only experience in various forms of writing, but vision and enthusiasm. He could inspire, and he had endless patience. He began with experimental classes in Edmonton primary schools, with the teachers sitting in — the techniques he demonstrated were as much for them as for the pupils. A questionnaire circulated at the end of the experiment showed the students enthusiastic and the teachers even more so.

Gillese went on to expand the extension courses in the high schools, continuing to draw on the experienced members of the branch. Marjorie Morgan instructed in fiction and radio writing, while Mary Dawe conducted the ten-week article-writing course. In 1972, he developed two-day writing seminars north in Grande Prairie, south in Red Deer and in Lethbridge.

That same year, the Division launched the Search-for-a-new-Alberta novelist, turning a deaf ear to the doubters. The government offered a prize of $1,000 for the best manuscript submitted by an Albertan who had not yet published a novel. A major Canadian publisher (Macmillan) would publish the manuscript with an advance on royalties of $1,500. Even runners-up could benefit, for the publisher might well discover other manuscripts to his liking, as indeed happened. That first Search turned up three publishable manuscripts: *Bird at the Window*, by Jan Truss, *Breakaway* by Cecelia Frey (both Calgary) and *Lonesome Hero*, by Fred Stenson of Twin Butte. Several other competitors had their manuscript accepted by other publishers.

Jan Truss had decided on sudden impulse to attend the two-day workshop in Lethbridge. Although she had written previously. she had never attempted a novel. Why not, someone asked, and she turned to. Ten months later, Truss received the $1,000 government cheque, plus a contract from Macmillan and $1,500 in advance royalties.

That first search drew ninety-eight entries from all parts of Alberta. In fact, the annual search attracted so many manuscripts that it became biennial, to give judges and the publisher breathing space. Two other competitions were initiated, for Non-fiction and for Regional History, to similar response.

Another important follow-up was the bimonthly *Alberta Authors Bulletin*, a shot in the arm for beginners (but read avidly by all Alberta writers) which proved so effective in driving home the lessons heard in the workshops, that a correspondence course in creative writing was established. Gillese's office was swamped, and a search was on for more writer-instructors, beyond the resources of the Edmonton branch, whose expertise was becoming strained to the breaking point. The popularity of the course and the early successes of the correspondents brought happy smiles to the director and the Minister.

"Younger authors need encouragement and help — and the companionship of their own kind," Gillese believed, and he arranged for the Banff Centre to provide scholarships for three young writers at the Centre's six-week course in creative writing. In addition, the Creative Writing Division provided small grants to help launch Alberta magazines.

The most spectacular success of the Search-for-a-new-Alberta-novelist came in 1976 to Pauline Gedge for her *Child of the Morning*. Gedge flouted the cardinal rule, "Write about what you know" to write about a long-dead pharaoh of Ancient Egypt — Hatshepsut, the first liberated woman — whom she knew thoroughly after intense research in University of Alberta library loans. This was not her first try for the award, but her third try was more than lucky. Not only did she win first place, but her book achieved runaway success in the United States and Europe. The search brought considerable renown to Alberta.

Why could not something similar be done in Ontario, wondered National President Cdr. C.H. Little (Ottawa). He therefore requested information on the founding and funding "so that the CAA could make representation to the government of Ontario for like action." The information was forthcoming, but the Ontario government already had plans of its own on a more modest scale. Ontario's Artist-in-the-Schools program, launched in 1975, included not only writers but artists from various other disciplines. Sundry Toronto branch members, and probably others took part in this continuing project.

The surging optimism and prosperity of the sixties carried on into the early seventies and witnessed a proliferation of writers' organizations, both national and provincial, resulting in the formation of The Writers' Union of Canada.

The notion of a union was not entirely new. William Arthur

Deacon had broached it in 1936, though without working out any details. His premise was that novice writers, eager to break into print, were giving their work away free to any good cause, though the charity thus serviced had to pay the printer and everyone but the willing freelance.

> One thing badly needed in this Association is a sense of personal worth and of joint interest — which is hard to arouse in a profession as competitive and as highly individualized as ours. It seems to me that the Association's prime function in future must be to build up some kind of protective measures. How far these are to follow the pattern of a labour union ... I welcome discussion from the members.

The Depression followed by five years of war combined to obliterate an idea to which there were no easy answers, and the matter scarcely rated discussion. Actually, it was too alien an idea for most of the membership. Nearly a decade later, Horace Brown (Toronto) raised the question again at the splendid 1946 convention.

> It seems to me that the CAA should be a Labour organization. It was formed to protect authors, but what can we do? As it is, we can only advise and make suggestions.

The *Canadian Forum* August 1946 issue, finally had a kind word, dipped in vinegar, for the CAA achievements re income tax and the standard contract, as it pontificated:

> Literature comes of age, not by improving its quality, but by adopting professional standards and ceasing to worry about its quality. Most Canadian literature is and always will be tripe, for the very simple reason that most literature of all countries in all ages is tripe. Any national group of authors will form a pyramid with a few serious writers at the top and a broad base of pulp-scribblers at the bottom. No literary critic would say that these were even earning an honest living; but commercially speaking, they sell their wares in the same market and are as much entitled to the name of authors as Mr. Callaghan or Gabrielle Roy. An author's association simply has to accept this fact, and, for the sake of its few serious writers, go ahead on trade union lines, working to get better publicity for its members, to equalize income tax so that it will be based on the average of several years instead of on the individual year, to standardize copyright laws, to arrange for pensions for elderly authors and scholar-

ships or prizes for young ones and so on. This last conference did begin to concern itself seriously with such matters, and the Canadian Authors Association will be a valuable asset to Canadian culture in proportion to its advance in the direction of an authors' union.

Most beginning writers, have a voracious appetite for discussion of markets and the scuttlebutt of editorial offices, and perhaps feel that craft should be the whole object of authors' meetings, not realizing that the established members are bored with the basic instruction craved by tyros.

When the Writers' War Committee was disbanded, the national executive could get on with other specific problems: Gwethalyn Graham on standard contract, Rod Kennedy on Income Tax, William Arthur Deacon on the Arts Reconstruction. Thus devoted work was going on outside branch meetings. Craft talks at convention were as down-to-earth as any novice could wish. Certainly the young writers' attitude more than ruffled feathers. It shook the entire Association. Times changed. The dinner jacket was laid away along with the pouter-pigeon corset. Branch programs dared to explore the confession magazine field, and escape literature. Older members mourned the passing of gracious ways.

In 1964, Ottawa branch president H.R. Percy was stung by a reporter's uninformed slur that the CAA was "only a bunch of old ladies crying over their rejection slips." Admittedly, the Association, now more than forty years old did number some elderly members. There was Christine Henderson in her late nineties, still writing acceptable poetry, and Margaret Furniss McLeod, over ninety, giving a series of radio talks on Prince Edward Island memories, (both Montreal); Mary Edgar, producing verse for the new Anglican hymnal, and Theodora Herapath (both Toronto and both in their eighties) turning out historical novels that sold reasonably well; Hubert Evans (Vancouver) and Jessie Beattie (Hamilton) both well up in years and though nearly blind, still adding to their long lists of books.

But there were also some members who stayed in the Association from force of habit, with little or no output. Some "Associates" never attempted to achieve "Active" status, and apart from having no voting privileges at annual meetings, were indistinguishable from the professionals.

Percy felt, and Ontario vice-president Allan Sangster agreed, that there should be greater differentiation. In fact, they suggested two parallel but affiliated organizations — the Associates forming, say, a Writers' Guild, and aspiring to join the senior body.

Delegates at the 1964 convention in Halifax would have none of it. There were swift rebuttals: (a) the Associates were learners who would gain knowledge of their craft through branch programs and rubbing shoulders with successful authors willing to offer advice; (b) they were infinitely useful when bodies were needed; (c) an Association of a thousand members would presumably have a stronger voice than one of a half that number; (d) the Association had no financial support other than members' fees.

The subject was dropped before the mutterings in corridors could split the Association irrevocably in an undesired way. It was therefore with a mixture of embarrassment and relief that Percy and some other members of the CAA attended the founding meeting of the Writers' Union of Canada in June, 1972. TWUC had solved the CAA dilemma by providing an organization to which professional writers could belong with pride, not cringing. If a touch of envy crept in, that was surely understandable, for the Canada Council had subsidized travel expenses of the new organization's founding members to Toronto from Atlantic and Pacific coasts. Professional writers built themselves an organization of fresh blood: youngish authors as willing to work for it as were those who had founded the Canadian Authors Association fifty years earlier.

Though not at the same cost of time and talent and cold cash. Many of the founders of the Writers' Union had received Canada Council grants, and knew the workings of official channels. Substantial annual grants have been forthcoming from federal and provincial bounty ever since, though the avowed intention is to become wholly self-supporting.

By the 1970s the idea of an artists' union was no longer bizarre. ACTRA (Association of Canadian Television and Radio Artists), formed in 1963, proved that a union had clout as an association had not, and that writers could be organized for their own good, especially when dealing with a single corporation, the Canadian Broadcasting Corporation (CBC). But a union of freelance writers with any number of bosses in the form of editors and publishers and such a wide variety of product? How could it be organized or controlled?

The Writers' Union solved one aspect, by originally limiting membership to those who had published a novel. This was quickly amended to cover non-fiction books, and then to authors of any Canadian book in print.

Still, the Writers' Union left out in the cold the non-professionals and writers in other genres. These formed their own specialized or provincially-sponsored organizations.

The pioneer in the latter field was SEC (*La Société des Ecrivains Canadiens*), which broke away from the Canadian Authors Association in 1936. The Saskatchewan Writers' Guild rose from the ashes of the CAA Regina branch, with modest government funding which was lately increased. In 1975, the Writers' Federation of Nova Scotia came into existence with substantial government support. Veterans of the Nova Scotia branch of the CAA assembled at the cradle to give the WFNS their blessing, albeit with misgivings as to how its youthful vigour — and bargain-basement fee — would adversely affect the senior Association. Other provincial groups gradually followed suit, even in Prince Edward Island.

In Toronto, other writers formed specialized national organizations for the benefit of other disciplines. ACTRA was the first of this type. The Canadian Copyright Institute gathered in representatives of the League of Canadian Poets, the Guild of Canadian Playwrights, PWAC (Periodical Writers Association of Canada) and CANSCAIP (Canadian Society of Children's Authors, Illustrators and Performers), as well as other creators of copyrightable material.

William Repka (Toronto) a long-time union man was deeply concerned over this fracturing of potential strength, and proposed an umbrella organization which would incorporate these similar but disparate groups in the manner of the Society of Authors (UK). An exploratory meeting was held with delegates from the various groups in the Canadian Women's Press Club which had recently changed its name to the Media Club. However, it soon became evident that each group was determined to remain autonomous, in short, preferred the status quo. Whether or not they realized it, all these organizations had benefitted from the spadework done by the Canadian Authors Association.

Repka lived to see at least a physical umbrella sheltering a handful of these organizations in 1979, through the Writers' Development Trust. Leases terminated for the Canadian Authors Association and for the Writers' Union, and it was necessary to find new inexpensive quarters. By renting space to several writers' groups, the Trust was able to acquire the first floor of a remodelled factory which has become a national Writers' Centre, complete with boardroom and photo-copier. The CAA office is small, congested, but adequate, after decades of shifting from city to city, from coachhouse to classroom to library basement, shedding possessions en route.

And the Association has benefitted by closer contact with other groups, not only in physical aspects but in stimulation of ideas. Cooperation may well be the clue to future action. In 1978, the WFNS and the CAA merged their annual meetings, to their mutual benefit and cost-paring. Plans are afoot to combine the sixtieth anniversary conference with *La Société des Ecrivains Canadiens* as in 1976.

It would appear that the Association has gone on a publishing binge during this past decade; four editions of the *Canadian Writers' Guide* were published with financial assistance of the Ontario Arts Council.

Having got the notion of a multi-cultural book to coincide with the Olympic Games held in Canada in 1976, Repka was loath to abandon the idea or waste the impetus. *The Spirit of Canada* eventually was published, a slim, handsome volume in tune with the prevailing winds of multicultural sentiment. By some quirk, not only were the contributors named, but also the would-be contributors. The verse of contributor James Moir (Calgary) so impressed a publisher that Moir was invited to submit enough poems for a book which was published a year later.

More tact was shown in the Association's *The Seasons of Children*, produced in celebration of the International Year of the Child, 1979. The competition drew a thousand entries from all parts of the country, providing a charming and popular anthology of prose, poetry and photos. Their elementary school held a party for four young Toronto contributors (Madeline Freeman's students), and the Honourable Pauline McGibbon, Lieutenant Governor of Ontario, invited the young writers to a reception. Many of the selections have been reprinted in new textbooks.

An extra fillip to the decade were the Literary Luncheons launched by Toronto literary agent Lucinda Vardey and Fred Kerner, Ontario vice-president, CAA. They began with Canadian-born John Kenneth Galbraith, outstanding American economist, and drew a good crowd in Casa Loma. All succeeding luncheons took place at a more central if less romantic venue, a downtown hotel. Simpson's Book Department collaborated, and audiences varied from 65 to 900. The latter tied-in with the very popular Tutankhamon exhibit at the Ontario Art Gallery. The most urbane speaker was undoubtedly Dr. Robertson Davies (Toronto) *Fifth Business*, while the one who "left 'em laughing" was Peter Ustinov, who had just published his autobiography *Dear Me*. The second season was even more successful than the first, both in terms of the CAA bank account and the publicity factor.

This was not the first time literary luncheons had drawn crowds. In the early sixties a series was held through the efforts of Helen O'Reilly, PR for a Toronto publisher, when the most outstanding author-speaker was Mazo de la Roche, whose wit and charm held listeners spellbound.

Edmonton, Calgary and Vancouver branches picked up the idea, each giving it a local twist. Edmonton held a tea in the local Hudson's Bay store, and exhibited not only books and their authors, but the story behind the book, from hand-written original manuscript to typescript, to galley proof, page proof, and to bound volume, sometimes in several editions, sometimes in translation into several foreign languages. Magazines were displayed, for instance the *Saturday Evening Post* containing Ross Annett's "Babe and Little Joe" yarns, complete with the illustrator's drawings and proofs of the colour plates.

Ella Jacoby Walker exhibited the original oil paintings illustrating her *Fortress North*. Sheila Mackay Russell contributed telegrams on the stage drama based on her *A Lamp is Heavy*. Barbara Villy Cormack showed material relating to her prize-winning *Local Rag*, and Eugenie Myles, of her *North Pole Boarding House*, ghost-written for a non-writing acquaintance.

There were samples of radio, TV and film scripts, and of Elsie Park Gowan's pageants plus photos of the actors. Perhaps the most notable success was an idea for a short story which John Patrick Gillese had jotted down on the back of a grocery store dodger. This grew into a short story published by *Country Gentleman*, and later became the book *Kirby's Gander* and a Hollywood film.

The event attracted enough customers to the store and sold enough books to keep the manager happy and eager for a repeat performance.

Epilogue

There come times in the life of any voluntary organization to assess its objectives anew and look back on its achievements, and to plot its future course. The aims of the Association were modest enough in 1921: "to act for the benefit of Canadian authors, and to procure adequate copyright legislation." The former has been fulfilled in nurturing Canadian writings through sixty years. Canadians are aware of their literature to an extent undreamed of in the beginning, though it still has far to go.

Copyright, the second objective, is still unfinished business, though nearing a conclusion, possibly within the next two years. University professors have been drawn into the act, and lawyers have turned up complexities never suspected. Some have suggested that "intellectual property" is not really property at all! The widespread use of photocopying, has furrowed many brows — and its misuse poses many special problems.

Canada has come from the family farm stage into the industrial, and embarked on the technological, foremost in some aspects, laggard in others. New technologies have sprouted, of which electric and electronic typewriters are merely footnotes, and word processors to correct one's spelling are an established fact. More devices will follow to bewilder and bedazzle in the next sixty years, devices that are not yet a gleam in an inventor's eye.

The Canada of 1981 is a far cry from that of sixty years ago. Today, federal and provincial governments — even some municipalities — take more than casual interest in cultural growth, including the discipline of writing. Libraries have expanded and multiplied, as have book stores. Canadian authors have become known nationally through radio and television interviews and government sponsored reading tours. Various periodicals devote their pages wholly to cultural reviews and news of the cultural scene.

We've come a long way.

What role will the Canadian Authors Association have to play in the near or distant future? It still has a viable part, though it may be recast as a bit player rather than the dramatic lead. Certainly it will carry on, in the service of both established and aspiring Canadian writers.

Appendix I

References

Chapter 3

Susan Sills. The Role of the Canadian Authors Association with Respect to the Licensing Clauses of Early Copyright Legislation and Canada's Adherence to the Berne Convention
Unpub. M.A. Thesis. Institute of Canadian Studies, Carleton University, 1977.

Excerpts throughout are taken from *The Canadian Author and Bookman,* and *Authors' Bulletin.*

The Canadian Author and Bookman 1919-1981:
Bound copies:
Main Reference Library, Toronto, Canada
Robarts Library, Thomas Fisher Rare Book Library, University of Toronto, Toronto, Canada (partial)
Microfilm:
Canadian Authors Association, 24 Ryerson Avenue, Toronto, Canada

Minutes and Records:
The Canadian Authors Association
Complete files at 24 Ryerson Avenue, Toronto, Canada M5T 2P3

Excerpts in Chapter 10 from:
A Life in Folklore by Dr. Helen Creighton (McGraw-Hill Ryerson Ltd, 1975).

A Slice of Canada by Watson Kirkconnell (University of Toronto Press, 1967).

Appendix II

Presidents and Places

Date	President	Branch	Convention Locale
1921	Dr. John Murray Gibbon	Montreal	Montreal
1922	Dr. John Murray Gibbon	Montreal	Ottawa
1923	Robert J.C. Stead	Ottawa	Toronto
1924	Dr. Lawrence J. Burpee	Ottawa	Quebec
1925	Dr. W.T. Allison	Winnipeg	Winnipeg
1926	Dr. W.T. Allison	Winnipeg	Vancouver
1927	Dr. Charles G.D. Roberts	Toronto	Ottawa
1928	Dr. Charles G.D. Roberts	Toronto	Calgary
1929	Dr. W.D. Lighthall	Montreal	Halifax
1930	Dr. W.D. Lighthall	Montreal	Montreal
1931	Dr. D.C. Scott	Ottawa	Toronto
1932	Dr. D.C. Scott	Ottawa	Ottawa
1933	Dr. C.W. Gordon (Ralph Connor)	Winnipeg	Quebec
1934	Dr. C.W. Gordon (Ralph Connor)	Winnipeg	Kenora
1935	Dr. Pelham Edgar	Toronto	Montreal
1936	Dr. Pelham Edgar	Toronto	Vancouver
1937	Leslie Gordon Barnard	Montreal	Toronto
1938	Leslie Gordon Barnard	Montreal	Ottawa
1939	Madge Macbeth	Ottawa	Halifax
1940	Madge Macbeth	Ottawa	Ste. Anne de Bellevue
1941	Madge Macbeth	Ottawa	Vancouver/ Victoria
1942	Dr. Watson Kirkconnell	Hamilton	Montreal
1943	Dr. Watson Kirkconnell	Hamilton	Toronto

1944	Dr. Watson Kirkconnell	Hamilton	Hamilton
1945	Roderick Stuart Kennedy	Montreal	Montreal
1946	Roderick Stuart Kennedy	Montreal	Toronto
1947	William Arthur Deacon	Toronto	Vancouver
1948	William Arthur Deacon	Toronto	Ottawa
1949	Will R. Bird	Nova Scotia	Halifax
1950	Dr. W.G. Hardy	Edmonton	Montreal
1951	Dr. W.G. Hardy	Edmonton	Banff
1952	Dr. Paul Kuhring	Montreal	London
1953	Dr. Paul Kuhring (Hardy)	Montreal	Toronto
1954	Dr. Frank Stiling	London	Banff
1955	Dr. Frank Stiling	London	Kingston
1956	Dr. Watson Kirkconnell	Nova Scotia	Halifax
1957	Dr. Watson Kirkconnell	Nova Scotia	Winnipeg
1958	H. Gordon Green	Montreal	Montreal
1959	H. Gordon Green	Montreal	Windsor
1960	Don W. Thomson	Ottawa	Victoria
1961	Don W. Thomson	Ottawa	Toronto
1962	Dr. Helen Creighton	Nova Scotia	Edmonton
1963	Dr. Helen Creighton	Nova Scotia	Ottawa
1964	Dr. R.S. Longley	Nova Scotia	Halifax
1965	Dr. R.S. Longley	Nova Scotia	Vancouver/ Victoria
1966	Vinia Hoogstraten	Winnipeg	Winnipeg
1967	Vinia Hoogstraten	Winnipeg	Montreal
1968	Dr. W.G. Hardy	Edmonton	Toronto
1969	Dr. W.G. Hardy	Edmonton	Edmonton
1970	M. Carol Wilson	Toronto	Halifax
1971	M. Carol Wilson	Toronto	Vancouver
1972	Cdr. C.H. Little	Ottawa	Ottawa
1973	Cdr. C.H. Little	Ottawa	Winnipeg
1974	Cdr. C.H. Little	Ottawa	Toronto
1975	Dr. Bruce Fergusson	Nova Scotia	Edmonton
1976	Dr. Bruce Fergusson	Nova Scotia	Montreal
1977	Dr. Agnes Nyland	Ottawa	Vancouver
1978	Dr. Agnes Nyland	Ottawa	Halifax
1979	Donald Wetmore	Nova Scotia	Ottawa
1980	Donald Wetmore	Nova Scotia	Winnipeg
1981	Donald Wetmore	Nova Scotia	Montreal

Appendix III

Governor General's Literary Awards

Year	Author	Title
1936	Bertram Brooker	Think of the Earth
	T.B. Roberton	T.B.R. — newspaper pieces
1937	Laura G. Salverson	The Dark Weaver
	E.J. Pratt	The Fable of the Goats
	Stephen Leacock	My Discovery of the West
1938	Gwethalyn Graham	Swiss Sonata
	Kenneth Leslie	By Stubborn Stars
	John Murray Gibbon	Canadian Mosaic
1939	Franklin D. McDowell	The Champlain Road
	Arthur S. Bourinot	Under the Sun
	Laura G. Salverson	Confessions of an Immigrant's Daughter
1940	Ringuet (pseud.)	Thirty Acres
	E.J. Pratt	Brébeuf and His Brethren
	J.F.C. Wright	Slava Bohu
1941	Alan Sullivan	Three Came to Ville Marie
	Anne Marriott	Calling Adventurers
	Emily Carr	Klee Wyck
1942	G. Herbert Sallans	Little Man
	Earle Birney	David and Other Poems
	Bruce Hutchison	The Unknown Country
	Edgar McInnes	The Unguarded Frontier
1943	Thomas H. Raddall	The Pied Piper of Dipper Creek
	A.J.M. Smith	News of the Phoenix
	John D. Robins	The Incomplete Anglers
	E.K. Brown	On Canadian Poetry
1944	Gwethalyn Graham	Earth and High Heaven
	Dorothy Livesay	Day and Night
	Dorothy Duncan	Partner in Three Worlds
	Edgar McInnes	The War: Fourth Year

Category	Publisher(s)
Fiction	Thomas Nelson & Sons (Canada) Ltd., Toronto
Non-fiction	Macmillan Co. of Canada Ltd., Toronto
Fiction	The Ryerson Press, Toronto
Poetry and Drama	MacMillan Co. of Canada Ltd., Toronto
Non-fiction	Thomas Allen Ltd., Toronto
Fiction	Jonathan Cape Ltd., London, and Thomas Nelson & Sons (Canada) Ltd., Toronto
Poetry and Drama	The Ryerson Press, Toronto
Non-fiction	McClelland & Stewart Ltd., Toronto
Fiction	Macmillan Co. of Canada Ltd., Toronto
Poetry and Drama	Macmillan Co. of Canada Ltd., Toronto
Non-fiction	The Ryerson Press, Toronto
Fiction	Macmillan Co. of Canada Ltd., Toronto
Poetry and Drama	Macmillan Co. of Canada Ltd., Toronto
Non-fiction	Farrar & Rinehart, New York & Toronto
Fiction	Oxford University Press, Toronto
Poetry and Drama	The Ryerson Press, Toronto
Non-fiction	Oxford University Press, Toronto
Fiction	The Ryerson Press, Toronto
Poetry and Drama	The Ryerson Press, Toronto
Non-fiction	Coward-McCann Inc., New York, and Longmans, Toronto
Non-fiction	Doubleday, Doran & Co., Garden City, N.Y.
Fiction	William Blackwood & Son, Ltd., Edinburgh, and McClelland & Stewart, Toronto
Poetry and Drama	The Ryerson Press, Toronto
Non-fiction	Wm. Collins Sons & Co. Canada Ltd.
Non-fiction	The Ryerson Press, Toronto
Fiction	Jonathan Cape Ltd., London, and Thomas Nelson & Sons (Canada) Ltd., Toronto
Poetry and Drama	The Ryerson Press, Toronto
Non-fiction	Harper & Brothers, New York and London
Non-fiction	Oxford University Press, London and Toronto

1945	Hugh MacLennan	Two Solitudes
	Earle Birney	Now is Time
	Evelyn M. Richardson	We Keep a Light
	Ross Munro	Gauntlet to Overlord
1946	Winifred Bambrick	Continental Revue
	Robert Finch	Poems
	Frederick Philip Grove	In Search of Myself
	A.R.M. Lower	Colony to Nation
1947	Gabrielle Roy	The Tin Flute
	Dorothy Livesay	Poems for People
	William Sclater	Haida
	R. MacGregor Dawson	The Government of Canada
1948	Hugh MacLennan	The Precipice
	A.M. Klein	The Rocking Chair and Other Poems
	Thomas H. Raddall	Halifax, Warden of the North
	C.P. Stacey	The Canadian Army, 1939-1945
1949	Philip Child	Mr. Ames Against Time
	James Reaney	The Red Heart
	Hugh MacLennan	Cross-country
	R. MacGregor Dawson	Democratic Government in Canada
	R.S. Lambert	Franklin of the Arctic
1950	Germaine Guèvremont	The Outlander
	James Wreford Watson	Of Time and the Lover
	Marjorie Wilkins Campbell	The Saskatchewan
	W.L. Morton	The Progress Party in Canada
	Donalda Dickie	The Great Adventure
1951	Morley Callaghan	The Loved and the Lost
	Charles Bruce	The Mulgrave Road
	Josephine Phelan	The Ardent Exile
	Frank MacKinnon	The Government of Prince Edward Island
	John F. Hayes	A Land Divided
1952	David Walker	The Pillar
	E.J. Pratt	Towards the Last Spike
	Bruce Hutchison	The Incredible Canadian
	Donald G. Creighton	John A. Macdonald, The Young Politician
	Marie McPhedran	Cargoes on the Great Lakes
1953	David Walker	Digby
	Douglas Le Pan	The Net and the Sword

308

Fiction	Wm. Collins Sons & Co. Canada Ltd., Toronto
Poetry and Drama	The Ryerson Press, Toronto
Non-fiction	The Ryerson Press, Toronto
Non-fiction	Macmillan Co. of Canada Ltd., Toronto
Fiction	Faber and Faber Limited, London, and The Ryerson Press, Toronto
Poetry and Drama	Oxford University Press, Toronto
Non-fiction	Macmillan Co. of Canada Ltd., Toronto
Non-fiction	Longmans Canada Ltd., Toronto
Fiction	Reynal & Hitchcock Co., New York, and McClelland & Stewart Ltd., Toronto
Poetry and Drama	The Ryerson Press, Toronto
Non-fiction	Oxford University Press, Toronto
Non-fiction	University of Toronto Press, Toronto
Fiction	Wm. Collins Sons & Co. Canada Ltd., Toronto
Poetry and Drama	The Ryerson Press, Toronto
Non-fiction	McClelland & Stewart Ltd., Toronto
Non-fiction	The King's Printer, Ottawa
Fiction	The Ryerson Press, Toronto
Poetry and Drama	McClelland & Stewart Ltd., Toronto
Non-fiction	Wm. Collins Sons & Co. Canada Ltd., Toronto
Non-fiction	University of Toronto Press, Toronto, and Copp Clark Publishing Co. Limited, Toronto
Juvenile	McClelland & Stewart Ltd., Toronto
Fiction	McGraw-Hill Co. of Canada Ltd., Toronto
Poetry and Drama	McClelland & Stewart Ltd., Toronto
Non-fiction	Rinehart, Toronto and New York
Non-fiction	University of Toronto Press, Toronto
Juvenile	J.M. Dent & Sons (Canada) Ltd., Toronto
Fiction	Macmillan Co. of Canada Ltd., Toronto
Poetry and Drama	Macmillan Co. of Canada Ltd., Toronto
Non-fiction	Macmillan Co. of Canada Ltd., Toronto
Non-fiction	University of Toronto Press, Toronto
Juvenile	Copp Clark Publishing Co. Limited, Toronto
Fiction	Collins Clear Type Press, London, and Houghton Mifflin, Boston
Poetry and Drama	Macmillan Co. of Canada Ltd., Toronto
Non-fiction	Longmans Green Canada Ltd., Toronto
Non-fiction	Macmillan Co. of Canada Ltd., Toronto
Juvenile	Macmillan Co. of Canada Ltd., Toronto
Fiction	Collins Clear-Type Press, London and Toronto
Poetry and Drama	Clarke, Irwin & Company Ltd., Toronto

	N.J. Berrill	**Sex and the Nature of Things**
	J.M.S. Careless	**Canada, A Story of Challenge**
	John F. Hayes	**Rebels Ride at Night**
1954	Igor Gouzenko	**The Fall of a Titan**
	P.K. Page	**The Metal and the Flower**
	Hugh MacLennan	**Thirty and Three**
	A.R.M. Lower	**This Most Famous Stream**
	Marjorie Wilkins Campbell	**The Nor'westers**
1955	Lionel Shapiro	**The Sixth of June**
	Wilfred Watson	**Friday's Child**
	N.J. Berrill	**Man's Emerging Mind**
	Donald G. Creighton	**John A. Macdonald, The Old Chieftain**
	Kerry Wood	**The Map-Maker**
1956	Adele Wiseman	**The Sacrifice**
	Robert A.D. Ford	**A Window on the North**
	Pierre Berton	**The Mysterious North**
	Joseph Lister Rutledge	**Century of Conflict**
	Farley Mowat	**Lost in the Barrens**
1957	Gabrielle Roy	**Street of Riches**
	Jay Macpherson	**The Boatman**
	Bruce Hutchison	**Canada: Tomorrow's Giant**
	Thomas H. Raddall	**The Path of Destiny**
	Kerry Wood	**The Great Chief**
1958	Colin McDougall	**Execution**
	James Reaney	**A Suit of Nettles**
	Pierre Berton	**Klondike**
	Joyce Hemlow	**The History of Fanny Burney**
	Edith L. Sharp	**Nkwala**
1959	Hugh MacLennan	**The Watch that Ends the Night**
	Irving Layton	**Red Carpet for the Sun**
	André Giroux	**Malgré tout, la joie**
	Félix-Antoine Savard	**Le Barachois**
1960	Awards given by Canada Council	

Non-fiction	Dodd, Mead & Co., New York
Non-fiction	University Press, Cambridge, and Macmillan Co. of Canada Ltd., Toronto
Juvenile	Copp Clark Publishing Co. Limited, Toronto
Fiction	Cassell & Co. Ltd., London
Poetry and Drama	McClelland & Stewart Ltd., Toronto
Non-fiction	Macmillan Co. of Canada Ltd., Toronto
Non-fiction	The Ryerson Press, Toronto
Juvenile	Macmillan Co. of Canada Ltd., Toronto
Fiction	Doubleday & Company, Inc., Garden City, N.Y.
Poetry and Drama	Faber and Faber Limited, London
Non-fiction	Dodd, Mead & Co., New York
Non-fiction	Macmillan Co. of Canada Ltd., Toronto
Juvenile	Macmillan Co. of Canada Ltd., Toronto
Fiction	Macmillan Co. of Canada Ltd., Toronto
Poetry and Drama	The Ryerson Press, Toronto
Non-fiction	McClelland & Stewart Ltd., Toronto, and Knopf, New York
Non-fiction	Doubleday & Co., Inc., New York and Toronto
Juvenile	Little, Brown & Co., Boston and Toronto
Fiction	McClelland & Stewart Ltd., Toronto
Poetry and Drama	Oxford University Press, Toronto
Non-fiction	Longmans Canada Ltd., Toronto
Non-fiction	Doubleday Canada Limited, Toronto
Juvenile	Macmillan Co. of Canada Ltd., Toronto
Fiction	Macmillan Co. of Canada Ltd., Toronto
Poetry and Drama	Macmillan Co. of Canada Ltd., Toronto
Non-fiction	McClelland & Stewart Ltd., Toronto
Non-fiction	Clarendon Press, Oxford, and Oxford University Press, Toronto
Juvenile	Little, Brown & Co., Toronto and Boston
Fiction	Macmillan Co. of Canada Ltd., Toronto
Poetry and Drama	McClelland & Stewart Ltd., Toronto
Romans et nouvelles	Institut Littéraire du Québec, Québec
Autres genres littéraires	Editions Fides, Montréal

Appendix IV

Canadian Authors Association Awards
funded by Harlequin Enterprises Limited, Toronto
Award: Silver Medal and $1,000.

Prose Fiction

1975	Fred Stenson	**Lonesome Hero**
1976	No Award	
1977	Carol Shields	**Small Ceremonies**
1978	Jane Rule	**The Young in One Another's Arms**
1979	Marian Engel	**The Glassy Sea**
1980	No Award	
1981	Hugh MacLennan	**Voices in Time**

Prose Non-Fiction

1975	Lena Newman	**The John A. Macdonald Album**
1976	John Mellor	**Forgotten Heroes**
1977	Bruce Hutchison	**The Far Side of the Street**
1978	Hans Selye	**The Stress of my Life**
1979	Sid Marty	**Men for the Mountains**
1980	Hal Lawrence	**A Bloody War**
1981	Pierre Berton	**The Invasion of Canada**

Poetry

1975	Tom Wayman	**For and Against the Moon: Blues, Yells and Chuckles**
1976	Jim Green	**North Book**
1977	Sid Stephen	**Beothuk Poems**

1978	Alden Nowlan	**Smoked Glass**
1979	Andrew Suknaski	**The Ghosts Call You Poor**
1980	Michael Ondaatje	**There's a Trick with a Knife that I'm Learning to Do**
1981	Leona Gome	**Land of the Peace**

Drama

1975	No Award	
1976	John Hirsch	**The Dybbuk**
1977	No Award	
1978	Rex Deverell	**Boiler Room Suite**
1979	No Award	
1980	Sheldon Rosen	**Ned and Jack**
1981	Ted Galay	**After Baba's Funeral and Sweet and Sour Pickles**

Appendix V

Vicky Metcalf Award Winners
Administration by
Canadian Authors Association
Awarded to a Canadian Author for a body of children's books

1963 Kerry Wood
1964 John F. Hayes
1965 Roderick Haig-Brown
1966 Fred Swayze
1967 John Patrick Gillese
1968 Lorrie McLaughlin
1969 Audrey McKim
1970 Farley Mowat
1971 Kay Hill
1972 William E. Toye
1973 Christie Harris
1974 Jean Little
1975 Lyn Harrington
1976 Suzanne Martel
1977 James Houston
1978 Lyn Cook
1979 Cliff Faulknor
1980 John Craig
1981 Monica Hughes

Vicky Metcalf Short Story Awards

1979 Marina McDougall   **Kingdom of Riddles**
1980 Estelle Salata   **Blind Date**
1981 James Houston   **Long Claws**

Index

315

317

318